THE MYTH OF THE SPOILED CHILD

Feel-Bad Education: And Other Contrarian Essays on Children and Parenting (2011)

The Homework Myth: Why Our Kids Get Too Much of a Bad Thing (2006)

Unconditional Parenting: Moving from Rewards and Punishments to Love and Reason (2005)

What Does It Mean to Be Well Educated?: And More Essays on Standards, Grading, and Other Follies (2004)

The Case Against Standardized Testing: Raising the Scores, Ruining the Schools (2000)

The Schools Our Children Deserve: Moving Beyond Traditional Classrooms and "Tougher Standards" (1999)

What to Look for in a Classroom . . . And Other Essays (1998)

Beyond Discipline: From Compliance to Community (1996)

Punished by Rewards: The Trouble with Gold Stars, Incentive Plans, A's, Praise, and Other Bribes (1993)

You Know What They Say . . . : The Truth About Popular Beliefs (1990)

The Brighter Side of Human Nature: Altruism and Empathy in Everyday Life (1990)

No Contest: The Case Against Competition (1986)

The Myth
of the Spoiled Child

Challenging the Conventional Wisdom
about Children and Parenting

ALFIE KOHN

Da Capo

LIFE
LONG

A Member of the Perseus Books Group

Editorial production by the Book Factory.

Cataloging-in-Publication data for this book is
available from the Library of Congress.
ISBN: 978-0-7382-1724-6 (hardcover)
ISBN: 978-0-7382-1725-3 (e-book)

Published by Da Capo Press
A Member of the Perseus Books Group
www.dacapopress.com

Da Capo Press books are available at special discounts for bulk purchases in the U.S. by corporations, institutions, and other organizations. For more information, please contact the Special Markets Department at the Perseus Books Group, 2300 Chestnut Street, Suite 200, Philadelphia, PA 19103, or call (800) 810-4145, ext. 5000, or e-mail special.markets@perseusbooks.com.

10 9 8 7 6 5 4 3 2 1

To M.W., whose marginalia always elevates what I started with.

Contents

Introduction

While chatting with a friend in his garden one day, the linguist George Lakoff came up with an interesting thought experiment. Was there, Lakoff wondered, a single question that one could ask people such that their answer would predict whether they were liberal or conservative on a range of political issues? Yes, his friend replied. Just ask them this: "If your baby cries at night, do you pick him up?"[1]

Lakoff tells this story at the beginning of his book *Moral Politics* to explain how he came to believe that our views on any number of topics—abortion, capital punishment, gun control, environmental regulation, foreign policy, immigration, and more—often bespeak a deeper "moral vision." And this vision, he maintains, can be described in terms of "models of the family." Conservative positions reflect what he calls a Strict Father model, while liberal positions point to a Nurturant Parent model.

Even after making my way through his 425-page book, I'm not entirely clear what status Lakoff meant to attribute to these views of parenting. Are they metaphors? (Elsewhere, he's written about how our thoughts and actions are shaped by metaphors we may not even be aware of using.) Or are one's attitudes about raising children actually supposed to be correlated with one's positions on all those political issues? And, if so, is there any evidence to support that hypothesis?[2]

Whatever their status, the models themselves are coherent and undeniably compelling—I'll say more about the Strict Father approach later—and it's fascinating to imagine that the way you treat your kids really can predict and explain your politics. Does a heavy-handed emphasis on obedience in the home foretell opposition to affirmative action? Are parents who talk things over with their children rather than spanking them more likely to favor tax incentives to promote renewable energy? The possibilities lend new meaning to Wordsworth's adage, "The child is father of the man."

There's just one problem with Lakoff's theory. An awful lot of people who are politically liberal begin to sound like right-wing talk-show hosts as soon as the conversation turns to children and parenting. It was this curious discrepancy, in fact, that inspired the book you are now reading.

I first noticed an inconsistency of this kind in the context of education. Have a look at the unsigned editorials in left-of-center newspapers, or essays by columnists whose politics are mostly progressive. Listen to speeches by liberal public officials. On any of the controversial issues of our day, from tax policy to civil rights, you'll find approximately what you'd expect. But when it comes to education, almost all of them take a hard-line position very much like what we hear from conservatives. They endorse a top-down, corporate-style version of school reform that includes prescriptive, one-size-fits-all teaching standards and curriculum mandates; weakened job protection for teachers; frequent standardized testing; and a reliance on rewards and punishments to raise scores on those tests and compel compliance on the part of teachers and students.

Admittedly there is some disagreement about the proper role of the federal government in all of this—and also about the extent to which public schooling should be privatized[3]—but otherwise, liberal Democrats and conservative Republicans, the *New York Times* and the *Daily Oklahoman*, sound the identical themes of "accountability," "raising the bar," and "global competitiveness" (meaning that education is conceived primarily in economic terms). President Barack Obama didn't just continue George W. Bush's education policies; he intensified them, piling the harsh test-driven mandates of a program called "Race to the Top" on the harsh test-driven mandates of "No Child Left Behind."[4]

Applause for this agenda has come not only from corporate America but also from both sides of the aisle in Congress and every major media outlet in the United States. Indeed, the generic phrase *school reform* has come to be equated with these specific get-tough policies. To object to them is to risk being labeled a defender of the "status quo," even though they have defined the status quo for some time now. Many of the people who *have* objected are teachers and other education experts who see firsthand just how damaging this approach has been, particularly to low-income students and the schools that serve them. But a key element of "reform" is to define educators as part of the problem, so their viewpoint has mostly been dismissed.

What's true of attitudes about education is also largely true of the way we think about children in general—what they're like and how they should be raised. Of course politicians are far less likely to speak (or newspapers to editorialize) about parenting. But columnists do weigh in from time to time and, when they do, those who are generally liberal once again do a remarkable imitation of conservatives.[5] Articles about parenting in general-interest periodicals, meanwhile, reflect the same trend. The range of viewpoints on other topics gives way to a stunningly consistent perspective where children are concerned.

That perspective sounds something like this:

- We live in an age of indulgence in which permissive parents refuse to set limits for, or say no to, their children.
- Parents overprotect their kids rather than let them suffer the natural consequences of their own mistakes. Children would benefit from experiencing failure, but their parents are afraid to let that happen.
- Adults are so focused on making kids feel special that we're raising a generation of entitled narcissists. They get trophies even when their team didn't win; they're praised even when they didn't do anything impressive; and they receive A's for whatever they turn in

at school. Alas, they'll be in for a rude awakening once they get out into the unforgiving real world.

- What young people need—and lack—is not self-esteem but self-discipline: the ability to defer gratification, control their impulses, and persevere at tasks over long periods of time.

These "traditionalist" convictions (for lack of a better word) are heard everywhere and repeated endlessly. Taken together, they have become our society's conventional wisdom about children, to the point that whenever a newspaper or magazine addresses any of these topics, it will almost always be from this direction. If the subject is self-esteem, the thesis will be that children have an oversupply. If the subject is discipline (and limits imposed by parents), the writer will insist that kids today get too little. And perseverance or "grit" is always portrayed positively, never examined skeptically.

This widespread adoption of a traditionalist perspective helps us to make sense of the fact that, on topics related to children, even liberals tend to hold positions whose premises are deeply conservative. Perhaps it works the other way around as well: The fact that people on the left and center find themselves largely in agreement with those on the right explains how the traditionalist viewpoint has *become* the conventional wisdom. Child rearing might be described as a hidden front in the culture wars, except that no one is fighting on the other side.

In order to write this book I've had to track down research studies on the relevant issues so as to be able to distinguish truth from myth. But I've also come across dozens of articles in the popular press, articles with titles like "Spoiled Rotten: Why Do Kids Rule the Roost?" (*The New Yorker*), "How to Land Your Kid in Therapy" (*The Atlantic*), "Just Say No: Why Parents Must Set Limits for Kids Who Want It All" (*Newsweek*), "Parents and Children: Who's in Charge Here?" (*Time*), "The Child Trap: The Rise of Overparenting" (*The New Yorker* again), "The Abuse of Overparenting" (*Psychology Today*), "The Trouble with Self-Esteem," (*New York Times Magazine*), and "Millennials: The Me Me Me Generation" (*Time* again), to name just a few.

If you've read one of these articles, you've pretty much read all of them. The same goes for newspaper columns, blog posts, and books on the same themes.[6] Pick any one of them at random and the first thing you'll notice is that it treats a diverse assortment of complaints as if they're interchangeable. Parents are criticized for hovering and also for being too lax (with no acknowledgment that these are two very different things). In one sentence, kids are said to have too many toys; in the next, they're accused of being disrespectful. Or unmotivated. Or self-centered. Anything that happens to annoy the writer may be tossed into the mix. Kids are exposed to too many ads! Involved in too many extracurricular activities! Distracted by too much technology! They're too materialistic and individualistic and narcissistic—probably because they were raised by parents who are pushy, permissive, progressive. (If the writer is an academic, a single label may be used to organize the indictment—"intensive parenting" or "nurturance overload," for example—but a bewildering variety of phenomena are offered as examples.[7])

In fact, the generalizations offered in these books and articles sometimes seem not merely varied but contradictory. We're told that parents push their children too hard to excel (by ghostwriting their homework, hiring tutors, and demanding that they triumph over their peers) but also that parents try to *protect* kids from competition (by giving trophies to everyone), that expectations have declined, that too much attention is paid to making children happy. Similarly, young adults are described as self-satisfied twits—more pleased with themselves than their accomplishments merit—but also as being so miserable that they're in therapy.[8] Or there's an epidemic of helicopter parenting, even though parents are so focused on their gadgets that they ignore their children. The assumption seems to be that readers will just nod right along, failing to notice any inconsistencies, as long as the tone is derogatory and the perspective is traditionalist.

Rarely are any real data cited—either about the prevalence of what's being described or the catastrophic effects being alleged. Instead, writers tend to rely primarily on snarky anecdotes, belaboring them to give the impression that these carefully chosen examples are representative of the general population, along with quotes from authors who accept and restate the writer's thesis about permissive parents and entitled kids who have never experienced failure.

Oddly, though, even as these writers repeat what everyone else is saying, they present themselves as courageous contrarians who are boldly challenging the conventional wisdom.

Perhaps the experience of reading all those articles—sloppy, contradictory, or unpersuasive though they may be—wouldn't have been so irritating if it were also possible to find essays that questioned the dominant assumptions, essays that might have been titled "The New Puritanism: Who Really Benefits When Children Are Trained to Put Work Before Play?" or "Why Parents Are So Controlling . . . and How It Harms Their Kids" or "The Invention of 'Helicopter Parenting': Creating a Crisis Out of Thin Air." If anything along these lines has appeared in a mainstream publication, I've been unable to locate it.

The numbing uniformity of writings on children and parenting, and the lack of critical inspection on which the consensus rests, is troubling in itself. When countless publications offer exactly the same indictment of spoiled children and entitled Millennials—and accuse their parents of being lax or indulgent—this has a very real impact on the popular consciousness, just as a barrage of attack ads, no matter how misleading, can succeed in defining a political candidate in the minds of voters. But of course what matters more than whether a consensus exists is whether it makes sense, whether there's any merit to the charges. And that's my task here: to dissect casual claims in light of the evidence.

Those claims can be sorted into three categories. Some of them are *descriptive statements*. (Permissiveness is widespread. Failure is useful. Kids today are more narcissistic than those of previous generations.) Some of them are *predictions*. (Children who are "overparented" will not fare well as adults. The absence of competition will foster mediocrity.) And some of them are simply *value judgments*. (Self-esteem ought to be earned. A parent's priority should be to make children more independent.) My goal will be to ask whether the descriptions are accurate, whether there are any data to support the predictions, and whether the values are defensible. I'm also intrigued by the worldview on which all these statements rest—along with the anger that often animates them—and what that tells us about ourselves.

In the first two chapters, I'll look at accusations that parents are permissive and children are spoiled—accusations that, as we'll see, have been around for quite some time, with each generation insisting that the problem has never been worse than it is now. To understand why so many people are eager to believe these complaints, we'll need to take some time to explore the nature of parenting itself and the version of it that actually helps kids to flourish.

In Chapter 3, we'll consider charges of "overparenting." As with permissiveness, absolutely no evidence exists to support the claim that this phenomenon is widespread. Where it does exist, moreover, the impact on children is troubling not because they are being indulged but because they are being controlled. The common stereotype of young adults being directed by helicopter parents also turns out to have virtually no basis in reality—in terms of either its pervasiveness or its effects.

The next two chapters consider a variety of situations in which children are supposedly protected from unpleasant experiences or allowed to feel more satisfied with themselves than they deserve. The claim is that kids are praised too readily, given A's too easily, and allowed to go home with trophies even when they haven't defeated anyone. Traditionalists have responded with fury at even modest efforts to scale back punitive practices as well as competitive activities that range from dodge ball to calculating high school students' class rank. This intense opposition, I'll argue, is based on three beliefs: that rewards are necessary to motivate people, that these rewards should be made artificially scarce and given only to winners, and that the best way to prepare children for future unhappiness and failure is to make them experience unhappiness and failure right now. Even though these assumptions prove false, each of them is driven by an ideological conviction that cannot be unseated by evidence—namely, that anything desirable should have to be earned (conditionality), that excellence can be attained only by some (scarcity), and that children ought to have to struggle (deprivation).

These value judgments inform the usual appraisal of what adults do for kids, but also of how kids think of themselves. Chapter 6 examines what's known about the psychological importance of self-esteem, and how that body of knowledge squares with traditionalists' efforts to discredit the concept. It then zeroes in on the major point of contention, which again concerns conditionality: What provokes particular outrage and ridicule is the idea that children might feel good about themselves in the absence of impressive accomplishments, even though, as I'll show, studies find that *un*conditional self-esteem is a key component of psychological health.

So, too, do the best theory and research challenge the claim that all children would benefit from more self-discipline. Chapter 7 examines this concept closely, reviewing the dynamics of self-control and exploring the ideology that leads so many people to demand that children work harder, resist temptation, and put off doing what they enjoy. Even if kids were as self-centered and spoiled as we're told they are, we might respond not by invoking the Protestant work ethic or with stricter discipline but by helping them to work for social change. Chapter 8 discusses ways we can promote a disposition to question things as we find them and refuse to go along with what doesn't make sense.

In the pages that follow, I want to invite readers who don't regard themselves as social conservatives to reexamine the traditionalist roots of attitudes about children they may have come to accept. And I want to invite all readers, regardless of their political and cultural views, to take a fresh look at common assumptions about kids and parenting. We've been encouraged to worry: Are we being firm enough with our children? Are we too involved in their lives? Do kids today feel too good about themselves? Those questions, I'll argue, are largely misconceived. They distract us from—or even make us suspicious about—the shifts that we *ought* to be considering. The sensible alternative to overparenting is not less parenting but better parenting. The alternative to permissiveness is not to be more controlling but more responsive. And the alternative to narcissism is not conformity but reflective rebelliousness.

In short, if we want to raise psychologically healthy and spirited children, we'll need to start by questioning the media-stoked fears of spoiling them.

CHAPTER 1

Permissive Parents, Coddled Kids, and Other Reliable Bogeymen

THIS TIME IT'S DIFFERENT . . . AGAIN

It's the sort of rhetorical cliché favored by high school orators and academics who are trying to spice up their plodding monographs: Offer an anonymous quotation that's directly pertinent to the topic and then reveal with a flourish that the source is actually decades, or even centuries, old. Ha! Gotcha!

This device, however, has the potential to be more than a source of mild entertainment. To read strikingly familiar observations or sentiments offered by people long dead is to be deprived of the myth of uniqueness, and that can be usefully unsettling. Whenever we're apt to sound off about how certain aspects of modern life are unprecedented in their capacity to give offense, the knowledge that our grandparents or distant ancestors said much the same thing, give or take a superficial detail, ought to make us stop talking in mid-sentence and sit down—hard.

Take education. Commentators and veteran teachers often announce— in a tone of either resignation or disgust—that the performance of our students and the standards to which they're held have become increasingly lax. Kids do the bare minimum and manage to get away with it. Heck, they're actually pleased with themselves—and celebrated by others—for their mediocrity!

"In recent years," one article observed, "parents have cried in dismay that their children could not read out loud, could not spell, could not write clearly," while "employers have said that mechanics could not read simple directions. Many a college has blamed high schools for passing on students . . . who could not read adequately to study college subjects; high schools have had to give remedial reading instruction to [students] who did not learn to read properly in elementary schools." On and on goes this devastating indictment of our education system. Or, well, perhaps not "our" education system, since few of us had much to say about school policy when this article appeared—in 1954.[1]

Comparable jeremiads were published, of course, in the 1970s and '80s (an influential example being the Reagan administration's deeply dishonest "Nation at Risk" report[2]), but couldn't one argue that those, like today's denunciations of falling standards, reflect the same legacy of multiculturalism, leftist education professors, and the post-Woodstock cultural realignment that brought down traditional values inside and outside of schools? Yes indeed, one could certainly make that argument. But defending it proves rather difficult given that people were attacking America's supposedly dysfunctional education system before Vietnam, before Civil Rights, before feminism—and were striking the very same tone of aggressive nostalgia.

So if pundits were throwing up their hands even during the Eisenhower era about schools on the decline and students who could barely read and write, the obvious question is this: When exactly *was* that golden period distinguished by high standards? The answer, of course, is that it never existed. "The story of declining school quality across the twentieth century is, for the most part, a fable," says social scientist Richard Rothstein, whose book *The Way We Were?* cites a series of similar attacks on American education, moving backward one decade at a time.[3] Each generation invokes the good old days, during which, we discover, people had been doing exactly the same thing.

Thus, middle-aged grumblers during the 1950s undoubtedly grew misty-eyed as they recalled *their* days in school—you know, back when excellence mattered and excuses weren't accepted. How inconvenient, then, to discover that, when they were children, adults had been out-raged that the judges of a college essay contest were forced to select "the essay having the fewest errors" (in 1911) and high school students missed two out of every three questions on a test of "the simplest and most obvious facts of American history" (in 1917).[4]

Did someone say "grade inflation"? Everyone knows that A's are handed out like fun-size candy bars on Halloween nowadays—a disgraceful dilution of rigorous standards that "got started in the late 60s and early 70s," as Harvard University's Harvey Mansfield tells the widely accepted story.[5] (Blame all the bleeding-heart radical professors hired and tenured during that period.) Hence a report from Harvard's own "Committee on Raising the Standard": "Grades A and B are sometimes given too readily—Grade A for work of not very high merit, and Grade B for work not far above mediocrity. . . . One of the chief obstacles to raising the standards of the degree is the readiness with which insincere students gain passable grades by sham work." Except that report was written in—you saw this coming, didn't you?—1894. Back then, letter grades were still a novelty at the university, less than one decade old, but Mansfield's ideological forebears were already complaining about how little the top grades had come to mean.[6]

"Nostalgia is only amnesia turned around," said the poet Adrienne Rich. Of course all this historical evidence doesn't mean that today's scolds, braying about our recent decline, will finally sit down and shut up. It just means they should.

"Before the days of dumbing down and propping up, we held high standards for children at home as well as in school." That declaration appears in a book published in 2003 called *The Epidemic: The Rot of American Culture, Absentee and Permissive Parenting, and the Resultant Plague of Joyless, Selfish Children.* (Once you've read the subtitle, you've read the book).[7] Like many other writings from the grouchy/wistful school of cultural criticism, it contends that education is just the beginning of our current problems. Indeed, the last few years have brought a boatload of polemics that focus less on how children are taught than on how they're raised. Given that the latter is our primary focus in this book, we might be forgiven for wondering what to make of claims that kids today are more spoiled than ever before and that parental authority has eroded over time. Is it possible that a response of "been there, seen that" is called for here, too?

Even without a trip to the archives, readers of a certain age will recall that condemnations of pervasive permissiveness are hardly new. For starters, the very same points being made today about pushover parents and their coddled offspring could be found in books published in the early 1990s (*Spoiled Rotten: Today's Children and How to Change Them*) and in the early 1980s (*Parent Power*). The latter was written by the Christian conservative John Rosemond, but at least three other books over the last few decades have used that same title, with its call for an unapologetic assertion of control.

A little earlier, in 1976, *U.S. News and World Report* ran an article called "Permissiveness: A 'Beautiful Idea' That Didn't Work." And a couple named Joseph and Lois Bird wrote, in their 1972 manifesto *Power to the Parents,* that "teaching the child responsibility . . . is not a popular idea" these days. "Most parents and teachers expect too little" from kids, they explained, with the result that we now have to worry not only about "the terrible teens" but also about "the rebellious preteens and the obstreperous grammar schoolers." The Birds hearkened back to a simpler time (though with no hint of when that was) during which "we knew what we believed in," before those "pseudo-psychologists" started telling us that children need more freedom.[8]

Not too long ago, *Time* magazine's cover featured an illustration of a smirking boy, his arms folded and a gold crown on his head, surrounded by an enormous collection of toys. "Do Kids Have Too Much POWER?" the cover demanded in boldface capitals. (Guess what the answer was.) The article reported that "80% of people think kids today are more spoiled than kids of 10 or 15 years ago."[9] But there's every reason to believe that a poll taken ten or fifteen years earlier would have found a large majority making precisely the same claim. When the author of a book called *Spoiling Childhood* warns, "We have entered an era of permissiveness in which the scales are tipped toward gratification,"[10] that can be true only if the word *era* denotes a period of at least forty years. Clearly, there's not much difference between what we're hearing today about how children are raised and what was being said before most parents of younger children were even born.

Here, though, just as with claims about education, the possibility exists that we're merely suffering from a lengthy interval of crumbling values and lax parenting, one that can be traced back to all those tie-dyed baby boomers who were allowed to do as they pleased and are now raising their own children the same way. Does it all get back to the tectonic shift of the late 1960s and early '70s? Did people raise their children responsibly before everything went to pot?

Like, say, in the *early* 1960s? Apparently not. Journalist Peter Wyden declared in *Suburbia's Coddled Kids* that it's become "tougher and tougher to say 'No' and make it stick." The cover of his book, published in 1962, depicted a child lounging on a divan, eating grapes while Mom fans him and Dad holds an umbrella to protect him from the sun.[11] (Perhaps the artist was the parent, or even the grandparent, of whoever created that *Time* cover illustrating how kids have never had so much power as they do *now*.)

Newsweek, meanwhile, which warned us a few years ago about the need to "just say no" to today's youngsters who "want it all," managed to scoop itself in the early 1960s with a cover that depicted a little girl with a miniature mother and father standing on her outstretched hands. It asked the ominous question, "Are We Trapped in a Child-Centered World?" The answer was conveniently supplied by *The Child Worshipers*, a 1963 book by Martha Weinman Lear: "We are living, like it or not . . . in a child-centered society"; in fact, "child worship is in some ways a national epidemic."[12]

Any chance that things were better in the mid-1950s (despite the failing schools)? Let's check in with Marguerite and Willard Beecher, authors of *Parents on the Run*:

Time was when parents had their own authority about the rearing of children. In those days, children were supposed to be "seen and not heard." The fear of parents and of God was instilled in them. There was no back talk and no nonsense. The homes of yesteryear were adult-centered. Today [in 1955] we have the child-centered home. In it there is little peace and quiet, and certainly not much respect for, or fear of authority. Today's comic-tragic home reveals the child is firmly and autocratically in command. Parents are barely tolerated around the house. Indeed, it is parents who are to "be seen and not heard."[13]

That denunciation was echoed by respondents to another poll, who lambasted contemporary (1950s) moms and dads for being "not strict enough," as well as by *Parents* magazine in a January 1950 article—"When and How to Say No"—that condemned parents for being "unable to take the responsibility for being grown up and making decisions."[14]

OK, so the problem didn't start with the peace-and-love generation. Here's a fallback hypothesis: Perhaps it began with Dr. Benjamin Spock, whose name in conservative circles has long been synonymous with permissiveness. If kids are insufficiently deferential, one author informs us, it's because of "the influence of progressive child-rearing experts and educators. This movement started with Dr. Spock."[15]

Alas, this explanation, too, suffers from a couple of rather serious flaws, beginning with the fact that Dr. Spock never really deserved his reputation. His famous *Common Sense Book of Baby and Child Care*, published in 1946, hardly reads as a manual for letting children do as they please. Spock's reputation for permissiveness was due mostly to his suggestion that parents should not impose a rigid feeding schedule on an infant—or potty-training demands on an unready toddler. In his approach to discipline and related topics, he was actually quite moderate. The famous distillation of his advice to mothers was "Trust yourself"—not "Trust your kids." "Don't say [to young children] 'Do you want to'—just do what's necessary," he advised. "It's easy to fall into the habit of saying to a small child, 'Do you want to . . . have your lunch?' . . . It is better not to give him a choice."[16]

Moreover, the book went through seven more editions during his lifetime, with its title shortened to *Baby and Child Care,* and he seemed to grow increasingly conservative as the years went by. Beginning with the second edition, in 1957, Spock took pains to emphasize his conservative credentials on the very first page: "Nowadays there seems to be more chance of a conscientious parent's getting into trouble with permissiveness than with strictness." Like so many others, Spock regarded that as a serious problem—and one that he, himself, clearly didn't create. By the third edition, he was even more worried about the possibility that children might be spoiled, and he recommended that parents just let them cry if they resisted going to sleep lest they become dependent on parental comfort. When he wasn't updating his book, Spock spent time rebutting the charge that he sanctioned permissiveness—beginning with a 1948 speech in which he denied being "foolish enough to say that a child does not need control . . . [as] some people imagine we have said," and continuing in a magazine article almost a quarter-century later that was titled "Don't Blame Me!"[17]

The other problem with the "it's Spock's fault" argument is that traditionalists were decrying what they saw as permissive parenting before this particular pediatrician ever set pen to paper. Shortly before his book was first published, an article in *American Home*—"I've Raised Three Selfish Little Savages"—blamed progressive child rearing for making the author's children believe "they have priority over everything and everybody."[18] Even earlier, during the 1920s, there had been a "great hue and cry about the loss of parental authority in the modern home."[19] Readers of *The Atlantic Monthly*, meanwhile, were treated to a stern rebuke directed to the younger generation. Sure, the author conceded, kids have always been pleasure seekers, but what we're currently witnessing "is different from anything we have ever seen in the young before." Parents teach "nothing wholeheartedly," and things now come so easily to children that they fail to develop any self-discipline. Forget about traditional values: Today, it's just a "*culte du moi*." That essay, by one Cornelia A. P. Comer, was published in 1911,[20] when Benjamin Spock was eight years old.

When Comer's piece was subsequently reprinted in an anthology, the editor added his own two cents. He confessed that "the older generation is bewildered. It cannot understand the freedom of youth. It agrees with foreign observers, that American children have the worst manners in the world; that they are thoroughly spoiled; and that, intent upon pleasure and oblivious to duty, they are driving straight to destruction." He added, "Though the world has certainly changed before, it never has changed at the whirling speed of the last half-dozen years"—that is, since 1915.[21]

This time, in other words, things really are different. That's what people today post on their blogs to get you to take their italicized complaints seriously, and it's what people were using fountain pens to communicate a hundred years ago for the same reason. Appeals to historical perspective apparently need to be put in historical perspective.

Set the Way-Back Machine even earlier and you'll find an English visitor clucking in 1832 about "the total want of discipline and subjection which I observed universally among children of all ages" in America.[22] In fact, it's difficult to know when these themes *weren't* being sounded. One writer in the 1640s decried children who carry their insolence "proudly, disdainfully, and scornfully toward parents."[23] And there are reports of people having said these sorts of things *thousands* of years ago. The following rant, for example, is widely attributed to the Greek poet Hesiod, who lived in the eighth century B.C.E.: "I see no hope for the future of our people if they are dependent on the frivolous youth of today, for certainly all youth are reckless beyond words. When I was young, we were taught to be discreet and respectful of elders, but the present youth are exceedingly [disrespectful] and impatient of restraint." And this, allegedly from Socrates: "Children today love luxury too much. They have detestable manners, flout authority, and have no respect for their elders. What kind of awful creatures will they be when they grow up?"[24]

True, even ample historical precedent doesn't rule out the possibility that parents *are* too permissive; theoretically, they might always (and everywhere) have been so. But the force of the argument one hears—in books and articles, at seminars and dinner parties—is that parenting is more that way now than it used to be. Back then, parents set limits and kids obeyed (which is uncritically assumed to be desirable). Back then, standards were high and students were motivated and self-disciplined. Thus, if it turns out that "back then" people were actually saying the very same thing, we've taken the first step to forcibly deflate this hot-air balloon.

ARE PARENTS PERMISSIVE?

To call attention to the vintage of our whines—or, if you prefer, how long our gripes have been fermenting—is just one of many possible responses when we hear sweeping claims about how children nowadays are spoiled because parents fail to set limits. A reasonably thoughtful person might point out that there are actually three assertions being made here: parents don't set limits, children act in a way we might describe as "spoiled," and the first problem causes the second.

Each of those claims needs to be proved; anecdotes, even the sort that make us shake our heads and click our tongues, simply aren't sufficient. There has to be some reason to believe that the stories we hear, or the behaviors we happen to observe, are representative of the population at large. And that, in turn, means we need to define more precisely what we're talking about. "Parents let their kids get away with murder" or "Kids are out of control" are not testable propositions—not just because they're vague but because they're infused with the values of the speaker, who is really saying, "Parents put up with behaviors that I think they should forbid" or "I disapprove of how some kids act." If we want to claim that more people act this way today than did those of prior generations, we need a clear way to circumscribe what we're looking for so we can compare data from different eras.

So how should we evaluate a complaint such as "We live in a child-centered society where children's wants and demands are increasingly being given priority"?[25] Our first response might be to ask how that assertion squares with deeply disturbing social indicators such as the high number of American children in poverty or the fact that juveniles are still tried and imprisoned as adults. More prosaically, we could point out that, as a culture, our attitude toward children appears to be ambivalent at best. Parents love their own kids but often have little patience with everyone else's. Sometimes we find children adorable, but more often we seem to regard them as nuisances. A "good" child is one who sits still and keeps quiet. Surveys of American adults consistently find what one newspaper report called "a stunning level of antagonism not just toward teen-agers but toward young children as well." Substantial majorities of our fellow citizens say they disapprove of kids of all ages, calling them rude, lazy, irresponsible, and lacking in basic values.[26]

In the 1930s, a researcher named Harold Anderson commented, "I think as a culture we have not yet learned to like children." One would have a tough time making a case that things have changed since then. In 2012, the late Elisabeth Young-Bruehl devoted an entire book to the "huge range of anti-child social policies and individual behaviors" still in place.[27] Child-centered? It's not clear that America today could be described even as child-*friendly*.

On the other hand, there has been a shift over a long period of time toward regarding children as individuals who possess intrinsic worth, as human beings who should be treated humanely. Children in the industrialized world today are much less likely to be forced to work, or to be viewed chiefly as economic assets, than they were as recently as the 1800s.[28] Similarly, they are less likely to be seen as sinful creatures whose wills must be broken than was the case a few centuries ago. In the New England of Puritan times, children were publicly flogged. Play was viewed as unacceptably frivolous, even for toddlers. Babies were described as "filthy, guilty, odious, abominable" beings and dealt with accordingly.[29] Indeed, infanticide was common throughout human history, with children routinely abandoned, tortured, and sexually abused. "Prior to modern times I have not been able to find evidence of a single parent who would not today be put in jail for child abuse or neglect," writes the historian Lloyd deMause.[30]

The answer to our question, then, depends on the time span we're considering and the definition we're using. Yes, there has been "greater expression of affection toward children and a greater interest in their development . . . over the past several centuries in industrial Western societies."[31] But that doesn't mean our culture is "child-centered" in the specific, and pejorative, way that phrase is often intended, with adults' needs and wishes made subservient to those of children.

And what if the question is whether parents today are more "permissive"? Again, we need to proceed carefully. Does that word refer to treating kids more humanely, giving them something to say about what happens to them, allowing them to be heard as well as seen, acknowledging their preferences rather than bending them to our will? Does it mean we're willing to take our cue from young children about when they're hungry or tired rather than making them eat or sleep when it's convenient for us? That we're willing to allow kids to fool around and have fun sometimes, and to comfort them when they're sobbing?

In fact, these do seem to be just the sorts of attitudinal changes to which the word *permissive* referred when it was first used. And in those days the general trend was indeed in that direction. One writer refers to "the ideology of permissive child rearing" that characterized advice to parents in the 1930s[32]—a decade that produced a book with the revelatory title *Babies Are Human Beings*. Another writer points out that what was described at the time as the "new permissiveness . . . reads today like common sense."[33] People were starting to talk about children's needs and to realize that they progress through stages of development such that they may not be ready to assume a given responsibility or acquire a proficiency just because we demand that they do so. However, this progress didn't take place in simple, linear fashion. The strictness that gave way to permissiveness was itself a reversal of an approach to child rearing during the nineteenth century that had been more responsive to children's needs.[34] Things had gotten worse before they got better again. And that reversal was later reversed once more: The 1950s brought retrenchment, as even some of these basic principles were once again viewed with suspicion.[35]

Today, the word *permissiveness* has a different meaning: It doesn't signify humane treatment or a willingness to nurse infants when they're hungry; it means coddling kids in a way that's unhealthy by definition. (Interestingly, the connotation of *coddle* also shifted. It once meant "to treat tenderly"; now it means "to overindulge.") Permissive parenting these days is understood by the general public as well as by developmental psychologists to refer to an approach in which demands and limits are rarely imposed and children are pretty much free to do what they like.[36]

So has any researcher tried to quantify the number of parents who could reasonably be classified as permissive in this sense? Most people who refer to an epidemic of permissive parenting just assume that this is true, that everyone knows it, and therefore that there's no need to substantiate the claim. My efforts to track down data—by combing both scholarly and popular databases as well as sending queries to leading experts in the field—have yielded absolutely nothing. I'm forced to conclude that no one has any idea how many parents could be considered permissive, how many are punitive, and how many are responsive to their children's needs without being permissive *or* punitive. (The tendency to overlook that third possibility is a troubling and enduring trend in its own right.) In short, *there is absolutely no evidence to support the claim that permissiveness is the dominant style of parenting in our culture, or even that it's particularly common.*

Notice, though, that many authors, journalists, and casual commentators aren't just saying that lots of parents fail to set limits. They're asserting that this is true today to a greater extent than it has been in the past, that permissiveness is, as *Time* magazine put it, a problem of "our age" because there has been an "erosion" of parental authority. Of course, if there's no good snapshot available of current parenting practices based on a representative national sample, we have no evidence about whether these practices have changed over the years—and, if so, in what direction.

A few decades ago, John Goodlad visited more than a thousand classrooms across the country in an effort to draw informed conclusions about the kind of education that's offered to most American children. He found that schooling was overwhelmingly traditional—fact-based, teacher- rather than student-centered—notwithstanding common claims that progressivism was running rampant.[37] It would be dauntingly ambitious to attempt such a comprehensive investigation of parenting practices. Such a study would have to overcome a long list of methodological challenges, beginning with how permissiveness should be defined and how to determine the way any given parent actually parents.[38] (Asking both the parent and the child often yields different responses,[39] and, interestingly, it's the child's that often proves to be more accurate and more relevant.[40]) But no one, as far as I can tell, has even proposed such a study.

Again, I came to this conclusion only after a reasonably exhaustive search. But that process yielded a couple of tantalizing false leads. For example, after I published an essay in which I mentioned the dearth of research on the question, a psychologist named Jean Twenge wrote to tell me I was wrong. She directed my attention to two academic journal articles by a sociologist named Duane Alwin,[41] which I quickly tracked down—only to discover that the word *permissiveness*, or even a discussion of the idea, didn't appear in either of them.[42] In fact, these articles were virtually silent on the question of how children are actually raised. Rather, their focus was on the qualities that parents of different generations desired in their children. Alwin concluded that parents have come to be less concerned about raising kids to be obedient people and more likely to want them to be able to think for themselves. Of course there's no reason to believe that these parents raised their children more permissively, or that doing so would have been a logical strategy toward that end.

Then I discovered a book written by a political consultant and pollster named Mark Penn that dealt with trends in popular opinion. One chapter was devoted to raising children, and it included some intriguing poll results:

> Fifty-five percent of parents say they're strict, compared to only 37 percent who say they are permissive. Fifty-two percent of parents (and 58 percent of older parents) say it's better to guide children with "discipline and structure" than with "warmth and encouragement." And by more than 2 to 1, American parents say it is more important to make their children good citizens than it is to make them happy.[43]

An opinion poll is not the same as a scientific study, but these numbers do seem to offer a solid challenge to the conventional wisdom about permissiveness.[44] When the pollster then asked people for their impressions of *other* parents, those results, too, were striking. "A whopping 91 percent say that 'most parents today are too easy on their kids,' compared to only 3 percent who say most parents today are too strict."

The vast majority of people, in other words, are saying, "Almost everyone is permissive except me." So what should we make of this finding? It's certainly possible that respondents are mischaracterizing how they raise their own children, perhaps because they're eager to describe what they're doing along the lines of what they think they *ought* to be doing—and in our culture strict discipline, not permissiveness, is regarded as the ideal. But it seems more reasonable to doubt the accuracy of people's perceptions of what's happening in other families—perceptions that reflect the uncritical assumption that permissiveness is widespread in our culture. This belief is called into question by what we know to be true of our own parenting, so we're forced to resolve the dissonance by regarding ourselves as an exception to what we continue to assume is the rule. (Either that, or we believe that other children require a degree of strictness that our own children do not.)

But Penn instantly arrived at the opposite conclusion: If most parents think that they're strict but that others are lenient, well, "they're only half-right—and it's about the others. Today in America, nearly *all* parents are more permissive with their kids than in generations past, despite their self-perceptions." How in the world does Penn justify his certainty about this? Just as Twenge's determination to believe that parents are permissive led her to cite irrelevant evidence (about parents' desire for their kids to be independent thinkers), so Penn managed to justify that same conclusion primarily on the basis of his own conservative attitudes. (That he's a consultant for Democratic candidates shouldn't be surprising: As I pointed out in the introduction, even political liberals often sound like Fox News hosts as soon as the conversation turns to children.)

Like so many others who complain about how much worse things are today, Penn offered nothing to support his assertion that parents are "more permissive . . . than in generations past"; he had virtually no data from earlier times to compare to the results of his one-shot poll.[45] And he chose to ignore the results of that poll because they conflicted with what he just *knew* to be true: "It has become socially unacceptable to discipline children. . . . In the old days, kids just got the rod, or at least the riot act. Now they get picked up, timed-out, and negotiated with at great length."

Here's where things get interesting—and useful for helping us to understand why so many people share Penn's perceptions. The notion that disciplining children is out of fashion has attained the status of a meme, widely circulated in books, articles, and blogs. So let's look more closely at each of the three phrases in that last sentence of Penn's. First, "picked up" refers to the fact that "sixty percent of the parents in our poll declared that 'babies should be comforted whenever they cry.'" That's exactly the response to a crying baby that's supported by developmental research,[46] so one might be dismayed that only three out of five parents accept this basic guideline of infant care. But Penn is evidently a fan of the long-discredited "let 'em cry it out" approach. What's more, he seems to view any departure from that approach as evidence of permissiveness.

Second, he refers to the popularity of giving children time-outs—that is, forcibly isolating them if a parent decides they have misbehaved.[47] This is not only an example of discipline but of *punitive* discipline. Because spanking isn't involved, however, we're supposed to conclude that "it has become socially unacceptable to discipline." Penn acknowledges that two-thirds of parents still approve of spanking, but, remarkably, this fact, too, is offered as evidence of permissiveness.[48] How? Because the approval rate was even higher a few decades earlier. (Note, too, that these numbers refer to *attitudes* about spanking. The proportion who actually engages in the practice appears to be higher still.[49])

Penn's last reason for pronouncing contemporary parenting permissive is that children are "negotiated with at great length." Here he refers to poll responses suggesting that many parents say that if they had a nine-year-old child "who screamed a curse word at you and said he/she hated you," or a fifteen-year-old who experimented with drugs, they would respond by having a conversation with the child to figure out what was going on. (In the first example, a substantial number actually said they would respond with punishment.) There is nothing in the responses to indicate that such conversations would assume the form of a "negotiation"—let alone that it would take place "at great length." Those are Penn's rhetorical embellishments, apparently intended to invite us to join him in rolling our eyes at the very idea that anyone would try to *talk* with a child who does something troubling rather than just resorting to punishment. And again, he believes that doing the former constitutes permissiveness.

I've reviewed Penn's account in some detail here partly because he's one of the few writers on the subject to present hard numbers, even if they are from a poll, but mostly because the spin that he gives to those numbers reflects a perspective that is widely shared and enormously revealing. Even in the absence of data—indeed, even in the presence of data to the contrary—many people are willing to pronounce our culture (though not themselves) appallingly permissive. If spanking enjoys anything less than universal support, if children are punished by any means other than spanking, if parents are willing to have a conversation with them when they do something wrong—well, that's all the proof we need.

The idea that we live in a permissive or child-centered culture also seems unshaken despite what things are like for children at school, where they spend a significant portion of their waking hours. There, a variety of behavior management programs—consisting of some version of bribes and threats—are employed to make students comply with rules that they almost certainly had no role in helping to formulate. The emphasis is not on promoting moral development but on eliciting compliance. More broadly, John Dewey's characterization of most schools remains accurate today: The "center of gravity" is outside the child. We say, in effect: This is the curriculum; this is how we will evaluate you; these are our rules and requirements, all of them having been set up long before we met you. Your needs and interests—or even those of an entire class—will have no bearing on what we do and what we demand.

Some of this is obviously a function of having twenty or thirty kids in a room and of the time and effort required to create a "learner-centered" environment. But not all of it can be explained that way, particularly since some teachers and schools have shown that it *is* possible to proceed more by asking than telling.[50] Rather, there is an ideology at work here that's similar to our approach to parenting—one defined by a fundamental lack of respect for children, by puritanical beliefs about the benefits of frustration and failure, by the assumption that children are best prepared for future unpleasantness by subjecting them to unpleasantness while they're small, and by a view of human nature that implies little can be accomplished without employing rewards and punishments as inducements to learn or to treat others kindly.

One may endorse or oppose this ideology, but how is it possible to suggest with a straight face that the main problem with American parenting or schooling is that punitive discipline is *rare* or that we're overly inclined to listen to our children's points of view? It's as though a maga-zine were to announce on its cover that people today spend an alarming amount of time reading for pleasure ("Bibliophilia Craze! Does It Spell Doom for Electronic Entertainments?") or that most of us are exces-sively careful to eat healthy foods in appropriate quantities ("Junk Foods a Distant Memory in Slenderized America"). The difference is that *this* weird inversion of reality regarding how we raise children isn't a curious anomaly that showed up in a single periodical. Somehow it seems to have become the conventional wisdom.

ARE YOUNG PEOPLE SPOILED?

A subset of adults has always viewed those who are significantly younger than themselves with something between impatience and contempt. Per-haps it's because "every generation in power has issues ceding that power to the next. Boomers [born between 1946 and 1964] were called hippies and dropouts [by their parents]. GenXers [born between the early 1960s and early 1980s] were labeled slackers. . . . [Yet] these two generations conveniently and hypocritically overlook their own youthful dalliances when judging this new cohort" known as Millennials.[51]

Of course there's no law against bellyaching—about how parents raise kids (the subject of the preceding section) or about the kids themselves (to which we'll turn our attention now). But bellyachers who wish to be taken seriously have their work cut out for them. They must first be clear about whom they're proposing to describe. School-age children? Teen-agers? Young adults? Second, in order to argue that things are worse now than then, they have to specify when "then" was. Are they comparing today's youth to those of a generation ago? Half a century ago? Third, exactly what characteristics are supposed to describe that cohort of tens of millions of youngsters: Are they spoiled? (And what, exactly, does that mean?) Self-indulgent? Self-centered? Selfish? Lazy? Do they think too highly of themselves? Are they narcissistic?

When you think about it, each of those labels denotes a different quality or set of qualities. Thus, if the goal is not just to hurl insults (like a 2013 *Time* cover story, which labeled Millennials "overconfident and self-involved," "stunted," "lack[ing] . . . empathy," "famous for . . . entitle-ment") but to offer a testable proposition for which data can be collected, it's necessary to define one's terms. Obviously *some* kids you've met, like some adults, could be described by any of those unpleasant adjectives. But how many more kids than adults, or how many more kids today as compared to kids at some point in the past, would have to be spoiled or self-centered or whatever? And *how* spoiled? And how exactly could that be proved?

Supporting data on any of these issues were pretty much nonexis-tent until a few years ago, when Jean Twenge and her colleagues began to publish papers in scholarly journals[52] as well as popular books[53] that purported to confirm just about any unfavorable description one might think of attributing to young people: greedy, lazy, selfish, superficial, you name it. The articles contain survey data; the books are polemics that re-flect her deeply conservative values about parenting, education, and other issues. Both offer a consistent message that kids today think too well of themselves, scoring higher on measures of self-esteem, self-confidence, and even narcissism than their counterparts did in earlier surveys. She also contends that young people today are more anxious and unhappy, which is a bit challenging to try to reconcile with her assertion that they like themselves more.[54]

Not surprisingly, Twenge's claims—and her catchy, snide label "Gen-eration Me"—have received an enormous amount of media attention. (*Washington Post*: "U.S. Teens Brimming with Self-Esteem"; *The Telegraph* [UK]: "Baby Boomer Parents Raising a Smug Generation"; *Time*: "The ME ME ME Generation.") Here, after all, was a social scientist saying she had proof that unflattering stereotypes of young people, the very stereotypes that had long been stoked by the media, were true. But a close reading of Twenge's articles leaves one with the impression that she has repeatedly cut corners in order to marshal support for her sour view of youth. In-deed, as soon as other researchers in her field, including experts in data analysis, inspected her publications, red flags began to pop up. And when they systematically reanalyzed her data, her claims essentially evaporated.

Given the attention that Twenge's assertions have attracted, it may be worth taking a few moments to explain exactly why her research proves unpersuasive. First of all, not only does she generalize (almost always un-favorably) about an enormous and diverse population of young people, but her definition of "young people" sometimes lumps high school students together with thirty-year-olds, as if they shared a single psycholog-ical profile. Second, the definition of "then" in her now/then comparisons keeps changing and is chosen with no apparent theoretical justification. Sometimes today's youth are compared to those who were surveyed in 1952, sometimes in 1975, sometimes in 1988, and so on.

But the problems with her methodology go deeper. Because it's dif-ficult to find a single survey taken by people of the same age at two dif-ferent points in time, Twenge combines multiple surveys despite the fact that they may have been constructed differently, and even though they may have been filled out by "convenience samples," meaning whichever college students happened to volunteer to answer some questions by their professor. There's reason to doubt whether any one of those samples represents all college students, and there's even more reason to doubt whether they represent everyone in that age group. (Only about 20 per-cent of eighteen- to twenty-four-year-olds attend four-year colleges.) Most dubious of all is the practice of tossing together several such sam-ples from different time periods and assuming, as Twenge often does, that they can be compared with one another, thus permitting the conclu-sion that, say, self-esteem is higher in college students today than it was two decades ago.[55]

When Twenge claims that young people today don't merely think more highly of themselves but are more *narcissistic*, a whole new set of problems appears. The psychiatric diagnosis of narcissism, which is dif-ferent from what most of us mean when we casually describe someone as narcissistic, is based on a combination of characteristics. Some of them are clearly pathological (exploitativeness, self-aggrandizement), some of them are merely obnoxious (self-admiration, a sense of entitlement), and some of them are actually associated with healthy functioning (lead-ership, confidence, self-sufficiency).[56] Depending on which features are emphasized, it's possible to find data to support virtually any generaliza-tion about "narcissism"—for example, to show that it's either positively or negatively related to self-esteem.[57] (If the relationship is negative, which isn't as surprising as you may think, then the assertion that young people today are both more narcissistic and possessed of higher self-esteem is problematic on its face.[58])

When Twenge claims to have discovered higher levels of narcissism in today's youth, she's talking about overall scores on the Narcissistic Personality Inventory (NPI)—a goulash of a questionnaire that's looking for both admirable and troubling attributes. It's not clear, then, that a rise in such scores would be worrisome even if it could be proved.[59] What's more, the increase she reports is actually quite small, representing only a few numerical points on the survey.[60] And that raises yet another objection: There's no agreed-upon number of positive responses that would officially qualify one as a narcissist—or, collectively, would signify that a given generation is narcissistic. What we do know is that, in absolute terms, most people don't score very high—they didn't then, and they don't now—so what we're really talking about are "degrees of low narcissism."[61] There's nothing in the data to support Twenge's (or the media's) dramatic claims of an "epidemic" of narcissism in today's youth.

But that's not all. When a group of researchers from three different universities added a new dataset to see if they could replicate Twenge's findings, not only did they find minuscule differences on the NPI between college students in earlier versus later samples, but it turned out that the only statistically significant difference that did show up was with women, who usually score lower than men. Combine that fact with what we know about the benign components of the measure and you start to realize that if this line of research really has turned up any meaningful change over the last couple of decades, it may be mostly an increased sense of self-confidence in young women.[62]

Because Twenge also claims that young people's *self-esteem* is on the upswing, those same researchers, in a separate study, looked for changes in the way high school students viewed themselves in 1977 and in 2006. They used a huge national dataset of more than four hundred thousand high school seniors over three decades who were asked the same questions. And again the researchers came up empty-handed, failing to discover any evidence of the rise that Twenge talks about—not just in self-esteem but also in egotism, self-perceived intelligence, or individualism.[63] For good measure, they checked to see whether adolescents in the 2000s were more unhappy, lonely, hopeless, or antisocial than those in the 1970s were. The results: No, no, no, and no.

As other experts have chimed in, the credibility of Twenge's claims threatens to melt away completely. One pair of researchers used the National Longitudinal Study of Youth (eight waves of adolescents and young adults assessed between 1994 and 2008) and the Americans' Changing Lives database (four waves of adults of different ages between 1986 and 2002). They found that self-esteem levels may be different for adolescents than for young adults, and for young adults than for older adults, but the levels for a given age group don't seem to be any different from one *time period* to the next. "The average self-esteem trajectory has not changed across the generations born in the 20th century."[64] (In the case of yet another claim by Twenge and her associates, that college freshmen today think more highly of their academic ability and creativity than freshmen did decades earlier, a scholar has posted the actual survey results over time so one can see at a glance just how misleading Twenge's conclusions are.[65])

Finally, a group of researchers at the University of Illinois undertook yet another reanalysis of Twenge's narcissism data and found "little or no trend over time. With the inclusion of still more data [from other student surveys], the evidence for Generation Me disappears." That they, like the other investigators, were unable to replicate Twenge's results didn't really surprise them, though. As they explained it:

> Every generation of young people is substantially more narcissistic than their elders, not because of cultural changes, but because of age-related developmental trends. . . . When older people are told that younger people are getting increasingly narcissistic, they may be prone to agree because they confuse the claim for generational change with the fact that younger people are simply more narcissistic than they are. The confusion leads to an increased likelihood that older individuals will agree with the Generation Me argument despite its lack of empirical support.

In other words, there's nothing unusual about today's cohort of young people. "Every generation is Generation Me. That is, until they grow up."[66]

Once Twenge's claims are revealed to be essentially without foundation, there is nothing left. No one has ever tried to quantify the extent to which children are spoiled, let alone to compare that number to children in earlier generations, which means we have no way to substantiate the hypothesis that any of those adjectives—self-indulgent, self-centered, self-aggrandizing, lazy, selfish, narcissistic, or spoiled—are more descriptive of today's children (or high school students, or young adults) than of those from *x* decades ago.

If we're trying to get a broader fix on young people, however, there are a couple of findings that may be relevant. One study that combined multiple samples of college students over about thirty years (a questionable technique, remember) reported slightly lower levels of self-reported empathy in 2009 as compared to 2000, but there was no change during the two decades before that.[67] On the other hand, 88 percent of college freshmen in 2011 reported having done volunteer work in the past year, up from 82 percent a decade earlier—and 69 percent a decade before that.[68] "Having a career that benefits society," meanwhile, was identified as a particularly important life goal by a significantly greater proportion of eighteen- to thirty-four-year-olds than by those who were at least thirty-five years old.[69]

Frankly, I have my doubts about the relevance and significance of any of these findings. The generalizations one chooses to apply to the younger generation seem to depend mostly on the worldview and experiences of the person doing the generalizing. As we've seen, older people have always insisted that children are unusually spoiled, or that young adults are unusually egocentric or entitled. One can make such a case today, just as one can make the opposite case—that today's youth are more tolerant than their parents were and admirably committed to making the world a better place. But the overriding reality is that there is almost certainly "more variation among members *within* a generation than there is *between* generations."[70]

Unfortunately, the naysayers are more numerous and more emphatic, and they have a habit of offering the most negative possible interpretation of qualities that could just as easily be seen as laudable, or at least developmentally appropriate for an emerging adult. Why should focusing on one's projects and goals be construed as noxious egocentricity? Why should having faith in one's capabilities, and high expectations about what life has in store, be interpreted as "entitlement" or inflated self-esteem?[71] To deride young people this way, as Twenge and many others do, is not only unfair—and unsupported by good data—but doubly unfortunate in that it may create a self-fulfilling prophecy: Fling derogatory labels enough times and the people at whom they're flung may start to internalize those assumptions and live down to expectations.

DOES PERMISSIVE PARENTING CREATE SPOILED KIDS?

Even if a lot of parents were permissive and a lot of children were self-centered, these phenomena are not necessarily related. Those who criticize what they see as an indulgent style of child-rearing are obliged to show, rather than merely assume, that it explains the characteristics in children they find troubling.

There's nothing new about trying to link undesired outcomes to insufficiently traditional parenting. Indeed, the entire 1960s counterculture was attributed to parents—well, let's just say "blamed on" parents, given the assessment of that counterculture by those who did the attributing. Specifically, the fault was said to lie with moms and dads who supposedly let their offspring have their way too often. This connection seems to have been sparked in the spring of 1968 by a *New York Times Magazine* essay called "Is It All Dr. Spock's Fault?" written by a young sociologist named Christopher Jencks. "The new ethos . . . on leading college campuses," he declared, is the result of "upper-middle-class children who . . . are mostly products of permissive homes."[72]

The trouble was, the homes that Jencks proceeded to describe—and it's not clear how common they actually were—didn't seem permissive so much as simply respectful of children. They were defined by hands-on parenting, but the active involvement consisted of justifying rules on their merits (rather than demanding absolute obedience), listening to kids' reasons, and involving them in decision making. As Jencks saw it, these parents still relied on discipline to elicit compliance, but it was a version based more on wielding disapproval and guilt than on the crude employment of power.

Furthermore, despite his article's title (which was likely supplied by an editor), Jencks didn't entirely condemn what was happening on college campuses or the new generation's resistance to authoritarian institutions.[73] But a parade of conservatives who appropriated his thesis certainly did. For example, Spiro Agnew, soon to be Richard Nixon's vice president, turned this issue into one of his signature campaign tropes, blasting student radicals as "spoiled brats who have never had a good spanking. . . . [Their] parents learned their Dr. Spock and threw discipline out the window."[74]

One inconvenient fact for such critics, which didn't escape Jencks's notice, is that some of the products of those allegedly permissive households ended up to the political right of their parents, challenging the established order as rebellious Goldwater conservatives. But an even more decisive rejoinder to the basic argument is that there wasn't a shred of evidence to support it; indeed, there were several good reasons to question its plausibility. Barbara Ehrenreich pointed out that the young activists "were far from being the stereotyped products of permissiveness. In fact, they were no doubt among the hardest-working, most disciplined members of their generation."[75] Moreover, a social scientist who reviewed some empirical investigations of the issue found that they "demonstrated rather clearly that the political activity of young people . . . shows no substantial relationship with 'permissiveness.'"[76]

People with a strong distaste for what they viewed as indulgent parenting couldn't substantiate their contention that it bred political radicalism, so eventually a new charge was dredged up: Such parenting was now said to have produced a generation of narcissists. (Similarly, we're told, "Today, punishment has a bad reputation" and the result is that we find ourselves with "self-indulgent, out-of-control children."[77]) Is there any evidence to support these claims? As we've seen, the contention that there is more narcissism or self-indulgence in this generation doesn't hold water, but it's still possible that, to whatever extent some young people do turn out that way, it's because of how they were raised.

Most writing about the childhood roots of narcissism is theoretical or based on clinical case studies. Psychoanalysts tend to argue that a lack of parental love and empathy, a diet of coldness and indifference, is what produces narcissists. Grandiosity is an attempt to compensate for the care one failed to receive as a child. By contrast, theorists who believe that a parent's approval should have to be earned, and should be used to reinforce desired behaviors, are inclined to think that "noncontingent" or excessive praise would permanently swell the little ones' heads.

It would be reassuring to be able to report that research offers a definitive verdict on the matter, but that's not the case. As I mentioned earlier, it's possible to "prove" that narcissism is a product of just about any parenting style depending on which aspects of the diagnosis are emphasized. Moreover, the handful of studies that have been conducted are small, and their methodology doesn't inspire a lot of confidence: One or two hundred college students are given a fifteen- or thirty-minute questionnaire that's designed to tap narcissistic qualities and that asks about how they were raised. That's pretty much it. Apart from the doubts one may entertain about the accuracy of a twenty-year-old's memories of early childhood, self-report measures are often problematic—and particularly so, for obvious reasons, when we're asking *narcissists* to describe themselves.[78]

In any case, the effects in most of these studies aren't particularly large, even when they reach conventional levels of statistical significance. When viewed together, moreover, the results are actually inconsistent. If there's any generalization to be made about this line of research, it's that children who score (a little) higher on measures of narcissism are at least as likely to have been raised by strict or cold parents as by permissive or overindulgent parents.[79] Meanwhile, "healthy, *adaptive* narcissism in young adulthood is predicted by early gratification of physical and psychological needs."[80]

And what about outcomes that are less serious than narcissism, even if they're still troubling? Can permissiveness be held responsible for these? Some proclamations along these lines seem like common sense, but that may be because they're based on circular reasoning: "Spoiling kids produces spoiled kids." Hard evidence is hard to come by, but one large study, published in *Pediatrics*, did turn up an interesting result. When parents of three-year-olds were questioned, there was indeed something they did that correlated strongly with the likelihood that their children, two years later, would be unusually loud, disobedient, argumentative, demanding, and mean. However, it wasn't indulgent parenting that contributed significantly to this profile of the classic spoiled kid. It was the use of spanking.[81]

By the same token, if we believed that young people lacked empathy, what generalization, if any, might we tentatively offer about how they were probably raised? Well, we've had the answer to that question for many years: Look for old-school parenting, precisely the sort that conservative critics of our "permissive" age recommend. It's easy to parody liberal "let's talk it out" child rearing, but the greater danger—and the far more common reality—is for kids to be bullied or bribed into obedience. The result is that they may never progress beyond the level of pure self-interest. (I'll say more in the following chapter about what *does* promote empathy and concern for others.)

It's also possible that self-centeredness is connected to the extraordinary emphasis on achievement and winning in contemporary America: schooling that's focused on mastering a series of narrowly defined academic skills in rapid succession, that's measured by nearly continuous standardized testing, that leaches from the school day into the evening with copious amounts of homework, and that's defined by a desperate competition for awards, distinctions, and admission to selective colleges, the point being not merely to do well but to triumph over everyone else. Indeed, research has long shown that competitive individuals—or people who have been instructed to compete—tend to be less empathic, less generous, and less trusting. That makes perfect sense when you think about it: If other people have been defined as obstacles to your own success, why would you be inclined to help them or see things from their point of view?[82]

If we're looking to identify likely sources of narcissism or egocentricity, we might do well to consider unresponsive parenting or achievement pressures. Here, too, there's probably no simple, satisfying cause-and-effect relationship. The one thing that *is* clear is that no persuasive reason exists to hold permissiveness responsible.

CHAPTER 2

Parenting in Perspective

One evening, as a group of us waited for a meeting to begin at the high school our children attended, a mother mentioned that she had figured out a way to make her daughter's phone shut down automatically at a certain hour, thereby preventing her from texting when, in the mother's opinion, she ought to be doing homework or sleeping. Somewhat un-diplomatically, I pointed out to this woman that she had excluded her daughter from any role in figuring out whether there really was a problem with her texting and, if so, how it might be solved. The mother shrugged off my comment. "Sometimes," she replied with an air of self-satisfaction, "you just have to be the parent."

That sentence was still echoing in my ears the next morning. The mom hadn't objected to the way I characterized her intervention. She seemed perfectly willing to acknowledge that she had used coercion to achieve her goal of restricted phone use. But rather than simply defending that way of handling the situation, she took the position that her approach de-fines the essence of the parent's role—a position I found more troubling than what she had done to her child's phone, or even to her child.

Parenting at its core—or at least at its best—is a process of caring, supporting, listening, guiding, reconsidering, teaching, and negotiating.

There will be days when we lack the time, the skill, or the patience to do these things properly. But if we resort to compelling children to do what we want, or using force (physical or digital) to prevent them from doing what we don't want, then we should be willing to admit that our response was less than ideal. There's a big difference, after all, between forgiving ourselves an occasional lapse and not even recognizing that what we did *was* a lapse.

Suppose, then, that this mom had said, "Sometimes you can't be the parent; you have to resort to being the dictator." I still might want to challenge her as to whether that's really true and ask her to reflect on all that's at stake: the need to help children take more responsibility for (and learn how to regulate) their own actions, the importance of inviting them to figure out how to persuade us that their position is reasonable, the urgency of making sure that we take them seriously and treat them respectfully. What's more, imposing our will on kids just teaches them to do the same with others when they find it possible and expedient to do so.

This mother might have disagreed with me about any of this, but if she at least had distinguished between a parent and a dictator (rather than equating the two), she would have avoided rationalizing her action by pretending that it was implicit in the very idea of parenting. Better yet, she might have put it like this: "Sometimes it's easier to impose our will on kids, but we have to resist that temptation . . . and be the parent instead."

IN DEFENSE OF "WORKING WITH"

So what does it mean to "be the parent"—or to be a *good* parent? These are critical questions in their own right, but they may also help us solve a puzzle suggested by the last chapter: If there's little support for claims about a rise in permissive parenting (or the number of spoiled or narcissistic children), how is it that such claims are widely accepted? Why are so many people willing, even eager, to believe them?

I'll be (relatively) brief in laying out a vision of high-quality parenting, mostly because I've done so at length in another book.[1] But let me say clearly at the start that by criticizing the critics, as I've been doing here—by challenging the casual assertion that most parents are too indulgent—I'm not defending mainstream approaches to parenting. While I don't endorse permissiveness (in the latter-day sense of non-interference), I suspect that most parents are so *fearful* of being permissive, or even of having other people accuse them of this, that they overcompensate by being excessively controlling.

In reviewing popular books and articles written for parents, I'm struck again and again by how their focus is on how to elicit compliance. There's considerable variation in the *strategies* they propose, from bullying to bargaining, from techniques frankly modeled on animal training to subtler forms of manipulation. But the animating question in such texts is rarely "What do kids need, and how can we meet those needs?" Rather, it's "How can you get your kid to do whatever you want?"[2]

The consumers of such advice seem to crave permission to feel good about making children feel bad. Thus, there's an inexhaustible audience for declarations that we're too permissive, that the main task for parents is to set more limits, impose more stringent regulations, devise more clever strategies for getting obedience—and to do so without regret. (Sample book title: *Don't Be Afraid to Discipline.*) We seem to want absolution for establishing this sort of relationship with our children, perhaps because we can't entirely silence our nagging—and appropriate—doubts about doing so.

Parenting authors are happy to oblige, telling us not to bother explaining the reason for our demands, to pay no attention to children's objections, even if they have logic on their side. "Don't take any crap from your kids when you make a decision. You're in charge," says Fred Gosman. "One should expect a child to simply do what he is told most of the time," says Robert Shaw. "Your word, not your reasoning, is what matters," adds Wendy Mogel. "Calmly ignor[e] his arguments."[3]

In short: I *am* the boss of you. Do whatever I demand, or else.

Some of us find this way of treating children intrinsically objectionable. But for anyone whose verdict depends on the result it produces, a mountain of research has established the detrimental impact of a single-minded focus on obedience, of relying on control and making children suffer when they act in a way that displeases the parent. Euphemisms and rationalizations aside, this is parenting defined mostly by power. And power is exactly what it teaches kids—with results that are all too apparent.

Elsewhere I've reviewed a number of studies on this topic—showing, for example, that children raised by parents who rely on punishment and coercion are especially likely to be disruptive and aggressive with their peers, even at the age of three, the consequence being that other children may not want to have anything to do with them.[4] Subsequent research has confirmed such findings, and the most interesting of the newer studies have looked at what parents did at one point in time and then evaluated how their children were faring years later (in an effort to sort out cause and effect).[5] Thus, a Canadian study investigated how two- to five-year-old children were being raised and then checked back after eight years had gone by. Punitive parenting, it turned out, was associated with higher levels of aggressive behavior, more anxiety, and also less helpfulness and sharing.[6] A US study discovered that stricter, less sensitive parenting produced children who were more likely to be overweight two years later, even after adjusting for family income.[7] And many other studies have found a variety of negative outcomes linked to the use of spanking in particular.[8]

What about permissive parenting? Assessing its effects is tricky because not all researchers distinguish between parents who can't be bothered to respond when their children do something wrong (or need help), on the one hand, and those who, with care and deliberation, choose a policy of minimal intervention, on the other. However, there is some evidence that even the former, which few of us regard as ideal, may be less damaging than authoritarian parenting. One study found that the extent to which children were punished was a powerful predictor of how aggressive and antisocial they were years later, whereas the use of "lax, inconsistent rules" was not.[9] Another study, which assessed older children and their parents, discovered that authoritarian parenting was associated with lower levels of "family satisfaction" but that permissiveness had no negative effect.[10]

The good news, though, is that it's not necessary to choose between punitive, power-based parenting and the kind of family environment in which there is a lack of structure (permissiveness) or a lack of parental involvement (neglect). I don't mean just that we can replace an either/

or choice with a continuum on which there are many gradations. That's certainly true, but a span between the extremes of "authoritarian" and "permissive" actually doesn't represent much of an improvement. What we need is a different approach altogether. Sometimes the alternative to black and white isn't gray; it's, say, orange.

Many theorists and researchers follow Diana Baumrind in nominating "authoritative" parenting as a third possibility, one that supposedly captures an optimal blend of warmth and support with firm control and predictable enforcement of rules. But I prefer not to use that term, mostly because it denotes more of a power-based approach to parenting than many people realize—apparently reflecting the traditional values that Baumrind personally endorses.[11] Furthermore, when you look closely at studies that purport to show the benefits of authoritative parenting, they have sometimes defined the term differently from the way Baumrind meant it. The positive results they report are due to an approach that features less (or even no) emphasis on control.[12]

Instead, I find it more useful to talk about "working-with"—as opposed to "doing-to"—parenting. This phrase emphasizes collaboration more than control, and love and reason more than power. It also includes these elements:

- accepting children unconditionally—loving them for who they are, not for what they do,
- providing regular opportunities for children to make decisions about matters that affect them,
- focusing more on meeting children's needs and providing guidance than on eliciting compliance,
- regarding misbehavior as an occasion for problem solving and teaching, rather than as an infraction for which the child should be subjected to punitive "consequences," and
- looking beneath a child's behavior in order to understand the motives and reasons that underlie it.

"Working-with" parenting overlaps with what other writers have called "autonomy-supportive," "responsive," or "empathic" parenting. It's quite different from a hands-off, disengaged style (permissiveness) as well as from an approach that emphasizes firm control, even when administered with warmth (Baumrind's authoritativeness). And it should also be distinguished from the sort of parenting that relies on subtle, often insidious, kinds of control: time-outs and other examples of what might be called "punishment lite," attempts to play on children's guilt, and the use of positive reinforcement (including praise) in place of threats—all to get kids to please us. As I'll argue in the next chapter, these, too, are forms of "doing to" parenting, particularly if they lead a child to believe that our love comes with strings attached.[13]

While definitions and emphases vary from one study to the next, there is by now an impressive body of research to show that something reasonably close to what I'm calling working-with parenting is not just benevolent but also beneficial. One study found, for example, that very young children were more receptive to what their parents suggested if the parents had been responsive to their needs earlier. Another showed that kindergarten-age children whose parents routinely provided them with explanations and choices were better adjusted several years later, both socially and academically, as compared with kids whose parents were more controlling. Yet another study discovered that the healthiest young adolescents, psychologically speaking, were those whose parents were accepting of them and avoided using love as a form of manipulation.[14]

One of the most powerful results of such parenting, though—and the most relevant to our concerns here—concerns children's connections with, and attitudes toward, others. A few years ago, my local newspaper featured a comment by an academic who writes about children's development, someone I knew slightly and regarded as generally thoughtful. He was quoted as saying, "You can make your kids self-centered by focusing too much on their needs." I wrote to him, mentioning that I had heard statements to that effect for many years but had never come across any evidence to support this view. I wondered whether he knew of some.

I suppose I shouldn't have been surprised that he never wrote back because, in fact, the available research strongly supports exactly the opposite position. Among its many advantages, warm, responsive parenting—the sort that is sometimes ridiculed and confused with over-indulgence—is particularly likely to help children become compassion-ate, generous, and empathic.[15] By contrast, power-based discipline and control, including punishment, often interferes with children's moral de-velopment, undermines their capacity to feel others' pain, and reduces the likelihood that they'll reach out to help.[16] Why? Probably because meeting children's needs frees them from being preoccupied with those needs (and, by extension, with themselves), the result being that they can be more sensitive to *others'* needs.[17] Warmth and acceptance may not be sufficient to guarantee that children attend to others' emotional states and take steps to assist them. But attacking "overindulgence," or urging parents to say no to their children or be less committed to mak-ing them happy, does absolutely nothing to promote caring or reduce self-centeredness.

IDENTIFYING ERRORS

With this brief account of working-with parenting—and the evidence that supports it—we're now in a better position to address the question of why so many people seem convinced that our culture has been en-gulfed by a tidal wave of permissiveness.

To begin with, certain conceptual confusions make such assertions look more plausible than they really are. A few of these are generic lapses in logic and thinking that social psychologists have been docu-menting for quite some time. Consider, for example, what's been called the *availability bias*: inferring a general rule from an example of some-thing just because it's particularly striking or close at hand. You witness a kid screaming at the mall while her parents do nothing and conclude, "People let their children get away with anything nowadays! When *I* was growing up . . . " Or you leap from the fact that you held the door open for a couple of teenagers and they failed to say thank you, to "the younger generation today is all about me, me, me."[18]

But why do we overgeneralize from some experiences and not oth-ers? One reason is suggested by *confirmation bias*: the tendency to notice and remember those events that validate what we already believe. As a result, we become even more committed to those beliefs—regardless of whether they're true. If you're convinced that teenagers are selfish jerks, or that parents are wishy-washy, you'll attend disproportionately to occurrences that support those beliefs while swearing that you're just an objective observer of reality. "A man hears what he wants to hear and disregards the rest," as Paul Simon put it.

A different sort of delusion, one more closely related to the "Generation Me" myth, occurs when your attitudes shift as your life changes, yet you find it easier to attribute those shifts to external forces: Hey, don't look at me; it's the world that's going to hell. "The belief that society is changing for the worse . . . has been evident in every generation of the United States since the late 18th century," one group of researchers wrote. What's interesting is that this belief actually reveals more about "unrecognized changes in the self" than it does about society. Young adults who become parents may suddenly become convinced the crime rate has increased, even when it hasn't. Older adults whose reflexes and coordination have declined may think other drivers have become more reckless, even when there's no evidence that's true. And the conviction that everything's getting worse is associated with people who, for whatever reason, have become more conservative.

"When people fail to realize that personal changes are the source of their perceptions of decline," the same researchers continued, "they are open to conservative movements that treat these perceptions as though they are real, offering their own explanations for decline and proposing reactionary solutions." There's no shortage of examples of this phenomenon, but the way children and parenting are viewed certainly number among the most compelling.[19]

Beyond these general glitches in logic, other errors are specific to parenting. These consist of failing to make important distinctions—treating separate ideas (about how parents or children act, or about how they *ought* to act) as though they were interchangeable. One example we've already encountered is mistaking differences among developmental stages (self-absorption in young people) for differences among cohorts (self-absorption in *today's* young people). Here are a few more.

Confusing two kinds of spoiling. Some parents shower their children with possessions, buying toys and clothes and digital devices for them even when their bedrooms are already crammed to the point of bursting. But that's entirely different from the kind of spoiling that interests us here, which is said to result from comforting babies when they cry, allowing children to challenge our requests, frequently acceding to *their* requests, and so on. To apply a single label ("spoiling") to both phenomena isn't just sloppy; it also increases the likelihood that responsiveness will be condemned along with materialism. As a matter of fact, some parents who give their children too many things also give them too little time and affection—a very different pattern from what's usually classified as permissiveness or indulgence.

Confusing respect with deference. Author Wendy Mogel can barely contain her indignation about parents who "actually feel guilty about demanding respect from their children"![20] Her twin assumptions, which many others hold as well, are that kids have an obligation to be respectful and that parents who fail to insist on this are permissive pushovers.

But what is meant by *respect*? (1) Does it refer to treating others decently rather than rudely? In that case, sure, everyone should be respectful of everyone else—although *demanding* this, let alone enforcing such demands with threats, is hardly an effective strategy for making it happen. (2) Does it refer to an appreciation for the qualities of a particular person, such as courage or compassion? If so, then it's absurd to insist that children feel this way about someone just by virtue of age or position. (3) Does it refer to showing deference and even fear? This is the only sense in which "respect" can be compelled, and on closer inspection it does seem to be what some people are looking for. "Your child has a chance to demonstrate how much she honors you by cooperating promptly and without a fuss."[21] This is a demand for mindless obedience dressed up with a word that's more . . . respectable. (As Albert Camus put it, "Nothing is more despicable than respect based on fear.")

Now imagine a parent who tries to teach children the importance of showing respect in sense 1 (for all people), who tries to prove worthy of respect in sense 2, and who avoids demanding "respect" in sense 3. Is such a parent admirable or a shameful example of how our culture has lost its way? Those of us who vote for "admirable" may notice how rarely respect (in sense 1) is shown *to* children. Face it: Kids' objections are routinely dismissed by adults; their perspectives are seldom taken seriously; they are interrupted at will and frequently addressed in a tone that parents would never permit anyone to use with *them*. Such treatment isn't just common; it's expected—to the point that it seems a little odd even to talk about "treating children (dis)respectfully." We're not used to applying that word to children, only to adults. By the way they treat children, many tradition- ally minded parents are also setting an example of disrespectful behavior *for* them—and are likely to be outraged if the children proceed to imitate what they've seen.

Confusing working-with parenting with permissiveness. Earlier, I argued that permissiveness and authoritarian parenting don't exhaust the possi- bilities. Just because we're strongly opposed to the first doesn't commit us to accepting the second. Similarly, just because a parent isn't at all author- itarian doesn't necessarily mean he or she is permissive. Yet many people make precisely these assumptions.

It takes talent and time, care and courage to raise one's children in the way that I've described as "working with," but I regularly receive mail from parents who strive to do so and are dismayed to find themselves accused of negligence. In a doing-to culture, such parenting is confused with letting kids do whatever they want. Likewise, those who *endorse* a respectful approach to parenting are tagged as apologists for permissive- ness, even though that is not at all their position.[22]

This confusion might also be described as the product of a false di- chotomy, one in which a complete absence of limits is assumed to be the only alternative to traditional parenting: If we're not dictating and pun- ishing, then we must be saying toddlers are free to choose not to use a car seat. And presumably a child can—and, it's assumed, in the absence of tight regulation and threats, *will*—lie, steal, hit, treat everyone mali- ciously, eat nothing but ice cream, and never go to bed. As one writer warns, "When we don't train our children to behave, they train us to be their servants."[23] If you stretch the definition of "permissive" until it includes everyone who avoids spanking, or everyone who tries to talk with children when things go wrong, then you end up concluding, with Mark Penn, that permissive parenting is the norm in our society. It's not unlike the way a dictator sees the world: Without martial law we have lawlessness; what you foreigners insist on calling "democracy" obviously isn't the former, so it must be just a fancy term for the latter.

By the same token, if there's no room on your mental map of parenting possibilities for treating kids with respect and trying to minimize the assertion of power, then you might be inclined to accuse parents who do so of "thinking that children and parents are equals" or "trying to be their children's friends." (This is a variation of the idea that to "be the parent" is to be authoritarian. If you're not authoritarian, you must be something other than a parent.) A child who wants to have some control over her life, meanwhile, may hear herself described as "manipulative," and a mom or dad who supports her desire becomes "indulgent."

Ironically, it's not only working-with parenting, but also the subtler methods of control I mentioned earlier, that are incorrectly characterized as permissive. Whatever one thinks of using guilt, or praise and other rewards, to control children, such techniques are a far cry from a working-with approach—and they are worlds apart from coddling. But that may not be clear to someone who equates discipline with yelling, hitting, or coercion.

UNCOVERING VALUES

The optimistic implication of the preceding section is that a fear of spoiling, or an accusation of permissiveness, may be based on a simple misunderstanding—a misconceived definition, the conflation of two distinct ideas, the reduction of a rainbow of possibilities to black and white. Thus, all we'd need to do is sort out the differences between working-with and laissez-faire, or between disparate meanings of "spoiling" or "respect," and the result will be fewer unfounded fears and accusations. Break out the champagne!

But of course there's more to it than that. In many instances what we're faced with are not just errors but strong ideological convictions—about how kids ought to act or the proper role of a parent. Those convictions, in turn, are rooted in basic assumptions about human nature that are not so easily dislodged.

Such values and assumptions express themselves in a variety of ways, beginning with deep-seated nostalgia—for a time when people sent handwritten thank-you notes and dressed up for airplane flights, when the kid next door offered to mow your lawn, when a roomful of students rose as one to greet their teacher with a chorus of "Good morning, Miss _____!" Indeed, most books that are filled with bitter complaints about spoiled, lazy, and materialistic kids consist of extended comparisons with the old days, when kids knew their place and worked hard.[24] But of course, as we've seen, people have always pined for the good old days. "Did our cave-dwelling forbears feel nostalgia for the days before they were bipedal?" one biologist asks wryly. "Were hunter-gatherers convinced that swiping a gazelle from a lion was superior to that newfangled business of running it down yourself? And why stop there? Why not long to be aquatic, since life arose in the sea?"[25]

Whence the perpetual appeal of yearning for an earlier time? One psychologist puts it down to the disorientation caused by rapid changes. An essayist, himself seventy-seven years old, observes that "grumpy old geezers have been complaining about the world going to hell in a handbasket . . . since time-keeping began." He speculates that they're attempting to "soothe their regret at leaving" that world.[26] But when children's behavior and parenting are singled out for critical attention, something else may be going on. We need to look carefully at the way things ostensibly used to be and ask why *they* are regarded as more desirable.

One feature commonly attributed to parents in the olden days is an insistence that children be "well behaved." An emphasis on this characteristic suggests that *behaviors*—outward appearance and conformity with established rules of conduct—count for more than a person's inner state. Kids are supposed to be polite, deferential, pleasant, self-controlled. They should avoid making a scene or developing a reputation as a troublemaker. Calls for a return to old-fashioned strictness are largely demands to create and enforce these qualities.

Put it this way: If you were to make an argument against doing-to parenting, it's unlikely that someone would challenge you by asking, "But if we stopped using rewards and punishments, how could we make sure that our kids will be happy, psychologically healthy, genuinely concerned about others, critical thinkers who will fight against injustice and work for social change?" Instead, you would probably hear, "No rewards and punishments?? Then how will we get our kids to do what they're told, follow the rules, and take their place in a society where certain things will be expected of them whether they like it or not?" Indeed, there is evidence that greater concern about social conformity translates into more punitive and restrictive parenting.[27] Conversely, as I'll argue in chapter 8, those who want to raise kids who are willing to be nonconformists when the occasion calls for it have yet another reason to reject a "doing to" parenting style.

Permissiveness is seen as objectionable because it's believed that kids left to their own devices won't turn out the way we'd like. It's a particular set of goals, in other words, that animates traditional discipline. These goals require that children be monitored carefully, told exactly what to do, rewarded when they comply and punished when they don't. This agenda suggests a fundamental distrust of children (and perhaps of people in general), which indeed seems to waft off the pages of many parenting resources as well as writings about character education and discipline at school.[28] The author of a book called *The Pampered Child Syndrome*, for example, describes kids as "experts" at exploiting us and twisting our good intentions to their own selfish purposes. We may "want our children to express their feelings and be heard," but that sentiment will just be interpreted by *them* to mean "I should never do anything unless I feel like doing it."[29]

If you believe that we need to crack down on young reprobates— and keep a close watch on *all* children since any of them will likely turn into a reprobate given half a chance—then you will be appalled by parents who allow children too much freedom. In fact, a child's demand for freedom strikes some people as disturbing in itself, which is why so many seem determined to take kids down a peg, rein them in, teach them their place. This impulse is sometimes rationalized as being for the benefit of the child ("Better to learn now that the real world isn't going to coddle you!"), but people who talk this way seem to harbor a resentment of children and a resistance to allowing them to make their own decisions that has very little to do with what's in the best interests of the children themselves.

To lay the groundwork for recommendations rooted more in "doing to" than "working with," it's necessary to convince oneself and others that children at present are not controlled enough. "Description is prescription," the conservative columnist David Brooks observed. "If you can get people to see the world as you do, you have unwittingly framed every subsequent choice."[30] If we can keep up the pretense that adults are too permissive with children, then we're more likely to accept the recommendation that what children really need is . . . more control.

Perhaps we can make sense of such attitudes by understanding them in a wider social context. Could it be that it's not only kids who are seen as too big for their britches, that they represent one of several constituencies that wants more than they've traditionally been permitted? Privileges have been reserved for some and not others, of course, so maybe parenting is just another stage on which the slow, fitful struggle to make our society more egalitarian and inclusive is played out. Time was when African Americans paid a steep price for being uppity and not knowing their place. Women were expected to be satisfied with second-class jobs and smaller paychecks; those who spoke out about lack of opportunities, or the assumption that they had to play a caretaker role even at work, were described as shrill and pushy—or worse. Gays had to keep their identity a secret, and their desire to marry their life partners prompted an outpouring of rage as if the institution of marriage itself would somehow be imperiled.

Alongside race, gender, and sexual orientation, there is age—with discrimination not only of seniors but of, well, juniors. Of course some limits, based on lack of maturity, are reasonable, but one of the most entrenched norms in our society is that kids should shut up and do what they're told; whether what they've been told is reasonable doesn't even figure into it. Thus, what is portrayed as narcissism or entitlement—and blamed on the reliable bogeyman of permissive parenting—may really constitute something as simple as a demand on the part of young people to have some say about their lives and to be treated with respect.

To identify the primary problem with parenting as overindulgence—which traditionalists have done for centuries—is not only to distort reality but to change things for the worse by encouraging an acceleration of harmful practices and *dis*couraging parents from doing what makes sense. We're left wondering how many children have failed to get what they need because their parents were terrified of being regarded as insufficiently firm.

CHAPTER 3

Overstating Overparenting

Contemporary parents, we're told, are screwing up their kids in two distinct ways. First, they give in too readily, let children get away with too much, and fail to set limits. Those, of course, are the charges that have occupied us up to this point in the book. The second complaint, to which we now turn our attention, is that parents are overly solicitous: They do too much for their kids, shielding them from the hard knocks of life. From this perspective, a wide-angle view of our society reveals a landscape dotted with millions of well-meaning but misguided moms and dads who are—pick your metaphor—hovering over their children, raising them in a bubble, or cushioning them from unpleasant circumstances. Again and again we're warned that kids are being "overparented" and therefore that they aren't prepared for the harsh realities of adulthood.

These two narratives are very different from one another. To say that parents are permissive with their kids ("Do whatever you want") is obviously not the same as saying that they're too involved in their kids' lives ("Here, let me do that for you"). Indeed, it takes some mental gymnastics to explain how they could be guilty of both, particularly if permissiveness is understood as a kind of "underparenting."

Viewed from another perspective, though, the two accusations may be related. What matters is the *reason* parents are thought to be too protective and involved. If it's because they want to indulge or coddle their kids, then that begins to look like a form of permissiveness. Whether that really is the best way of understanding what's going on is a question to which we'll return. But regardless of whether the two narratives can be reconciled, one feature they clearly share is popularity. Both have been repeated so frequently that their accuracy has come to be taken for granted.

That's certainly true of the accusation that parents involve themselves too closely in their children's lives and don't allow them to fail. It's common to come across—in fact, it's hard to avoid—hyperbolic references in the media to "kids who leave for college without ever having crossed the street by themselves" and "'Lawnmower Parents' [who] have 'mowed down' so many obstacles (including interfering at their children's workplaces, regarding salaries and promotions) that these kids have actually never faced failure."[1] Just in the couple of years before this book went to press in 2013, articles about overparenting appeared in *The Atlantic,* the *New Yorker, Time, Psychology Today, Boston Magazine,* and countless newspapers and blogs.

In each case, just as with condemnations of permissiveness, the phenomenon being attacked is simply assumed to be pervasive; there's no need to prove what everyone knows. The spread of overparenting is vigorously condemned by journalists and social critics, but mostly on the basis of anecdotes and quotations from other journalists and social critics. On the relatively rare occasions when a writer invokes research in support of the claim that overparenting is widespread (or damaging), it's instructive to track down the study itself to see what it actually says.

A case in point: In 2013, several prominent American blogs, including those sponsored by *The Atlantic* and the *New York Times,* reported an Australian study purportedly showing that parents were excessively involved in their children's schooling. But anyone who took the time to actually read the study realized that the authors had just asked a handpicked group of local educators to tell stories about parents whom they personally believed were doing too much for their children. There were no data about what impact, if any, this practice had on the kids, nor was there any way to draw conclusions about how common the practice was—at least beyond this small, presumably unrepresentative sample. More remarkably, only 27 percent of the educators in the sample reported having seen "many" examples of this sort of overinvolved parenting. (This low number somehow did not make it into any of the press coverage.) If anything, the effect of the study was to raise doubts about the assumption that overparenting is a widespread problem. But the study's very existence allowed bloggers to recycle a few anecdotes, giving the appearance that fresh evidence supported what they (and many of their readers) already believed.[2]

Another example: In 2010, Lisa Belkin, a writer for the *New York Times Magazine,* devoted a blog post to an article in a California law review that declared a tilt toward excess "has dominated parenting in the last two decades." But how did the authors of the law review article substantiate that remarkable assertion? They included a footnote that referenced a 2009 *New York Times Magazine* column written by . . . Lisa Belkin.[3]

It's striking that evidence on this topic is so scarce that academic journals must rely on opinion pieces in the popular press. But in this case, the popular press was actually claiming that the trend had already peaked.[4] That was true not only of Belkin's column ("Could the era of overparenting be over?") but of a *Time* cover story ("The Growing Backlash Against Overparenting") that was cited by an essay in another academic journal. The latter essay began with the sweeping (and rather tautological) statement that an "epidemic" of overparenting was "running rampant"—which is exactly what its sources claimed was no longer true.[5] So who's right? There are, as far as I can tell, no good data to show that most parents do too much for their children. It's all impressionistic, anecdotal, and, like most announcements of trends, partly self-fulfilling.

Here's one more illustration of the misleading way in which those already committed to the overparenting story cite research to bolster their position. It's commonly claimed that children whose parents do too much for them will grow up with a sense of entitlement. Thus, given the supposed spread of overparenting, our society has raised a generation of obnoxiously entitled young people. A few years ago, a prominently placed article in the *New York Times* made just this claim, focusing on how students expect high grades as their due. The apparent justification for publishing this complaint as a news story was a "recent" study on the subject.

But that study, which at the time was actually more than a year old, had merely distributed questionnaires to students at a single university. Moreover, even if one took the results seriously, they had the effect of undermining the very conclusion they were being used to support, just like the Australian report. On all but one item on the questionnaire, a majority of the students—in most cases, a substantial majority—gave a negative answer to the questions intended to measure academic entitlement. Nevertheless, the *Times* invited readers to conclude that kids today feel entitled, presumably just because any of the students had said yes to any of the questions.[6] (Judging by the unusually large number of outraged letters to the editor published a few days later, readers didn't need much prompting to share this view.)[7]

Neither that study, nor the one published in Australia, has anything to teach us about the extent of overparenting or entitlement—except, perhaps, that neither phenomenon may be as common as is widely believed. But the articles that *mentioned* these studies, like many other publications taking the same position, do reveal something important: the strength of the ideological commitment that leads people to complain about an epidemic of overparenting.

AN ANATOMY OF INTRUSIVE PARENTING

Any serious discussion of this topic must begin by acknowledging that children benefit, psychologically and in other ways, from having parents who are closely connected to them and involved in their lives. This, according to a solid foundation of research, is true not only in early childhood but through adolescence and beyond. Warnings about the harms of overparenting often gloss over the fact that there's far more danger to children in having parents who aren't sufficiently involved in their lives.[8]

So why is disproportionate attention paid to the possibility of being *too* close? It could be due to the premium that our culture places on the value of self-sufficiency. We are deeply attached to the idea of not being too attached. We see creativity as a characteristic of separate selves rather than groups, and the heroes glorified in popular culture are mostly loners. Inevitably this value system colors our approach to parenting. When you think about it, the developmental milestones we celebrate are those dealing with the child's capacity to do things without assistance, not about her growing capacity for more sophisticated connection to others. The parent's job is to promote this independence, and the constant fear is that a child will be too clingy, will want to be carried rather than walk on his own two feet (first literally, then figuratively), will continue to need a parent's help at an age when we think he should be able to—and should want to—do that task alone. (At the end of this chapter, I'll focus on the version of this indictment that pertains to older adolescents and young adults.)

Few of us stop to question this reflexive equation of maturity with independence. That's why I found it surprising, even somewhat bracing, when Marilyn Watson, a developmental theorist and educator whose work I've long admired, suggested that parents should sometimes make a point of doing things for their children that the children are able to do for themselves. This advice reflects a commitment to balancing our support for the child's growing competence with the value we place on our relationship with the child and the trust she has in us, acknowledging the developmental importance of secure attachment. It's also a vote of confidence that kids will continue to acquire skills, and to enjoy demonstrating what they're capable of doing, even if they aren't always expected to fly solo as soon as they can. "Of course we can do too much for children, depriving them of the opportunity to stretch themselves," she concedes. "But we can also be too afraid that if we help our children or do things for them, they will take advantage of our largess and be 'spoiled.' What a terrible message of mistrust."[9]

To some extent, then, good parenting is about providing support, not just assisting with separation—and we ought to be skeptical about the cultural values that relentlessly privilege the latter over the former. Nevertheless, it is possible that some parents get carried away with providing support, so it's reasonable to ask whether overparenting is a legitimate cause for concern. The trouble is, as with claims about permissiveness, we can't say whether something is damaging or widespread until we're clear about exactly what the term means. "Overparenting," of course, is bad by definition: The prefix *over-* implies excess. But it's hard to determine how much harm it really does, or even how many people are guilty of it, until we've figured out how much parenting is too much. Or whether that's even the best way to frame the question.

Is there an ideal amount of closeness or involvement in a child's life? No, not that we can specify regardless of age or temperament. Some kids need more support even when they're older; others not only don't require it but actively resist it. And the demands of each situation also matter. We're likely to keep closer tabs on our children when they're in an unfamiliar neighborhood, or when the activity they're engaged in is intrinsically riskier.

Then, too, there's the possibility that we apply different standards depending on whom we're judging. What those people over there do with their children may seem to me like hovering, even though when I act in a very similar way with *my* children, I'm convinced that what I'm doing is perfectly appropriate—indeed, wonderfully loving. Thus, if it's hard to be sure whether a given interaction, or a pattern of interactions in a particular family, constitutes overparenting, how in the world can we apply that term to an entire culture?

Some books and articles stretch the concept to include parents who err on the side of keeping their children safe. But do we really want to condemn as excessive the use of safety helmets, car seats, playgrounds designed so kids will be less likely to crack their skulls, childproof medicine bottles, and baby gates at the top of stairs? One writer criticizes "the inappropriateness of excessive concern in low-risk environments," but of course reasonable people often disagree about what constitutes both "excessive" and "low risk." Even if, as this writer asserts, "a young person growing up in a Western middle-class family is safer today than at any time in modern history," the relevance of that relative definition of safety isn't clear. Just because fewer people die of disease today than in medieval times doesn't mean it's silly to be immunized. And perhaps young people are safer today *because* of the precautions that some critics ridicule.

Nor is it clear that the desire to protect children is new. "We want to believe there was a time when it was all very different—when kids could be kids, and parents weren't too risk averse to let their offspring grapple with the world's harshness," one journalist writes. "This is the idea embedded in much of the criticism one hears about contemporary child rearing." But historians have shown that "parents in the Middle Ages worried about their kids no less than we worry about ours today," and by the nineteenth century there is evidence of bars being placed on windows to protect toddlers from falling out as well as "leading strings" so that young children couldn't wander off during walks.[10]

Perhaps the question "How much protection—or involvement in a child's life—is too much?" is misconceived. It may be the *kind* rather than the *amount* to which we should pay attention—a distinction overlooked by an awful lot of people who write about the subject. One group of researchers defines overparenting as "a form of developmentally inappropriate parenting that is driven by parents' overzealous desires to ensure the success and happiness of their children." That form of parenting, they add, usually reflects "benevolent intentions," and the behaviors involved "may indeed be adaptive at modest levels." The same is true of the closely related phenomenon of *helicopter parenting*, a made-for-the-media phrase if ever there was one, which denotes "a version of overparenting in which parents demonstrate excessive involvement in their children's lives . . . [that fails] to allow for levels of autonomy suitable to their child's age."[11]

But here, too, the water quickly becomes muddied. How do we know when an intervention is "excessive" or "developmentally inappropriate," or how much autonomy *this* child needs or wants? Again, appropriateness may vary depending on the circumstances as well as the child's personality. So maybe the definition of problematic parenting isn't a function of how much, or even how, the parent gets involved. Maybe it has more to do with why. There are different reasons for helping or hovering, and some of them are healthier than others. With parents, as with children, to focus only on what we can see and measure is to ignore the all-important motives for what people do.

Suppose you or I conclude that a particular parent down the street phones or texts her child more often than necessary to assure his safety or is a little too involved with his homework. Can this be attributed to a legitimate difference in opinion about the risks of a trip downtown, or about how important it is that the child turn in a high-quality school assignment? Or are we looking at something more psychologically complex and potentially worrisome, such as the belief that the more you do for your children, the better you are as a parent? Worse, consider moms and dads "whose own self-esteem is crucially dependent on their child's success"—quoting here from an essay called "Overparenting and the Narcissistic Pursuit of Attachment."[12] Some parents use their children to meet their own emotional needs—and may be unaware that they're doing so.

In short, rather than just asking whether parents are doing too much for their kids, it may be more relevant to ask *for whom* they're doing it. At first glance it may seem as though these parents are guilty only of putting their children's "happiness ahead of [their] own" and are "heavily invested in their childhood at the expense of [the parents'] own lives."[13] But look again: Conspicuously sacrificing everything for one's children, such that one's very life seems to revolve around them, actually turns out to be rather egocentric. Parents who are plagued by doubts about their own worth may be so consumed with getting what *they* lack, psychologically speaking, that it becomes impossible for them to see their children for who they are and what they need—or who they aren't and what they don't need. "There is no parent more vulnerable to the excesses of overparenting than an unhappy parent," as Madeline Levine, a psychotherapist, has observed.[14]

CODDLED—OR CONTROLLED?

The genuinely troubling phenomenon of using one's child to shore up one's own sense of self accounts for only some fraction of what's commonly called overparenting. No one knows how common that version is, yet most articles and books on the subject feature such extreme examples of overparenting and then imply, or even state explicitly, that this type is rampant.

It's also common, as with discussions of permissiveness, to offer claims (without any evidence) that overparenting is more widespread today than ever before—or even, as one article asserts, that we're currently witnessing "the first generation of children raised by intensive parents."

Often, too, we find very different things lumped together as instances of "overparenting"—for example, efforts to protect kids from physical harm, to replace competitive with cooperative activities, and to induce children to work harder in school—as if these were instances of a single trend.

Given this record of sweeping statements and sloppy analysis, perhaps we shouldn't be shocked to find that, when such writings get around to discussing the *effects* of overparenting, the case once again tends to be built on anecdotes, quotes from a few observers who share the writer's opinions, and, once in a while, a citation to a book or study that turns out to have been addressing something rather different.[15]

We need to pose the question carefully: What are the effects on children of a certain degree of overparenting, or a certain kind, or a certain set of motives for it—and how do we know? The two disturbing outcomes proposed most often are entitlement and anxiety. Let's look at each in turn.

The suggestion that kids whose parents hover and protect them will engender a feeling of entitlement is rather like the claim that kids raised in a permissive environment will grow up to be narcissistic: While superficially plausible, there's not much evidence to support it. I could find only one study that investigated the possibility of a connection, and it turned up a weak association between a self-report measure of overparenting and a sense of entitlement in young-adult children.[16]

But the concept itself turns out to be more complicated than most people realize. Just as not all aspects of narcissism are pathological, so entitlement seems to come in different flavors—for example, "exploitive" and "non-exploitive," according to one team of researchers. The latter means you think you have a right to positive outcomes, but you don't take advantage of others in order to get them. Indeed, such individuals "may feel entitled to get things they want at least partially because they are willing to put in the necessary effort to obtain them." And it's this variant, which is rather innocuous even if it includes "unrealistically high aspirations," that may be widespread. There's no evidence that exploitive entitlement is common in young people, and, as we saw, there's only weak evidence that it's due to having been overparented.[17]

But does this way of raising children contribute to anxiety? Here's what some relevant studies found:

- Intrusive, infantilizing parenting was associated with separation anxiety among a small group of children who were already predisposed to be anxious.
- What investigators regarded as parental overinvolvement at age four was a modest predictor of anxiety in the same children at age nine.
- A review of forty-seven studies concluded that childhood anxiety seemed to be associated with any of several parenting styles: rejection or withdrawal, hostility, or overinvolvement. The most striking findings, though, were that (1) the lowest levels of anxiety were found among children whose parents actively supported their autonomy, and (2) all the parenting variables put together explained a very small percentage of the differences in anxiety rates.[18]

There are two important qualifications to these results. The first is straightforward: *Overinvolved parenting may be a reaction to children's expressions of anxiety more than its cause.* Most adults tend to offer help and reassurance to kids who seem less sure of themselves. As the lead author of that second study explained to an interviewer, other research has shown that when parents of confident kids were paired with children who were more anxious than their own, they gave those children more help. "There is potentially something in a child's behaviour that brings out the protective instincts in parents."[19] While it's been established that some forms of parenting do contribute to certain outcomes in children, cause and effect are hard to tease apart when we're talking about intrusiveness and anxiety.[20]

The other qualification is particularly intriguing, and its implications extend far beyond the question of anxiety. In fact, they reach to the very heart of the idea of overparenting. When you look closely at the studies, it turns out that what's classified as "overparenting" or "intrusive parenting" might better be understood as excessive *control* of children.[21] That also appears to be true of the disturbing subset of overparenting that I described earlier, in which parents' own psychological needs determine the way they act with their kids.

This offers a different lens through which to view all those warnings that parents do too much for their children and have become overly involved in their lives. Until now, I've been suggesting that we should question generalizations about how many parents act this way. Now I want to add that we should also question the assumption that parents who *do* act this way are mostly being indulgent and trying to make things too easy for their children. Perhaps what's really going on is more about controlling than coddling. In that case, what we're talking about might be described not as a variation of permissiveness but as virtually the opposite of that: a variation of the sort of traditional parenting for which many conservative critics of indulgence seem to be nostalgic, distinguished by a lack of respect for kids' needs and preferences. Maybe that approach was never discarded after all; many parents just switched to a slightly different, more intrusive version.

One struggles to find convincing evidence that overparenting conceived as indulgence is harmful. But overparenting conceived as control is decidedly bad news. In chapter 2, I outlined the benefits of a "working with" approach to raising children. The flip side is that a "doing to" approach, which relies on control, has a number of disadvantages even when it doesn't reach levels that could be described as abusive or authoritarian. In *The Psychology of Parental Control*, psychologist Wendy Grolnick reports that "controlling parenting has been associated with lower levels of intrinsic motivation, less internalization of values and morals, poorer self-regulation, and higher levels of negative self-related [emotions]."[22] When parents are controlling about their children's academic performance, the effects on the children's achievement—and on their *interest* in learning—are usually detrimental.[23]

It's worth keeping these findings in mind the next time you hear someone try to rationalize his or her need to control children:

"Hey, kids need limits."
"You know, they secretly appreciate the security of being told what to do."
"They'll thank me later for pushing them to do their best."

While there is surely a role for structure and predictability in children's lives, those concepts are often invoked to justify what is more accurately described as control, which *isn't* appreciated by, or healthy for, children. Indeed, research has found that parental control appears to be destructive for kids of all ages, including young adults—and also across ethnic groups and cultures.[24] One interesting example, though by no means the only one,[25] is a study of Chinese-American families published in 2013, which found that children raised by "tiger" parents (characterized by extreme control and a relentless demand for high achievement) were more likely than those raised by more supportive parents to be depressed, to describe themselves as pressured, and to feel resentment toward their parents. They also ended up having lower grades.[26]

Control can take different forms, however. Some theorists distinguish between *behavioral control*, which means exactly what it sounds like, and *psychological control*, which is subtler but more intrusive and perhaps even more damaging.[27] Psychologically controlling parents don't just coerce children to make them act (or stop acting) in a particular way; they attempt to take over their children's very selves. Kids are made to feel guilty when they do something contrary to the parent's wishes. Love and acceptance are made contingent on pleasing the parent. Care, in effect, is turned into "positive reinforcement." When the child is well behaved or impressive, there are plenty of hugs, smiles, high-fives, and "Good job!"s. But when the child doesn't do what the parent wants, the love is withdrawn and the atmosphere turns chilly. This strategy can be diabolically effective because the child becomes, in effect, a wholly owned subsidiary of the parent. It's harder to fight this than it is to rebel against the overt regulation of one's behavior.[28]

An impressive collection of research has illuminated a long list of effects of such manipulation. In 1996, Brian Barber, the topic's leading researcher, mentioned "dependency, alienation, social withdrawal, low ego strength, inability to make conscious choice, low self-esteem, passive, inhibited, and overcontrolled characteristics, and depressed affect."[29] Since then, the evidence to confirm those initial results has grown, and so has the list itself. Children raised with this sort of control may also develop "maladaptive perfectionism."[30] And they're affected not only psychologically "but also [in] their functioning in school and social relationships."[31]

It's not that such parents don't provide love; it's that they use their love as a lever. Indeed, one study found that things were even worse when the parent was more affectionate because of the controlling context in which affection was given.[32] This strategy amounts to a violation of psychological boundaries, so children come to feel "enmeshed" with the parent and sometimes develop a fear of abandonment. That fear, in turn, may lead them to become extremely dependent—or, paradoxically, it may drive them to become "pathologically *in*dependent" because they feel "an unhealthy need to prove themselves and to differentiate themselves from others."[33]

And speaking of paradoxes, being on the receiving end of this kind of control can leave one with a sense of grandiosity but, at the same time, a lower feeling of self-efficacy, which means the child is less confident about his or her ability to accomplish things. The use of praise ("conditional positive regard") to control a child—which means selectively reinforcing the behaviors and attitudes the parent desires—"creates a continual longing for the missing *un*conditional parental appreciation and affection," which is to say, the kind of love that doesn't have to be earned and isn't used to control.[34] "Probably all of us know what it is like to be accepted conditionally," two other researchers commented, "but for low-self-esteem individuals, this may be a predominant state of mind."[35] In simple language: People who felt they had to earn their parents' love are likely to feel lousy about themselves.

Some social critics have employed other terms to refer to psychological control and have warned about its implications. One writer talked about "love-oriented" (as opposed to "fear-oriented") discipline as being "actually more totalitarian—the child no longer has a private sphere, but has his entire being involved with parental aspirations." This raises the question of who, beyond the parents, is likely to benefit from inducing children to internalize those aspirations as well as favored rules, norms, and values. A pair of social scientists pondered the political and economic implications of socializing children to "*internalize* authority and . . . implement goals and objectives relatively alienated from their own personal needs."[36]

This isn't to suggest that most parents are driven primarily by a desire to turn their children into compliant workers who will do whatever they're told without having to be monitored. I think it's safe to say there's no single, simple explanation for why some parents resort to a pattern of psychological or behavioral control.[37] More broadly, the question of why we raise our children as we do has challenged theorists and researchers for many years. There does seem to be agreement that our parenting style is heavily influenced, but of course not completely determined, by how *we* were raised. For example, if we experienced our parents' acceptance as conditional on how we acted, and consequently grew up with doubts about our own worth, then we may be inclined to offer our children the same kind of love with strings attached—which amounts to a form of psychological control.[38] Indeed, two studies have found that parents whose feelings of self-worth varied with their kids' successes were apt to be more controlling than other parents, particularly if they had reason to expect their children would be judged.[39]

Even if we can't say for certain what predisposes parents to control their children, it's clear that control takes place in different ways and for different reasons. Kids can be restricted and restrained, commanded and compelled. My central point is that excessive involvement or protection is just one more variation on that same basic theme. Doing too much for one's kids, in other words, may really be just another way of doing things *to* one's kids.

To be sure, there's also an element of solicitousness in overparenting. But what defines a problematic concern for one's children (and involvement in their lives) isn't that it's overdone so much as *why* it's overdone. And that brings us back to the parent's need for control. You can see this most starkly when the involvement is conditional, such that "warmth and love are only provided when the child remains within close parent-child boundaries." Such parents may "anticipate their child's increasing independence with feelings of resentment and anxiety."[40] And even when that doesn't seem to be the case, the intense involvement still has a stifling, coercive feel to it.

How we frame and make sense of parental behavior has enormous practical implications. If overparenting is defined simply as getting too close to children, spending too much time with them, or solving too many of their problems for them, the prescription that follows is simple: Back off. Do less. And if overparenting is also viewed as a kind of coddling in which parents are protecting kids from failure, then it might make sense to say, "*Let* them fail sometimes."

But these responses are both simplistic and wrongheaded. In the first case, we need to remember that too little involvement in kids' lives is even more problematic than too much. In the second case, the idea that letting kids fail will teach them to become more resilient so they can deal more successfully with future failure is driven more by ideology than by solid science.[41]

If, by contrast, overparenting is understood mostly as an exercise in control, then "Back off" or "Let them fail" misses the point entirely. Those responses are animated more by traditionalists' antipathy to making things too easy for children than by an accurate assessment of what they need. The appropriate response is not to do less for kids but to actively support their desire for having some say over their own lives (and also to meet their needs for empathy, guidance, and unconditional love).

Consider again the controversy about permissiveness. What if—and this is purely a speculative exercise—the indictment of parents as being too easy on their kids led some to become even more controlling than they already were? (No one wants to be thought a pushover.) And what if that control sometimes took the form of overparenting? In that case, parents would likely be criticized again—not for controlling their children but for hovering too close and being too protective. And their reaction this time might be to play a smaller role in their children's lives, to offer less help and guidance.

Both prescriptions (stricter discipline; less involvement) are misguided, I believe. And both criticisms (too permissive; too intrusive) lead us to provide our children with less of the "working with" approach that's more likely to promote psychological health. All of this becomes easier to see once we've understood overparenting as an example of "doing to"—which is to say, a type of control.

HELICOPTER PARENTING—COLLEGE EDITION

Reporters and researchers have treated helicopter parenting (HP) of older adolescents and young adults as something separate from overparenting more generally. Before we examine some of the underlying beliefs here, let's take a moment to investigate what we really know about parents who are closely connected with their children in, and out of, college.

It's not very hard to find someone with a secondhand story concerning a dad who phoned the dean about a trivial problem or a mom who's overly involved with junior's love life (even if from a distance). But is there any reason to believe such incidents are common? A team of researchers representing five universities began their 2012 report on the topic as follows: "Popular media outlets are rampant with stories of helicopter parents who smother overly dependent grown children . . . yet studies examining such intense parental support are scant."[42] Indeed, even academic articles tend to offer generalizations about the scope of the problem based on popular media coverage, which, in turn, rests mostly on anecdotes.

It does appear that most parents are in touch with their college-age children on a regular basis.[43] But we need to make a distinction that's ignored by a lot of articles on the subject: Communicating isn't the same thing as intervening on your kid's behalf. In fact, those two activities aren't necessarily even correlated.[44] And the latter—frequent (or "excessive") intervention—actually seems to be fairly rare. A national survey found that only 13 percent of college freshmen and 8 percent of seniors said a parent had frequently intervened to help them solve problems. (Another 25 percent of freshmen and 21 percent of seniors said a parent had sometimes intervened.[45]) "Helicopter parents? Truly, there aren't that many of them," one university administrator told the *Chronicle of Higher Education* in 2008. "The popular image of modern parents as high-strung nuisances who torment college administrators . . . doesn't match reality."[46]

Such parents certainly don't seem to be tormenting their children. An overwhelming majority of the ten-thousand-plus University of California students who were surveyed in 2009 said their parents weren't involved in their choice of courses or their major. "While students view their parents as supportive of their academic endeavors, they generally do not view them as encroaching on their academic decision-making in college," these researchers concluded. Moreover, surveys of students by psychologists who are looking for the effects of that type of parenting typically haven't found evidence that it's especially common. One study determined that

only 10 percent of the students who filled out the questionnaire had helicopter parents; in another, average levels of HP were described as "relatively low" (registering about six on a fifteen-point scale).[47]

Alarming media reports have also suggested that parents hover when
their young-adult children enter the workplace, but the available evidence casts doubt on that claim, too. Michigan State University researchers found that 77 percent of the 725 employers they surveyed "hardly ever
witnessed a parent while hiring a college senior" but noted that it was the
aberrant incidents of involvement that "yielded the most interesting anecdotes for media stories" and gave the impression that helicopter parents
were lurking behind every water cooler.[48] And what about "intense parental support of grown children" outside of college and the workplace?
According to the only study on the topic I could find, just one in five or
six parents seemed to be intensely involved in their children's lives.[49]

If there's a study showing that HP—of college students, young employees, or adult children in general—is anywhere near as common as
we're led to believe, I haven't been able to locate it. But what about the
effects of such parenting when it does occur? Does the evidence support
the objections we so commonly hear?

Three studies have raised concerns about the more extreme versions
of HP. In each of them, questionnaires were given to about three hundred students at a single college, with no attempt to find a representative
sample. Conclusions were drawn based on whoever happened to sign up
for the study. And each used a different measure of helicopter parenting,
which means it's tricky to compare the results of the three studies. One,
whose results hadn't been published as of this writing, found that the
small percentage of students at a New Hampshire college who seemed to
have helicopter parents described themselves as more anxious and less
open to new ideas than did other students. (Whether that difference was
statistically significant, particularly given that only about thirty students
had such parents, wasn't clear from a reporter's description of the research.[50]) The second study, from Tennessee, reported that students who
described having a lower sense of "well-being" were slightly more likely
to describe their parents as having been intrusive or controlling when

they were growing up.[51] And the third, by Virginia researchers, found that helicopter parenting was related to higher levels of depression and lower levels of life satisfaction.[52]

Both of the qualifications I mentioned in connection with research on overparenting in general apply here, too. First, the items on these questionnaires primarily seem to be gauging how *controlling* the parents were. In fact, the Virginia researchers noted that their "measure of helicopter parenting behaviors appears to reliably capture the construct of behavioral control" and argued that a key reason HP seemed to have negative effects had to do with undermining the students' sense of autonomy. Again, the problem is control, not indulgence.[53]

The second qualification is what leads me to say that HP *seemed* to have negative effects. It's not at all clear that HP caused the problems with which it was associated. The Tennessee researchers acknowledged that "students with low levels of well-being, as well as high levels of anxiety or depression, may *view* their parents as more intrusive," while the Virginia researchers admitted that "when parents perceive their child as depressed, they may be more likely to 'hover.'"[54] Either of these interpretations is entirely plausible: Pre-existing unhappiness may have drawn the parents in, or it may have led the students to interpret their parents' actions as excessive. These are very real possibilities, yet invariably they're mentioned in a single throw-away sentence buried in the articles' discussion sections. If they're true, then the study offers no evidence at all that HP has negative effects—and all the press coverage of such research, which claims that HP makes kids unhappy, would be completely without merit.

But even if these studies can be taken at face value, they—and other research—have also *disconfirmed* certain beliefs about detrimental effects:

- The New Hampshire study found no association between HP and a sense of entitlement or exploitive behavior.[55]
- The Virginia study found no association with anxiety.
- A study of adults in their twenties discovered—"contrary to hypothesis"—that those who still lived with their parents "did not display a more dysfunctional dependent orientation" than those who were living on their own.[56]

- A Utah study found no connection between HP and students' self-worth, sense of identity, or even the extent to which they felt like an adult, although there was a negative relationship with their reports of how reliably they attended classes and completed their assignments.[57]
- In an amusing example of unintentional debunking, an education periodical published an assertion on its front page that "Millennials have had helicopter parents who have protected them" from having to struggle, thereby depriving them of critical life skills, the result being that fewer students finish college these days. Three pages later in the same issue, another article (by the same reporter) carried the headline: "K-12 and College Completion Rates Set Record."[58]

The case *against* HP isn't particularly compelling, then, but what may be more surprising is that there's a case to be made *for* it—that is, for parents to be actively connected and involved with their young-adult children, even to an extent with which many people are uncomfortable. The National Survey of Student Engagement, which included more than nine thousand students at twenty-four colleges and universities, didn't find a lot of HP going on, but the students who did have such parents reported "higher levels of [academic] engagement and more frequent use of deep learning activities."[59] Jillian Kinzie, a researcher involved with that project, confessed that when she saw those results, her first reaction was, "This can't be right. We have to go back and look at this again." But the benefits did indeed prove impressive. As the survey's director, George Kuh, told a reporter, "Compared with their counterparts, children of helicopter parents were more satisfied with every aspect of their college experience, gained more in such areas as writing and critical thinking, and were more likely to talk with faculty and peers about substantive topics."[60]

Nor is this the only finding of positive effects. In a preliminary data analysis, the researcher who conducted the New Hampshire study found indications that "helicopter parenting appears to be associated with young adults who have the capacity to love, feel supported, and who seek out social connections."[61] Another study revealed that the more contact freshmen had with their parents, the less likely they were to engage in binge drinking.[62] As Stephanie Coontz, the director of research for the Council on Contemporary Families, summed things up, "In the majority of cases, this increased closeness between parents and kids is found among healthy students, not unhealthy ones."[63]

You may or may not be surprised to learn that even when children are well into their twenties, parental involvement generally continues to be helpful. Here are the researchers who conducted that 2012 study of grown children: "Although the popular media lament parental dependency as detrimental to the current generation of young adults, the findings from this study provide a contrasting and more nuanced view. Frequent parental involvement, including a wide range of support, was associated with better well-being for young adults," including "clearly defined goals and higher life satisfaction."[64]

Support (not limited to money) from one's parents may be helpful, if not critical, when students graduate with a crushing load of debt. Cultural norms, too, have been changing, with people less likely to marry and have children right away.[65] When it's a struggle "to figure out what it means to be an adult in a world of disappearing jobs, soaring education costs and shrinking social support networks," a close connection to the people who raised you can be vital.[66]

Yet mass-media accounts continue to portray that connection as objectionable. A *Time* cover story in 2013 claimed "more people ages 18 to 29 live with their parents than with a spouse," and introduced that rather misleading statistic by declaring that "their development is stunted."[67] No evidence was offered to support this dire conclusion because none exists; it reflects nothing more than the personal disapproval of the writer. By contrast, Richard Settersten Jr., a professor of social and behavioral health sciences, argues that "the support of parents—emotionally and financially—is the single most important predictor of the success of young adults." In fact, he adds, "if you want to see just how much involved parenting matters, track the lives of young people who don't have it. . . . In obsessing about helicopter parents, we're focused on the wrong end of the spectrum."[68]

"Excessive" parent involvement—and attempts to spare children various types of unpleasantness at school and at play—are strongly condemned for reasons that go beyond the likely effects. Imagine, if you will, someone who rolls her eyes at a college student for checking in with a parent several times a week about minor matters, or who criticizes the student's parent for e-mailing a college administrator in an attempt to fix some problem. (Such criticisms are more often heard from people who do not themselves have children in college.[69]) "Give me a break!" snorts our critic. "The kid is legally an adult! It's time for him to learn how to make his way in the world. If Mommy or Daddy keeps running interference, how is he ever going to learn to solve his own problems? Parents who hover may think they're helping, but they're actually making things worse for their kids by keeping them dependent."

Now let us suppose that we reply by pointing out that there's actually no evidence to support that prediction of dependency, and indeed, there is reason to believe close contact and even intervention may be positively beneficial. Would that revelation be likely to silence this critic? My experience suggests not. While objections to overparenting are often framed as empirical predictions (here's what will happen), they often seem to be fueled more by basic values (here's how I think parents *should* act). As regards HP, the central conviction is that *kids ought to become independent as soon as possible.* A parent's job is to give them the skills they'll need to make it on their own and then strongly encourage them to do just that.

While I won't argue that this view is flat-out wrong, I think it needs to be defended rather than treated as a self-evident truth. If parents are overly involved because *they're* unwilling to let go—if, that is, they're cultivating a child's dependence to meet their own emotional needs—then, yes, that's a problem. But if that's not the case, then the "kick 'em out of the nest" view merits our skepticism for three reasons.

1. *Attacks on helicopter parenting sometimes reflect a scornful attitude about young people.* Those who demand that emerging adults hurry up and emerge already often seem to regard them as self-indulgent slackers and moochers. Their opinion isn't really driven by what young people need, in other words, but by a particular belief about what young people are like (specifically, what's wrong with them). There's always a receptive audience for media coverage along these lines, such as the cover of yet another issue

of *Time* magazine, this one depicting a young man sitting in a sandbox. The accompanying headline lamented, "They Just Won't Grow Up."[70]

2. *Maturity isn't the same as self-sufficiency.* I argued earlier that many people define healthy growth in terms of how much progress a child has made at separating from parents. That's particularly true where adolescents are concerned; it's widely believed that this is the stage of life whose main business is individuation. But the field of developmental psychology has moved toward adopting a more nuanced view. It's now understood that the quality of relationships, including those with one's parents, continues to matter, even past childhood. To insist that college students "handle difficult decisions and unfamiliar environments on their own . . . minimizes the importance of family connectedness in early and middle adulthood."[71] There's more to growing up than just going out on your own, and parents must walk a fine line, supporting self-sufficiency but also maintaining connection. That means responding to what one's child needs rather than applying a simple, single-minded principle—"promote independence"—which is the essence of most advice on the topic.

Within the field of *motivational* psychology, meanwhile, some theorists draw a distinction between independence and autonomy. A child whose autonomy is supported is one who is allowed "to act upon [his or her] true interests and values." That's quite different from encouraging *separation* from parents or freedom from their influence. Some very healthy, autonomous young people aren't particularly independent.[72] Conversely, not all independent young people are—or are helped to become—psychologically autonomous. Parents may push their children to be self-sufficient despite the children's need for continued guidance and support. One group of researchers points out that if, for example, parents insist that their college-age child "discuss academic problems with [his or her] professor," that might promote independence but could be "perceived as unsupportive or even controlling."[73]

3. *Not everyone shares "our" values about growing up.* Independence is closely connected to an individualistic worldview, and that worldview is far from universal. It's more commonly endorsed by men than

women, and more commonly found in the West than the East, in industrialized than nonindustrialized societies, and among professionals than working-class people. Regarding college students in particular, "traditional understandings of parental involvement presented in education are based on the practices of White, middle-class parents," ignoring the "cultural values of many ethnic minority groups, which focus on centrality of the family and interdependence."[74]

The cultural bias that seems to fuel the popular condemnation of HP—and perpetuates norms that favor independence over interdependence, particularly at the most selective colleges[75]—has a very real impact on students' well-being. "Levels of parental involvement that may be considered 'excessive' for some students could for other students represent an important source of academic and social support."[76] Surveys confirm substantial differences by class and ethnicity in how much contact and intervention kids want from their parents as well as how much they get.[77]

A fascinating series of studies published in 2012 by a multi-university research team revealed that "predominantly middle-class cultural norms of independence that are institutionalized in many American colleges and universities" are particularly ill suited for young adults who are the first in their families to attend college. These norms "do not match the relatively interdependent norms to which many first-generation students are regularly exposed in their local working-class contexts prior to college." The result of this mismatch is to create a hidden academic disadvantage for these students, one that adversely affects their performance.[78] Given the expectations of self-sufficiency that permeate our institutions—"learn to do for yourself"—connections with, support from, and maybe even interventions by parents become that much more important to help students persist and succeed in a challenging environment. Simplistic and sometimes unpleasant denunciations of HP are particularly unfortunate, in other words, when no attention is paid to differences among students and their backgrounds.

One last point. In any consideration of what sort of parenting role best serves a given student, we shouldn't forget to ask, "But what does the student want? How do things look from his or her perspective?"—a question that appears in remarkably few discussions of the topic. "It's only helicopter parenting if parents are more involved than their college students want or need them to be."[79] If kids balked at how often their parents were in touch with them, or objected to how much their parents were involving themselves in academic and social decisions, then critics would (with some justification) complain about these folks who ignore their children's desire for distance. But in fact the majority of kids *don't* mind. Most students say either that they're happy with the level of their parents' involvement or that they'd like them to be even more involved.[80] Some critics simply pivot, however, attempting to turn that preference for connection into the basis of a new complaint: Look how dependent they've made their children![81]

With most issues involving parenting and education, the impact of what we do is a function of how the children think and feel about what's done to them, not by the behaviors themselves. It may be easier to measure behaviors (how we act), but it's the perspective of those on the receiving end of those actions that determines the effect. The key variable that predicts whether parental support will prove beneficial isn't how much of it is offered but whether that support is welcomed by the recipient or viewed as an imposition.[82]

CHAPTER 4

Getting Hit on the Head Lessons

Motivation, Failure, and the Outrage Over Participation Trophies

Not long ago, several elementary schools took a fresh look at the game called dodge ball and decided that their physical education programs would be better off without it. Many p.e. teachers had been unenthusiastic about an activity that doesn't teach useful skills or offer a good workout; most players at any given time are just standing around. The more compelling objection, though, was that kids are required to hurl an object at one another as hard as possible. "Dodge ball is one of those games that encourages aggression and the strong picking on the weak," as one professor of health and physical education put it.[1] Is an activity that turns children into human targets really consistent with the values that schools say they're trying to teach?

People who favor keeping dodge ball in schools might have replied that the game isn't all that different from other competitive sports (although perhaps that's less a defense of dodge ball than a reason to rethink those other sports as well). Or they might have tried to make a case that the problems aren't inherent to the game and could be addressed by changing how it's played. But efforts to get rid of dodge ball, which received considerable media attention, produced a response that relied less on reasoned opposition than on incredulity, rage, and sneering contempt, even from normally equable writers[2] and mainstream sources.

An editorial in the *Los Angeles Times* was fairly typical. It ridiculed people who wanted to protect children's "hurt feelings" or make them include everyone in their games. For adults to try to minimize the nastiness that kids may experience—not only deliberate exclusion but also physical aggression—is to fail to prepare them for the real world, the editorial declared. It's never too early for children to learn that "someone always gets picked last." To protect their "tender egos"—a phrase used facetiously, not compassionately—by barring dodge ball is to deprive them of an important lesson about what life (in the editorial writer's experience) is really like.[3]

Something about the issue hit a nerve, but it wasn't because of a deep attachment to the game itself. In fact, that same white-hot anger shows up whenever anyone proposes to minimize unpleasantness for children, especially if it involves moderating the impact of activities that pit them against one another or questioning the usefulness of punishment.

Consider a Florida school board that was asked by its own curriculum specialists to eliminate the practice of giving zeroes to elementary school students for individual assignments. When averaged in with other marks, a single zero can drag down a child's overall grade disproportionately and irreversibly. Moreover, as the superintendent pointed out, "after a few zeroes, a child can 'shut off' and not recover." But as soon as this idea was floated, board members received a flood of mail, all of it excoriating the proposal. Some members didn't even wait to hear from their constituents; they instantly announced their opposition on the grounds that tempering this punitive policy would lower standards. "The kids need to learn to study and do their homework and earn the grades they deserve," one member declared. The zeroes remain.[4]

In Massachusetts, meanwhile, a middle school principal became uncomfortable with the tradition of holding a special evening awards ceremony to which only students who made the honor roll were invited.

"Honors Night, which can be a great [source] of pride for the recipients' families," he said, "can also be devastating to a child who has worked extremely hard in a difficult class but who, despite growth, has not been able to maintain a high grade-point average." He didn't propose eliminating the honor roll or even the public recognition of students who were on it. He suggested only that the event be folded into a daytime assembly that included arts and athletic awards, which the entire student body attends. (Indeed, part of the principal's reasoning was that students who weren't on the honor roll might be "motivated" by watching their classmates receive recognition.) But even this modest change elicited furious opposition from parents as well as unpleasant coverage on Fox News and conservative websites. One parent's comment was typical of the reaction: "I think the school should be committed to excellence and not mediocrity. . . . They shouldn't cancel [Honors Night just] because somebody's feelings could be hurt. Life is a competition, and they should start competing."[5]

In defending his proposal, the principal insisted somewhat defensively that it didn't amount to "the dumbing down of America. This isn't everyone getting a trophy." Here he was comparing the modified awards assembly to something that serves as a cultural lightning rod. Few practices involving children attract more scorn than giving some kind of trophy or recognition to all the kids who participate in an athletic contest rather than reserving prizes for the conquering heroes. It's not clear how common such participation trophies really are, but the depth of rage stirred up by the idea is both indisputable and fascinating. It began when the Internet was in its infancy,[6] and it has reached the point that an online forum about virtually anything having to do with parenting or education is likely to include at least one comment that strays from the topic at hand to sound off angrily about "trophies just for showing up." (The last time I checked, that phrase alone produced more than 250,000 hits on Google.) A typical blog post, titled "Sorry, Just Because You Tried Hard Doesn't Mean You Deserve a Prize," waxes nostalgic for the days when "to get an ice cream after the Little League baseball games, you had to win the game." In an opinion piece published in the *New York Times* under the headline "Losing Is Good for You," a journalist complains that kids will have no "impetus for improvement" if everyone gets a trophy.[7] It's an issue, in short, that boils the blood of social conservatives—and unmasks people *as* social conservatives who might not have thought of themselves that way.

These four controversies, two involving academics and two involving sports, illustrate how accusations about indulgence, which we've been examining in the context of parenting, have leached into areas like education and recreation. The argument here is that by protecting kids from unpleasantness we deprive them of beneficial experiences with failure and allow them to feel more satisfied with themselves than they deserve, thus blurring the sharp line that divides winners from losers—and excellence from mediocrity—at school and at play.

Three separate issues can be identified in these criticisms, all of them involving motivation. The first concerns rewards (what you get for what you do), the second concerns competition (arrangements in which some kids must defeat others), and the third concerns failure (and its alleged role in preparing children for life's challenges). In each case, the argument has two dimensions, as we noticed with helicopter parenting. There's an empirical claim—what's true, or what's likely to happen—that in theory can be proved or disproved with evidence. And there's a prescriptive claim, based on the speaker's preferences and values, which can't. Both sets of beliefs need to be inspected carefully, the point being to determine whether the first are accurate and the second are reasonable.

This chapter addresses empirical claims for each of the three topics— rewards, competition, and failure. The following chapter explores the underlying values.

"WHY WORK HARD IF EVERYONE GETS A REWARD ANYWAY?"

That rhetorical question (posed by a blogger) implies that people do their best only when offered a reward for exemplary performance—and, conversely, that motivation dissipates or even disappears if a reward is *not* offered or if it isn't made contingent on how well one did. There is supposed to be a quid pro quo arrangement for receiving a sticker, an A, a bonus check, or some sort of recognition. If something interferes with that arrangement, people won't be inclined to strive, to succeed, to do what's expected of them, or to act morally.

The widely held belief that humans are motivated by the prospect of receiving rewards is based, it turns out, on an antiquated version of psychology constructed largely on experiments with lab animals. To describe all the research over the last few decades that has revealed its multiple flaws would require a book in itself. But that book has already been written, so I'll just summarize the arguments here.[8]

The idea that we do things mostly, or perhaps even exclusively, to obtain rewards assumes that there is a single thing called "motivation" that is present or absent, that can rise or fall. But in fact different *kinds* of motivation exist, which behave differently and have different sources. "Extrinsic" motivation refers to an outcome outside of the task in which one is engaged; one might be induced to read, for example, to get a prize or someone's approval. It's all about the reward. "Intrinsic" motivation, on the other hand, means wanting to do something for its own sake—to read just to acquire information or because it's exciting to see what direction the story might take.

Thus, what matters isn't how motivated people are, but *how* people are motivated. And intrinsic motivation is real, pervasive, and powerful. Every time a child loses herself in creating an elaborate Lego structure, or asks for markers so she can draw a dinosaur, or writes a poem just for the hell of it, or persists in asking "But why?" so she can understand something more fully, we're looking at another example of intrinsic motivation. The same is true of adults: We pour our time and love into our avocations—activities for which we will never be compensated—nicely making the point that money often is not the point. (One thinks not only of the usual range of hobbies but also of raising children, an activity reasonably certain to produce a net loss.) And we typically try to do these things *well*, despite the absence of any extrinsic inducement.

Even our work is usually about more than just earning a living: We may complain about the daily grind, but studies show that we're often absorbed in our work and happy with it on a moment-by-moment basis.[9]

In short, regardless of age or setting, we frequently act out of curiosity or passion, animated by the sheer joy of pushing our limits or making sense of the world. Every example of this offers yet another refutation of the sad, cynical belief that people make an effort only in exchange for money, a pat on the head, or some other version of a doggie biscuit.

Those who hold that belief, and consequently feel compelled to offer rewards to children, implicitly discount the power of intrinsic motivation—or perhaps even doubt its existence. Similarly, those who compulsively praise children for helping or sharing seem to imply that the act was a fluke: Kids must be "reinforced" for doing something nice because otherwise they'd never act that way again. (A habit of offering squeaky "Good job!"s often betrays a dark view of children and perhaps of human nature.) Those who defend merit pay or incentive plans in the workplace, meanwhile, apparently believe that employees could have been doing better work all along but simply refused until it was bribed out of them. A strong belief in the need to dangle rewards in front of people to "motivate" them—or a fear of failing to do so—implies that people lack not just skills but the desire to acquire them. And that view of our species isn't just insulting, it's inaccurate.

Still, everyone isn't intrinsically motivated to do everything. Wouldn't children refuse to engage in some activities unless goaded by an extrinsic inducement? No doubt. But when this happens, one of two things is often true. The first possibility is that children *used to* take pleasure from doing it—until they were rewarded. Intrinsic and extrinsic motivation aren't just different, you see. They tend to be inversely related. Scores of studies have shown that *the more you reward people for doing something, the more they tend to lose interest in whatever they had to do to get the reward.* Incentives, in other words, are actually corrosive. Give a child an "A" for learning something and he's apt to find that topic—and perhaps learning in general—a little less appealing than he did before. (He'll also come to find it less appealing than does a child who was never graded to begin with). Offer a reward, including praise, for an act of generosity, and kids become a little less likely to help next time if they don't think they're going to get something out of it. Far from proving that rewards are necessary "in the real world," the moral of this line of research is that rewards create their own demand. And the problem isn't that we're setting the bar too low and giving out goodies too easily; the problem is with rewards, per se, and the damage they do to intrinsic motivation.

The second possibility when kids seem "unmotivated" and appear to require an extrinsic inducement to do something is that the something they don't want to do isn't particularly engaging. What we're talking about here isn't the child's motivation but the adult's demand for obedience. On those occasions when it's true that children wouldn't do *x* if (a) they weren't rewarded for doing it, or (b) they got a reward irrespective of whether or how well they did it, the problem might well be with *x* itself. Rewards aren't necessary to promote learning, but they may be necessary to make kids memorize a list of facts for a quiz. Rewards aren't necessary to make kids concerned about the welfare of other people (indeed, they tend to *undermine* that concern), but they may be necessary to make kids shut up and do what they're told.

Even on those occasions when people do seem to depend on rewards, then, this may reflect the harm done by rewards in the past or a problem with the task. In any case, that dependence is far less broad and deep than is often assumed—which means that the fear of not offering a reward for doing something well is largely misplaced.

FROM REWARDS TO AWARDS

An award is just a reward that has been made artificially scarce: If you get one, then I can't. A good grade is a reward, and the primary effect of inducing students to try to get one is that they're less likely to ask the teacher "What does that really mean?" and more likely to ask "Is that going to be on the test?" That's bad enough. But when students are graded on a curve, it has been decided in advance that even if all of them do well, all of them can't get A's. Now we're talking not only about extrinsic inducements (rewards) but about competition (awards). And the negative impact on learning is even more pronounced.

Competition, which has been described as America's state religion, is an arrangement in which people are pitted against one another—at work, at school, at play, and even at home. Later I'll explore the larger worldview on which it rests. For now, let's just consider the hypothesis that competition is useful, if not necessary, for motivating people to do their best—and, conversely, that people won't challenge themselves in an environment where everyone can succeed.

Because an award is a type of reward, the disturbing evidence I just summarized about extrinsic motivators also applies to competition. In fact, a separate body of research suggests that competition is uniquely counterproductive. Typically, its effect is to undermine self-confidence, relationships, empathy and the inclination to help,[10] intrinsic motivation, and, perhaps most surprisingly, excellence. Contrary to popular belief, competition usually does not enhance achievement, even on straight-forward tasks. And when the tasks are more complex—for example, when they involve creativity—study after study shows that the *absence* of competition is more likely to produce better results. That's true in part because a competitive environment (I can succeed only if you fail) strongly discourages the arrangement that *does* help people do their best: cooperation (I can succeed only if you also succeed).[11]

When we set children against one another in contests—from spelling bees to awards assemblies to science "fairs" (that are really contests), from dodge ball to honor rolls to prizes for the best painting or the most books read—we teach them to confuse excellence with winning, as if the only way to do something well is to outdo others. We encourage them to mea-sure their own value in terms of how many people they've beaten, which is not exactly a path to mental health. We invite them to see their peers not as potential friends or collaborators but as obstacles to their own success. (Quite predictably, researchers have found that the results of competition often include aggression, cheating, envy of winners, contempt for losers, and a suspicious posture toward just about everyone.) Finally, we lead children to regard whatever they're doing as a means to an end: The point isn't to paint or read or design a science experiment, but to win. The act of painting, reading, or designing is thereby devalued in the child's mind.

Our culture remains in thrall to the dogma that competition builds character, that it teaches skills (which ostensibly couldn't be acquired by engaging in noncompetitive versions of the same activities), and that it motivates people to do their best. But by now the empirical evidence of competition's destructive effects is impossible to deny. Moreover, it appears that the problem isn't due to the age or personality of the competitors, the type of activity, or the way the contest has been structured. The problem is competition itself.

Remember the Massachusetts principal who attempted to moderate the exclusivity of his school's academic awards assembly? His decision to give out awards in front of the whole student body ("look what they did that you didn't") may well accentuate the competitive nature of the occasion. The effect of an awards assembly on the kids who leave empty-handed is either nil (for those who don't care) or cruel (for those who do). Anyone who believes that watching someone else get an award will "motivate" a student to improve has, at the very least, failed to distinguish between intrinsic and extrinsic motivation. Mostly, though, such a belief is laughably unrealistic.

Anyone who was familiar with the research on competition wouldn't ask where, when, or in front of whom the academic awards should be handed out. Rather, he or she would want to know why a school committed to excellence (let alone to creating a caring community) would give out awards, period. If the argument for doing so—and the outrage over any attempt to make the process a little less harsh—is based on the empirical belief that it's productive to make kids try to defeat one another, then the argument is without foundation.

And here's the kicker: Ultimately, even the winners lose. The effects on how kids feel about themselves, about one another, and about learning—and the long-term impact on the *quality* of that learning—are just as unfortunate for those who get an award as for those who don't. The reason to eliminate rituals like awards assemblies isn't just that they're mean to the losers, but that they're counterproductive for everyone.

The outrage over participation trophies—again, to the extent it's really based on an empirical belief—is similarly misconceived. It's assumed not only that we should have kids play competitive sports—recreation in our culture having been limited largely to games in which one group must struggle for dominance over another—but that we should drive home the competitive impact of that struggle, making things even more unpleasant for the losers.

If popular assumptions about the benefits of competition turn out to be dead wrong, then the relevant question isn't "How many trophies should we give out?" but "Why do we have trophies at all?" And, while we're at it, we could ask, "What might minimize the inherently ugly effects of competition (rather than maximize them, which is the effect of giving trophies only to the victors)?" Or, better yet, we might explore alternatives to competitive sports—which George Orwell once called "war minus the shooting"—in which kids can get exercise, have fun, acquire skills, and interact with their peers in a cooperative rather than adversarial activity.[12]

In any number of arenas, we find a convergence of rewards and competition. One writer, for example, asks, "If you get the prizes no matter the outcome, what motivates a person to try hard and win?"[13] This is basically the same question that headed the preceding section, except now the desired outcome isn't just to "work hard" but to triumph over other people who are also working hard. If we don't make the losers unhappy, why would anyone want to make an effort?

Consider the practice of ranking high school students by their grade-point averages and publicly recognizing the victor in this contest as the valedictorian. The vicious competition and resentment that ensue, as a handful of academic overachievers battle it out over tiny differences in GPA, has led some schools to identify a batch of high-scoring kids rather than a single valedictorian, or to stop ranking students entirely. Predictably, this has stirred up a furious reaction. A *Newsweek* columnist pointed to one district's move away from class rank as proof that "you can't tell anyone anymore that they're no good—or less good than their peers."[14]

A review of editorials and letters to the editor on this topic suggests that those in favor of identifying a valedictorian rely principally on two arguments: When we recognize a single student for exceptional achievement, we demonstrate our support for excellence and hard work; and such an arrangement is good preparation for life, which is competitive. These points are often accompanied by sarcastic references to the hurt feelings of "the losers"—which, of course, includes every student but one—and how misguided it is to be swayed by those feelings.

Here are six quick responses:

1. The differences in grade-point averages among high-achieving students are usually statistically insignificant. It's therefore both pointless and misleading to single out the "top" student or even the ten top students.

2. Ranking students provides little if any practical benefit. Class rank has much less significance to college admissions officers than does a range of other factors, and the proportion of colleges that view it as an important consideration has been dropping steadily. As of 2005 nearly 40 percent of high schools have either stopped ranking their students or don't share that information with colleges—with no apparent effect on students' prospects for admission.[15]

3. What's being rewarded isn't always merit or effort but some combination of skill at playing the game of school (choosing courses with a keen eye to the effect on one's GPA,[16] figuring out how to impress teachers, etc.) and a willingness to sacrifice sleep, health, friends, a sense of perspective, reading for pleasure, and anything else that might interfere with one's grades.

4. If the chance to be a valedictorian is supposed to be a motivator, then the effect of class rank is to *de*motivate the vast swath of students who realize early on that they don't stand a chance of acquiring this distinction.

5. What we're talking about here is *extrinsic* motivation, which ultimately harms everyone, including the valedictorian. Research by educational psychologists suggests that grades typically do three things: They reduce students' interest in learning, they lead students to prefer less challenging tasks, and they encourage students to think in a more superficial fashion.[17] The effect of class rank, honor rolls, and grade-based scholarships—all of which are essentially rewards for having been rewarded—is to exacerbate all three of those effects by making grades even more salient.

6. Pitting students against one another for the status of having the *best* grades adds the arsenic of competition to the strychnine of extrinsic motivation. It not only makes the high school experience

unnecessarily stressful but simultaneously undermines the sense of community and support that can help students get through those years intact.

PAIN: BETTER GET USED TO IT

The upshot of the previous two sections is this: Even if we thought it would be productive to subject kids to unpleasant experiences, neither rewards nor competition *is* productive, let alone necessary. To that extent, efforts to minimize those experiences don't really constitute overprotectiveness on the part of parents and educators—just good sense.

But let's take a step back and ponder that phrase "subject kids to unpleasant experiences" in more general terms. We often hear an argument that runs as follows: If adults allow (or perhaps even require) children to play a game in which the point is to slam a ball at someone before he or she can get out of the way, or hand out zeroes to underscore a child's academic failure, or demand that most young athletes go home without even a consolation prize (in order to impress upon them the difference between them and the winners), well, sure, they might feel lousy—about themselves, about the people around them, and about life itself—but *that's the point*. It's a dog-eat-dog world out there, and the sooner they learn that, the better they'll be at dealing with it.

The corollary claim is that if we intervene to relieve the pain, if we celebrate all the players for their effort, then we'd just be coddling them and giving them false hopes. A little thanks-for-playing trophy might allow them to forget, or avoid truly absorbing, the fact that they *lost*. Then they might overestimate their own competence and fall apart later in life when they learn the truth about themselves (or about the harshness of life). We do them no favors by sheltering them from the fact of their own inadequacy or from the cruelty that awaits them when they're older.

That's why a teacher-blogger had no reservations about describing herself as coercive, insisting her approach is justified because, first, "the role of school is inherently to prepare students for adulthood," and second, "when we become adults, life itself is coercive by nature. Most everything we do, we do with some amount of coercion present, in one form or another."[18] Now take this logic one more step. If children are going to have teachers who coerce them, then parents should start coercing them even before they start school. One parenting author offers the cautionary tale of a boy who was distressed when his preschool teacher punished him; the fault, according to the author, lay with his parents who hadn't "prepared him for the real world" by punishing him earlier.[19]

In sum, the best way to get children ready for the painful things that may happen to them later is to make sure they experience plenty of pain while they're young.

When the premise is spelled out so bluntly, it sounds ridiculous. But that summary captures a mindset that is widely accepted and applied. I call it BGUTI (rhymes with duty), which is the acronym of Better Get Used To It. It brings to mind a Monty Python sketch that featured "getting hit on the head" lessons. When the student recoils and cries out from the pain, the instructor says, "No, no, no. Hold your head like this, then go, 'Waaah!' Try it again"—and gives him another smack. Presumably this is extremely useful training . . . for future experiences of getting hit on the head.

We smack elementary school students by subjecting them to grades and standardized tests. There is absolutely no evidence that kids of that age derive any benefit from either of these practices, but the practices nevertheless persist and are rationalized on the grounds that, because children will encounter them when they're older, they had better start getting accustomed to them now.[20] So, too, for homework, which, according to the available research, provides no advantages whatsoever, either academic or attitudinal, when assigned to elementary school students. Yet even many educators who know this is true fall back on the justification that homework—time-consuming, anxiety-provoking, and pointless though it may be—will help kids get used to doing homework when they get to high school. One researcher comes close to saying that the more unpleasant (and even unnecessary) the assignment, the more valuable it is by virtue of teaching children to cope with things they don't like.[21]

Or consider an English instructor named Mark Bauerlein, who argues against making high school more engaging and relevant. Why? Because college, too, will be boring. Success, he says, requires the "ability to slog through" whatever is required. "In adjusting curriculum and pedagogy to student interest, educators may raise certain secondary school results but, ironically, stunt students in preparation for the next level of their education." Rather than making school better, we should just teach students the "skill of exerting oneself even when bored." After all, the more people who adopt this BGUTI view, the more boredom they're likely to face later.[22]

This reasoning is often applied outside of school as well. In an article about devices used to monitor and control children while they use technology, a father shrugs off any concern that his daughters will conclude he doesn't trust them: "They should learn that they will be monitored throughout their lives: 'It's not any different from any employer.'"[23]

BGUTI actually takes two forms. The positive version holds that it's beneficial for children to have unpleasant experiences of the type they'll presumably encounter later. The negative version says that the *absence* of unpleasant experiences—or the presence of experiences that are "unrealistically" supportive or reassuring—is harmful. Thus, if children are spared from having to do things that cause them anxiety, if they're permitted to revise and resubmit a school assignment without penalty or introduced to cooperative games (where the point is to accomplish something together rather than trying to defeat one another), a typical response is "That's not how things work in the real world!"

Underlying such a comment are a couple of assumptions. First, it's taken for granted that life is pretty damn unpleasant, a belief that may be most informative for what it tells us about the experiences and attitudes of the people who offer this objection. The claim, for example, that kids ought to be forced to compete because "life is competitive" is based on a partial truth. Life actually consists of some activities that entail competition, some that involve cooperation, and some that require neither. So why prepare children mostly for adversarial encounters? If the goal were really to get them ready for what they're likely to experience, wouldn't there be a comparable emphasis on helping them learn how to collaborate and empathize? Yet rarely do we hear people complain that kids mostly taught to compete are being ill prepared for the real world.

The second assumption is that childhood is—and should be—mostly about preparation for what comes later. It doesn't matter if you're miserable now because what you experience as a child isn't important in its own right. Everything is about the payoff, which doesn't come until some (unspecified) period during adulthood. School, for example, may be awful for you—it may squelch your excitement about learning—but that's okay because the purpose of education is to acclimate you to gratuitous unpleasantness. Anyone who finds this premise unsettling, anyone who agrees with John Dewey that education is a process of living and not merely a preparation for future living, would object to BGUTI even if experiencing pain as a kid *did* succeed in diminishing the effects of pain as a grownup.

But does it? Often we hear people say things like "In life, everyone doesn't get a trophy" or "When you grow up, people aren't going to think you're special." But those are grumbles, not arguments. In themselves, they don't offer any reason not to give everyone a trophy or to treat children as if they were special. We need to focus on the primary empirical claims driving BGUTI: that bad experiences really are useful preparation for subsequent bad experiences, and that children who are treated too well, or who don't experience enough frustration, will suffer later when they're treated less kindly by others. What matters is whether those statements are true.

Let's concede that a hypothetical child who managed to succeed in every one of his endeavors, or who always got everything he desired, might find it hard to cope if things suddenly turned sour. But are we entitled to conclude from this fanciful thought experiment that parents and teachers should deliberately stand back rather than help out? I'm not aware of any evidence to support the hypothesis that a relatively bump-free childhood leads to adjustment difficulties down the line.

On the other side of the ledger, long-term follow-ups of people who attended nontraditional schools—the sort that afford an unusual amount of autonomy and/or nurturing—suggest that the great majority turned out well and seemed capable of navigating the transition to traditional colleges and workplaces.[24] Second, even if early, supportive experiences were responsible for some children's developing unrealistic expectations about themselves or the world—and I don't know of any evidence to substantiate that connection—research challenges the belief that those young people implode once they're unceremoniously brought back to earth.

Take students who thought they would graduate from college but didn't end up doing so. Some would argue that "teenagers' achievement expectations are related to their sense of entitlement" and when they "fail to achieve the level of education to which they feel entitled, they are likely to respond with anxiety or depression." But that doesn't appear to be true. In fact, "higher expectations are associated with fewer symptoms of depression in adulthood" and, overall, there were "almost no long-term emotional costs" when expectations weren't realized. That finding confirmed another, more general study in which young adults were asked, "Have things worked out the way you thought they would since high school?" Despite the fact that many respondents answered no, "None of the interviews was characterized by fatalism, resignation, or even notable distress."[25]

If it doesn't hurt to expect too much, we're left wondering why it would help to be brought down to earth even before one had the chance to soar. Anyone who supports BGUTI-inspired practices has an obligation to explain how exactly this is supposed to work. What's the mechanism by which the sting of a zero, or the smack of an undodged ball, or the silence of a long drive home without a trophy, is supposed to teach resilience?

And how hurtful does an experience have to be before an adult is allowed to step in to help? Not so long ago, humiliation—even physical abuse—at the hands of bullies was regarded as a rite of passage that kids were expected to deal with by themselves—without assistance from "overprotective" teachers and parents. The talk about toughening them up and forcing them to learn how to handle problems on their own isn't so different from the BGUTI rhetoric that's still used today to justify painful experiences.

When I hear people complain that kids are being spared the necessity of hard work, sheltered from the inevitability of competition, deprived of the benefits of skinned knees, and so on, I'm tempted to respond with satirically feigned heartiness:

Damn right! And you know what else these touchy-feely parents are doing? They're *reading* to their kids at night! Not only that, but they'll read any book the kid demands—because of course their precious little angels are the center of the universe, right? I'll tell you what, though: Those tykes are going to be in for a rude shock when they get out into the real world and discover that no one's going to crawl into bed with them and read aloud while they just lie there and do nothing. Sorry, Charlie— that's not the way life works. If you want to know what a book's about, you're going to have to damn well find out for yourself!

BGUTI proponents often give the impression that the sin being committed by overzealous adults is leaving kids *unfamiliar* with the tough challenges they'll face later. This raises three questions.

1. Are children, including those raised in very supportive families or taught in progressive schools, really unaware of the larger culture in which they live (in all its unloving particulars)? Without evidence of this ignorance, the whole argument falls apart.

2. If the goal is familiarity, wouldn't a single exposure to any given practice be sufficient to ensure it won't catch them by surprise when they're older? Why would we need to keep clobbering them with grades, contests, and the like day after day, year after year?

3. What reason is there to believe that mere familiarity with something equips one to deal with it productively? "Our kids must experience disappointments to develop skills in handling failure and imperfection," one writer asserts.[26] But the fact of being disappointed neither imparts a skill nor promotes a constructive attitude. Of course one could argue that we need to *teach* such skills to, and *promote* resiliency among, children—or at least those children who seem to lack them. But that's not what the BGUTI contingent is saying. They're arguing for giving homework and tests to all young children, or separating them into winners and losers, because these tykes need to get used to such things—as if exposure itself will inoculate them against the negative effects they would otherwise experience later. If we were interested in helping

children to anticipate and deal with unpleasant experiences, it might make sense to *discuss* the details with them and perhaps guide them through role-playing exercises. But why would we *subject* kids to those experiences? After all, to teach children how to handle a fire emergency, we talk to them about the dangers of smoke inhalation and advise them where to go when the alarm sounds. We don't actually set them on fire.

But the key point is this: From a developmental perspective, BGUTI is flat-out wrong. *People don't get better at coping with unhappiness because they were deliberately made unhappy when they were young.* On the contrary, what best prepares children to deal with the challenges of the real world is to experience success and joy, to feel supported and respected, to receive loving guidance and unconditional care and the chance to have some say about what happens to them. This is the foundation that allows one to see what's wrong with unsympathetic people and coercive institutions, to realize that grades or punishment or competition is not a necessary part of life, and to imagine alternatives. Most of all, positive emotional experiences give kids the confidence and psychological stability to weather the bad stuff. That's what all the research about effective parenting (pp. 40–41) teaches us: Loved, empowered kids are in the best position to deal constructively with unloving, disempowering circumstances.

IS FAILURE BENEFICIAL?

The case for BGUTI is, to a large extent, a case for failure. The argument is that when kids don't get a hoped-for reward, or when they lose a contest, they'll not only be prepared for more of the same but will be motivated to try harder next time. Overcoming failure is also believed to be the key to character, and character is the chief ingredient of success. Hence the indignation about indulgent parents: If adults intervene to help children succeed, or soften the distress caused by failure, that means they're preventing them from confronting the full force of their deficient performance.

The purveyors of this narrative, as of the others we've been examining, are not limited to self-identified social conservatives. A 2013 essay (on a mainstream magazine blog) titled "Why Parents Need to Let Their Children Fail" cued an enormous online amen chorus. Similarly, a columnist for a prominent magazine for teachers and school administrators insisted, "We need to be sure that [students] sometimes encounter frustration and failure" because "how can they learn to overcome adversity if they haven't experienced it?" And the journalist Paul Tough informed us, "If you want to "develop [kids'] character, you let them fail and don't hide their failures from them or from anybody else."[27] A casual Web search produces tens of thousands of similar declarations.

Unlike the charge that kids are spoiled, which has been around forever, there was a time when it would have seemed surprising to make a case for failure—an example of what reporters call a "man bites dog" story—because it upends the expected order. It's logical to think that success is good and failure is bad; we want to help kids succeed and reassure them about their capabilities. But listen to this: Failure can actually be helpful! It's possible to feel *too* good about yourself! Parents may be hurting their children by helping them! These messages presumably raised eyebrows at first because they were unexpected and counterintuitive. Except now they aren't. As I noted in the introduction, people are still telling this story as if it represents a bold challenge to the conventional wisdom, but the fact is that almost everyone else has been saying the same thing for some time now. It has *become* the conventional wisdom. Indeed, the notion that failure is beneficial, or that kids today have inflated self-esteem, is virtually the only message on these subjects that we're likely to hear.

The corresponding advice—*let* them stumble!—is offered in response to our alleged tendency to overparent, our failure to let children fail. So let's begin by asking whether this assumption is really true. The idea that kids lack experience with failure and frustration is really just another way of saying that things are too easy for them. (Perhaps it's not so different after all from the age-old complaints that they're spoiled.) But have you ever met a child who doesn't regularly experience failure and frustration? I haven't. People who describe kids as entirely satisfied and successful are inadvertently confessing how little they understand of the inner life of children and perhaps how little they remember of their own childhoods.

One need only watch a child carefully—or, if the occasion presents itself, ask her directly—to get a sense of how often she tends to fall short of her own or others' expectations, how often she's disappointed with how things worked out, how often she doesn't get what she wants, how often she finds herself on the receiving end of critical judgments from her peers or adults, how desperately she wishes she could perform as well as _____ (that kid she knows who seems to do things effortlessly). And her frustrations are doubtless compounded if all these feelings aren't taken seriously by adults. Which they often aren't.

The key question, though, is how likely it is that failure will be constructive, and whether our chief concern should be to make sure children have more opportunities to screw up. Undoubtedly many very successful people have encountered setbacks and deprivation on the way to triumph. Such inspirational story arcs are a staple of popular entertainment, in fact. But that doesn't mean that most people who encounter setbacks and deprivation go on to become successful.[28] We rarely hear about all those folks who tried and tried and tried, displaying awesome grit and gumption, but never made a go of their business, never sold their app, were never discovered by a talent scout, never had a chance to smugly recount their earlier setbacks and deprivation to an interviewer—for the simple reason that they're still having them.

Here's what we learn from psychology: What's most reliably associated with success are prior experiences with success, not with failure. Although there are exceptions, the most likely consequence of having failed at something is that a child will come to see himself as lacking competence. And the result of that belief is apt to be more failure. All else being equal, a student who gets a zero is far more likely to give up (and perhaps act up[29]) than to try harder. The late psychologist Arthur Combs put it this way:

> It is a common fallacy among many lay people and some teachers that,
> since the world is a very hard place and people sometimes fail, children

should be introduced to failure early. . . . But the position is based on a false premise. Actually, the best guarantee we have that a person will be able to deal with the future effectively is that he has been essentially successful in the past. People learn that they are able, not from failure, but from success. While it may be true that toughness and adequacy come from successfully dealing with problems, the learning comes not from experiencing failure but from successfully avoiding it.[30]

We may *wish* that a child who can't seem to get on base, or spit out a list of facts from memory during a test, or coax anything more than a hideous shriek from his violin will react by squaring his shoulders, reciting the mantra of *The Little Engine That Could*, and redoubling his efforts until, gosh darn it, he turns things around. But wishing doesn't make it true. That turn of events remains the exception rather than the rule. It's true that kids learn from failure, but what they're likely to learn is that *they're* failures.

To make sense of this, we need to understand something that's often ignored by people who insist on the benefits of experiencing failure: *Trying to succeed isn't the same thing as trying not to fail.* The first isn't always constructive, but the second is pretty reliably destructive.[31] Some of the greatest names in psychology—including Kurt Lewin in the 1930s and David McClelland in the 1950s—emphasized the all-important difference between being motivated to approach success and being motivated to avoid failure. When you actually do fail, it tends to trigger the latter: an avoidance mentality. The goal isn't to accomplish great things but to cover your butt, save your reputation, and preserve a positive view of yourself.

In a typical experiment, children are asked to solve problems that are rigged to ensure failure. After that, they're asked to solve problems that are clearly within their capabilities. What happens? Even the latter problems now tend to paralyze them because a spiral of failure has been set into motion. This doesn't happen in every case, of course, but for at least half a century researchers have been documenting the same basic effect with children of various ages.[32]

The fundamental difference between approaching success and avoiding failure will be missed by anyone who tends to focus only on what can be observed and measured. The decisive factor isn't what happened but how an individual—in a certain social context—*interprets* what happened. It's not just behaviors that matter, in other words, but attitudes, goals, perspectives, and feelings. On the one hand, this means that not every dropped stitch, botched chord, or "death" at a given level of a video game will register in the child's mind as a spirit-crushing Failure. After all, any attempt to master a skill will involve setbacks along the way. That's the good news.

The bad news is that under certain conditions (which I'll describe shortly), the objective fact of coming up short may indeed be experienced by children as failing in a meaningful way. And that does prove damaging—partly, as Deborah Stipek of Stanford University explains, because it changes their understanding of *why* they succeed and why they fail. Specifically, kids who have learned to see themselves as failures are "more likely to attribute success [when it does happen] to external causes, and failure to a lack of ability" as compared to "children who have a history of good performance."[33] A kid who doesn't do well assumes that if he *does* succeed, he must have just gotten lucky—or that the task was easy. And he assumes that if he fails again, which he regards as more likely, it's because he doesn't have what it takes: intelligence, athletic ability, musical talent, whatever. This quickly turns into a vicious circle because attributing results to causes outside of one's control makes people feel even more helpless, even less likely to do well in the future. The more they fail, the more they construct an image of themselves—and a theory about the results—that leads to still more failure.[34] All of this helps to explain why, as the educational psychologist Martin Covington put it, "simply increasing the pressure on students to try harder in the face of failure"—for example, by "rewarding hard workers and punishing the indifferent"—"is to invite disaster."[35]

And it's not just achievement that suffers. Kids who fail also tend to lose interest in whatever they're doing (say, learning), and they come to prefer easier tasks.[36] Both of these outcomes make sense, of course: It's hard for a child to stay excited about something she has reason to think she can't do well, and it's even harder for her to welcome a more difficult version of whatever she was doing. In fact, failure often leads kids to engage in something that psychologists call "self-handicapping": They deliberately make less of an effort in order to create an excuse for not succeeding. This lets them preserve the idea that they have high aptitude. They're able to tell themselves that if they *had* tried, they might have done much better.[37]

What all this means is that when kids' performance slides, when they lose enthusiasm for what they're doing, or when they try to cut corners, much more is going on than laziness or lack of motivation. What's relevant is what their experiences have been. And the experience of having failed is a uniquely poor bet for anyone who wants to maximize the probability of future success.

So how can we predict when failure is likely to do less damage? Different aspects of a situation and different characteristics of an individual help to determine how a given experience will be perceived and therefore what impact it's likely to have.

- Was it an unusual occurrence, or is failure so common for the child that he's come to expect it and therefore to infer that he's incompetent?
- Was the failure accidental, or was the child deliberately given too difficult a task in the hope that he would somehow be a better person for failing at it?
- Was failure intrinsic to the task itself (falling off the bike) or was it defined on the basis of someone else's judgment (getting a bad grade)?
- Was the failure just one element of a long-term activity that the child sees as meaningful and enjoyable, or was it a stand-alone event?
- Was the failure part of a process (learning to write or dance), or a summative outcome at the end of that process (a poor result on a test; an unsuccessful audition)?
- Has the child been helped to think about managing failure, or is it assumed that failure, per se, will benefit him?
- How did the child feel about himself before he failed? (As we'll see in chapter 6, people are *least* likely to persist in the face of failure

if they start out with low self-esteem.) Has he been raised with un-conditional care and the kind of autonomy support that produces a sense of efficacy—or in a "doing to" environment characterized by rewards and punishments?

- Did the child fail in a supportive environment where setbacks are viewed as no big deal? Or was the impact of the failure com-pounded because it took place in the context of intense pressure to succeed—or, worse, losing to someone in a public competition?

What leads kids to say, "This isn't worth it" or "I'm no good at this"—in other words, what's *least* likely to turn the experience of failure into something productive—are things like grades, contests, rewards, and punishments. These things draw attention to *how well* kids are doing—or, more ominously, how well they're doing compared to everyone else—as opposed to helping them focus on *what* they're doing. Ironically, the former are often favored by the same people who extol the motivational benefits of failure.

Under certain circumstances, then, it is possible for a child to pick herself up and try again, just the way we might hope. But it's still not the likeliest outcome. And the news is even worse if we're concerned not only about achievement but about kids' psychological health. Even someone who really does buckle down and try harder when she fails may be doing so out of an anxious, compulsive pressure to feel better about herself rather than because she takes pleasure from what she's do-ing. Even if it does occur, is success really worth that price?

Finally, if we take the advice of all those articles that urge us to step back and let our children stumble, the important question isn't what message we meant to communicate ("You can do it!") but what message the kids are likely to receive ("Mom could have helped me but didn't"). Not every instance in which a parent holds back will generate resent-ment or disappointment, of course. As we saw in Chapter 3, the amount of help kids need and welcome varies widely. But if we respond less to those individual needs than to a one-size-fits-all commitment to pro-moting self-sufficiency, or an abstract conviction that failure is good for kids, then we may damage the relationship we have with our children.

(In fact, we may be affecting the way they view themselves as a result of that relationship: "Does she not love me enough to help? Am I not *worth* helping?") A decision not to step in when kids are obviously frustrated and feeling inadequate is unlikely to make them more self-sufficient or self-confident. Instead, it's apt to leave them feeling less supported, less secure about their own worthiness, and more doubtful about the extent to which we really care about them.

The notion that kids need even more opportunities to fail is incredibly simplistic and often flatly false, in part because the whole BGUTI mindset is misguided. Like so many assertions about the motivational power of rewards and competition, it just doesn't stand up to the best psychological theory and research.

CHAPTER 5

The Underlying Values

Conditionality, Scarcity, and Deprivation

Let's review. Amazing accomplishments routinely take place in the absence of rewards. Competition isn't necessary to promote excellence and often holds people back from doing their best. Exposing children to unpleasant experiences is not a constructive way to prepare them for the possibility that they will encounter more unpleasant experiences when they're older. Frustration and failure have a tendency to elicit more of the same. And there is no evidence to suggest that children who receive recognition just for playing, or support just for trying, will develop unrealistic expectations, a sense of entitlement, or a sudden lack of interest in doing well.

What's particularly striking about these findings is how little they seem to matter. At some point one starts to realize that many traditionalists aren't just offering predictions about what *will* happen to children later (if we do this rather than that); they're telling us what we *ought* to do with children now. If their empirical assertions turn out to have little support, they merely shift gears and emphasize that losers *shouldn't* get trophies. For Pete's sake, they *lost*! They're *supposed* to go home empty-handed!

More generally, one finds an almost palpable outrage over the possibility that kids will get off too easy, or feel good about themselves without having *earned* that right. This anger—which, incidentally, I have never witnessed from people on the other side of the argument, such as supporters of participation trophies or opponents of dodge ball—contributes to the impression that what's at issue here are deeply held values. The economist Paul Krugman once pointed out that "the great divide in our politics isn't really about pragmatic issues, about which policies work best"; it's about differences in conceptions of morality and justice.[1] So, too, for disputes involving children.

Three features of the powerful reaction I've described are worth noting. First, it's liable to be triggered by very modest changes (or even just proposals for change): getting rid of school-sponsored dodge ball but not all competitive sports; eliminating zeroes for children's individual assignments, not grades, per se; putting an end to separate gatherings for elite students, not to awards assemblies across the board. Second, critics seem to take on faith that such changes are widespread. (Typical assertion: Today's teens have been "bathed from the cradle in affirmations and awards meant to boost their self-esteem."[2]) As with claims about permissiveness and overparenting, no evidence is ever presented to show that the practices being disparaged really are pervasive, even when it's something as easily quantifiable as the use of participation trophies. Finally, published criticisms are often distinguished by vitriolic sarcasm—mocking references to how we're protecting "the precious snowflakes of the world" or children's "tender self-esteem." The point, presumably, is that children are not as precious or tender as they're made out to be. Moreover, that case is made through ridicule rather than by demonstrating that the activity in question actually doesn't harm them.

Each of the empirical claims explored in the last chapter has a corresponding "shadow" value that I'd like to try to illuminate now. Behind the claim that rewards are required to motivate people is a commitment to *conditionality*. Behind the claim that competition produces excellence is a commitment to *scarcity*. And behind the claim that failure or unhappiness offers useful preparation is a commitment to *deprivation*.

CONDITIONALITY

If I give you a hug for no reason other than that I'm fond of you or hand you a banana just because I know you like them, those are not rewards. To qualify for that term, the item must be offered conditionally—based on my approval of something you did or how well you did it. You must "do this" to "get that."

Many people find it extremely upsetting that anyone might receive something desirable—a sum of money, a trophy, a commendation—without having done enough to deserve it. It's outrageous, we're told (in this case by *Newsweek*), that some children get "awards, gold stars, and happy-face stickers for the most routine accomplishments of childhood." Even recess in the primary grades is often defined not as a chance to play, a break to which all children are entitled, but as a reward for having lived up to the teacher's expectations—a privilege that ought to be withheld from children who don't merit it.

The insistence on attaching strings to whatever we offer isn't justified only by appealing to the ostensible effects on future behavior. Rather, it's assumed that we have a *moral* obligation to reward those who are deserving and, equally important, to make sure the undeserving go conspicuously unrewarded. Hence the fury when, for example, children who didn't defeat their peers are given a trophy anyway. Everyone at the game knows full well who won, but the losers must not receive anything that even looks like a reward.[3]

And it's not just treats or trophies that must be earned. Children shouldn't be allowed to feel good about themselves—or "special"—without being able to point to tangible accomplishments. (In the following chapter, I'll say more about the conservative assault on the concept of self-esteem and particularly on any version of it that isn't sufficiently conditional.) This basic message often shades into a disparagement of children or young adults in general. For example, a 2012 commencement speech delivered by an English teacher, in which he told the graduates, "Do not get the idea you're anything special. Because you're not," was noteworthy mostly for the explosion of (overwhelmingly positive) attention it attracted, including nearly two million views on YouTube, a decision by a local newspaper to publish the complete transcript, and a book deal. A vast segment of our culture believes that kids are too highly valued, that they haven't paid their dues and need to be put in their place.

The idea that good things must always be earned, and that any compromise on that principle means that we're spoiling or overprotecting children, might be said to live at the intersection of economics and theology. This is where lectures about the law of the marketplace meet sermons about what we must do to earn our way into heaven. Here, almost every human interaction, even among family members, is regarded as a kind of *trans*action. In explaining her opposition to the idea of expressing unconditional love for one's children, the influential developmental psychologist Diana Baumrind declared, "The rule of reciprocity, of paying for value received, is a law of life that applies to us all."[4] No one (even children) is entitled to get something (even love) for nothing.

Just as things that are desirable must be classified as rewards so they can be parceled out conditionally, so it follows that when people do something bad, bad things must be done to them. "The essence of punishment is that it involves suffering, or in [the seventeenth-century Dutch philosopher] Grotius's terms, 'The infliction of an ill suffered for an ill done,'" according to the criminologist Philip Bean. "The suffering created by punishment is not incidental, but the deliberate work of persons who claim the right to inflict it."[5] This holds true even when children are involved and even when the punishment is described euphemistically as a "consequence." In effect, a tit-for-tat view of justice is married to a market-exchange view of life.

Now one problem with punishment is that it really doesn't work very well. Practically speaking, it's remarkably ineffective—even counterproductive—with respect to any goal other than eliciting temporary compliance. Punishment fails to promote ethical growth, responsibility, or concern for others' well-being. What it does tend to promote are intense feelings of resentment, a concern with figuring out how to avoid being caught (rather than with doing the right thing), a belief that power allows one to get one's way in life (by making weaker people suffer), and a nearly exclusive attention to self-interest.[6]

There are several reasons why punishment persists despite its disappointing, if not alarming, track record. The one I want to identify here is that for some people its track record is irrelevant. They punish not to promote ethical growth but because they see it as appropriate, even a matter of duty, to do so. Its purpose is retribution, not improvement. When children misbehave (however the adult chooses to define that), they should be made to suffer—just as those who accomplish something should be rewarded. In short, conditionality is often seen as a moral imperative, not just a way to bring about certain results.

Praise

The crusade against perceived entitlement, and in favor of conditionality, is on display in rants like one in the *Washington Post* about how "everywhere you turn these days, adults are passing out stars, stickers and trophies to children for not doing much more than showing up."[7] But it's become just as common to denounce what we *say* to children as what we give them—in particular, what's described by traditionalists as excessive or empty praise. I find this last example particularly interesting because for the past couple of decades I, too, have offered a critical account of praise, but from a very different direction.[8] As a result, I've had the odd experience of seeing my work cited approvingly by people whose views and values are diametrically opposed to my own.

As I see it, praise is a verbal reward, often doled out in an effort to change the behavior of someone with less power. (It's managers who praise employees, teachers who praise students, parents who praise children—rarely the other way around.) It's a "doing to" intervention, one likely to be experienced as manipulative regardless of the intentions of the person who offered it. It's a pat on the head—"pat" being short for "patronizing"—that's offered when the person with less power impresses or pleases the person with more. And that's true regardless of whether the less-powerful person is praised for his ability or for the effort he's made.[9]

Unlike feedback, which is purely informational, praise is a judgment. And positive judgments are ultimately no more constructive than negative ones. The primary effect of offering them is to make children dependent on getting more such expressions of approval. Like other extrinsic inducements, moreover, praise tends to undermine intrinsic motivation and, often, the quality of people's work or learning.[10]

But beyond its practical effects, I find praise troubling because children are likely to conclude that they're valued—and, by implication, valuable—only when they live up to someone else's standards. The message is that attention, acknowledgment, and approval are offered only when the child does a "good job." As we saw earlier in the context of psychological control, praise is tantamount to what psychologists call "conditional positive regard." It's not only different from, but antithetical to, the *unconditional* care that children need: to be loved for who they are and not merely for what they do. It makes perfect sense, then, that positive reinforcement was developed as a technique to elicit certain behaviors, not to promote healthy development.

The suggestion that there might be anything problematic about telling children you like what they've done will strike many people as counterintuitive, even unnerving. But if you've ever come across an article that's critical of praise, chances are it didn't sound anything like what I've just described. Instead, it probably said something like this: "We congratulate children for every little thing they do—to the point that praise has become meaningless. By over-celebrating their accomplishments, we lead them to believe they're more talented than they really are." What's thought to be wrong with praise is that it, like other rewards, is given out to the undeserving—just one more symptom of a culture of overindulgence and overparenting. The solution is to be more parsimonious, more stringent in our expressions of approval. Set the bar higher. Demand that kids do more before we praise them.

In other words, make our approval of them even more conditional.[11]

A central weakness of this common conservative critique is that praise actually doesn't represent indulgence or excessive encouragement. Rather, like most of what's classified as overparenting, it just extends the old-school "doing to" model of raising children and teaching students. That becomes clear if we stop focusing on how often or how easily kids are praised, and instead ask *why* they're being praised. What are the intentions of the adult? The answer, once again, is that the point is often to control children. Control, we may need to remind ourselves, doesn't always take the form of punishment and coercion. Sometimes it's expressed by means of a sugary "Good job!" The latter is obviously less harsh, but the point is still to produce whatever behavior is favored by the parent or other authority figure. To that extent, children's *resistance* to being controlled may explain the research showing that praise tends to be counterproductive (apart from eliciting temporary compliance, which any reward or punishment can sometimes manage).

To listen to adults as they dole out a verbal reward to a child is to hear another example of how approval is contingent on the child's performance or behavior. Traditionalists, by contrast, listen to the same utterances and think, "But that kid wasn't very impressive! He should have to do more before we say nice things to him." This reaction isn't based on evidence that it's beneficial in a practical sense to set more stringent standards for praising kids. It's based on the belief that there's something morally wrong with giving anything to children that the speaker believes they haven't earned.

SCARCITY

Just as the hypothesis that rewards are required to motivate people often rests on the conviction that people *should* be rewarded for doing something well (and not rewarded when they don't), so the hypothesis that competition is productive goes hand-in-hand with the belief that the struggle to be number one is desirable regardless of its effects. In our culture it's not enough to achieve; one must triumph over others. Even when it's possible for many people who are engaged in an activity to do it successfully, we're encouraged to think of success as a scarce commodity. In fact, if people aren't sorted into winners and losers, that's taken as evidence that we've "lowered our standards."

This scarcity model is rarely questioned or even named. But it permeates our society to the point that it's hard to find recreational activities for children that don't pit them against one another, either individually or in groups. Sure, we think it's nice if they acquire skills, get some exercise, and maybe even have fun. But at the core of these games is an imperative to prevail over the other team, to achieve a status that one side can acquire only if the other does not. The (symbolic) spoils go to the conquerors—and only to them.

Again, the attachment to this arrangement that many people feel isn't based primarily on the testable proposition that making kids compete will improve their performance. Rather, excellence has been *defined* as something that everyone can't attain. This may explain why the word "competitive"—applied to a corporation, a school system, or an entire country—has become an honorific, a synonym for high quality. Doing well is conflated with beating others.

What follows from all of this is an interesting bit of circular logic. Because we're committed to this ideology, we set up a vast array of competitive activities. Within those activities, success does indeed require winning. Good tennis players are those who beat other tennis players, and a good shot during play is one the opponent can't return. But that's not a truth about life or about excellence—it's a truth about tennis. We've created an artificial structure in which one person can't succeed without doing so at someone else's expense, and then we accuse anyone who prefers other kinds of activities of being naïve because "there can be only one best—you're it or you're not," as the teacher who delivered that much-admired you're-not-special commencement speech declared. You see the sleight of hand here? The question isn't whether everyone playing a competitive game can win or whether every student can be above average. Of course they can't. The question that we're discouraged from asking is why our games are competitive—or our students are compulsively ranked against one another—in the first place.

It's remarkable how empirical evidence tends to be shunted aside in discussions of this topic. You can cite study after study that shows people tend to do better on most tasks when they're working with, rather than against, one another—only to be met with the accusation that you "don't value excellence" or are "dumbing down" whatever institution is involved. You can point out that turning an activity into a contest tends to prevent all children, including the eventual winner, from doing their best, but that doesn't matter once it has been decided that excellence cannot be attained by everyone. Each must strive against the others so that only one will end up on top. That struggle, and that result, are thought to be at the core of what excellence *means*.

This is not just another instance of BGUTI. The objection to making things "too easy" for children is based partly on the belief that they need to learn to cope with bad things. But from the perspective I've been describing, competition *isn't* bad, even if losing is unpleasant. One of its supposed virtues is that the process of sorting people into winners and losers reveals, and forces us to acknowledge, a natural distribution of ability. Talent, like successful outcomes, is thought to be scarce. Inequality is a defining feature of life, something to be emphasized and celebrated.

That belief helps us to make sense of the contempt showered on anyone who suggests that we should stop keeping score at young children's games, eliminate (or even just modify) awards assemblies, recognize kids for effort, or create more inclusive activities. "Why should an awards ceremony be about discrimination, excellence, and making choices when, instead, it can be about inclusion?" a *Chicago Tribune* reporter sarcastically demands.[12] To smooth over the rough edges of competition is seen as tantamount to claiming that everyone is equally able, whereas, we're repeatedly informed, the truth is that only a very few are special and worthy of commendation.[13] Competition illuminates and accentuates the differences in talent and accomplishment among us.[14]

In response, I would begin by pointing out that not even the most committed opponents of competition believe that all people are equally talented. I certainly don't. By the same token, we can be reasonably sure that no child who received a trinket after losing a contest walked away believing that he (or his team) had won—or that failing is just as good as succeeding. (A twenty-four-year-old writer, describing how Millennials are faulted for everything under the sun, points to an article filled with the usual blather about their lack of motivation due to having received too many trophies, and offers this deadpan response: "It's true. I remember when I got a trophy for soccer in second grade and assumed I was set for life."[15]) The fact that participation trophies have never been convincingly shown to have any negative effects at all[16] provides further evidence that the outcry over them has its roots in ideology more than in practical objections.

Giving trophies to all the kids in order to minimize the destructive effects of competition is a well-meaning attempt to exclude fewer children from these noxious distinctions—a tiny step in the right direction. But it doesn't begin to compensate for all the ways that children are made to feel inadequate on a daily basis at school and at play. In fact, adding more trophies distracts us from the problems inherent in competition itself and its message that each kid must succeed by making others fail. In other words, "trophies for everyone," like effusive praise, troubles me for the opposite reason that it offends conservative critics.

As for the tendency to emphasize differences in ability: List a hundred capabilities—writing poetry, sensing how others are feeling, hitting balls with sticks—and you'll find a range of aptitude in any population. Some kids have to work harder than others to do any given thing well. We know it, and they know it. But that's not an argument for calling attention to those differences, let alone for making children try to defeat one another. On the contrary, we ought to assist those for whom things come less easily, thereby reducing the salience and significance of kids' relative standing. Better yet, we can help the kids themselves to reframe the differences in how good they are: If Allison grasps certain concepts faster than Allen does, it's not that Allison wins and Allen loses, but that Allison is lucky enough to be able to help Allen improve. Later, at another task at which *he* excels, he can return the favor.[17]

Grade Inflation

Where young people are concerned, the best illustration of an ethic of scarcity may come from the classroom rather than the playing field. I'm thinking of the widespread assumption that grades are inflated—accompanied by the belief that this is a very bad thing. Academe's usual requirements for supporting data and reasoned analysis seem to have been suspended where this issue is concerned. The idea that grade inflation is out of control has largely been accepted on faith and, in some quarters, feeds indignant expostulations about a diminished commitment to excellence and, of course, kids' sense of entitlement.

There are two problems with this claim right off the bat: First, it's not clear that grades are actually rising.[18] Second, even if they were, that doesn't prove they're inflated. (One would have to demonstrate that those higher grades are undeserved, which means ruling out any number of alternative explanations.[19]) The bottom line is this: No one has ever demonstrated that students today get A's for the same work that used to receive B's or C's. We simply do not have the data to support such a claim, and that claim is the linchpin of the belief that grades are inflated.

It's telling, though, that many critics don't even bother to assert that grades have risen over time or are too generous. They simply point to how many students get A's right now—as if a sufficiently high number was objectionable on its face. Some find it disturbing if "too many" good grades are given out because it then becomes harder to spread out students on a continuum, ranking them against one another for the benefit of post-college constituencies. One professor asks, by way of analogy, "Why would anyone subscribe to *Consumers Digest* if every blender were rated a 'best buy'?" But how appropriate is such a marketplace analogy? Is the professor's job to rate students like blenders for the convenience of employers? Or is it to offer feedback that will help students learn more skillfully and enthusiastically? (Notice, by the way, that even consumer magazines don't grade on a curve. They report the happy news if it turns out that every blender meets a reasonable set of performance criteria.)

What we're really looking at here is, again, a commitment to scarcity. "The essence of grading is exclusiveness," says Harvey Mansfield, a Harvard professor, who adds that students "should have to compete with each other." It doesn't matter whether they're all learning more or working harder, adds Richard Kamber, who, like Mansfield, is a tireless critic of the putative "epidemic" of grade inflation. "If grades are to have any coherent meaning, they need to represent a relative degree of success."[20]

The key word here, of course, is "relative." In other words, students should be sorted, with grades used to announce how well they're doing compared to one another, rather than providing information about absolute accomplishment. And if they've already been sorted by the admissions process so that elite institutions contain the very best students, well, they ought to be sorted again *within* those institutions. No matter how well they all do, the game should be rigged so that only a few can get A's. To put it differently, the question guiding evaluation ought not to be "How well are they learning?" but "Who's beating whom?" A school's ultimate mission therefore wouldn't be to maximize everyone's success but to ensure that there will always be losers.

This view, while rarely stated explicitly, is what drives denunciations of grade inflation. I find it both intellectually and morally deficient. What statisticians call a normal distribution (also known as a bell curve) may sometimes—but only sometimes—describe the range of knowledge in a roomful of students at the beginning of a course. But when that course is over, any responsible educator hopes that the results would skew drastically to the right, meaning that most students have learned what they hadn't known before. He or she would want *all* students to wind up with A's—if grades have to be given out at all. Conversely, as a group of education theorists argued, "It is not a symbol of rigor to have grades fall into a 'normal' distribution; rather, it is a symbol of failure—failure to teach well, failure to test well, and failure to have any influence at all on the intellectual lives of students."[21]

Making sure that students are continually re-sorted, with excellence turned into an artificially scarce commodity, is really rather perverse when you think about it. In any case, relative success—how many peers a student has bested—tells us little about how much she knows and is able to do. And such grading policies tend to create a competitive climate that's counterproductive for everyone because it discourages a free exchange of ideas and destroys any sense of community, which is conducive to exploration. Based on what we know about the effects of extrinsic motivation, the real threat to excellence isn't grade inflation at all; it's grades. And the more we're preoccupied with limiting the number of A's, the more attention students are led to pay to grades—rather than to the learning itself.

People who are focused on relative success have a curious understanding of "high academic standards." They seem to use this term not in the context of students' skill at formulating questions, the incisiveness of their thinking, or their ability to look at problems from multiple perspectives. Rather, it refers to how few high grades are given. Stringent grading, a more "rigorous" course or school, is assumed to be better not because it's associated with other intellectual outcomes but because that's how *better* is defined.

Conversely, no matter how high the quality of students' thinking, from this perspective we've abandoned our commitment to excellence if a lot of those students receive A's. This attitude perfectly captures the scarcity mentality, the assumption that education, like life itself, is a race in which most cannot prevail. Once again, that's not based on the *reality* that everyone can't win but on an *ideology* that confuses succeeding with winning.

DEPRIVATION

Alongside conditionality and scarcity we find the ideological engine behind BGUTI—namely, a determination to make sure that things aren't too easy for kids. The premise here is not only that deprivation, struggle, and sacrifice are useful preparation for life's hardships, but that there's simply something objectionable about sparing kids from having to cope with deprivation, struggle, and sacrifice.[22]

I'm reminded of a famous ad campaign to sell Listerine mouthwash, which was based on the assumption that because it tasted vile, it obviously had to work well. The flip side of this way of thinking is that we ought to be wary of anything that's too appealing. "Feel-good" and "touchy-feely" have become all-purpose epithets to disparage whatever seems suspiciously pleasurable. This is particularly true in education, where these terms are often applied to authentic ways of evaluating learning (in place of standardized tests), a course of study that emphasizes creativity (rather than the memorization of facts), and having students learn in cooperative groups (instead of alone or against one another).

Here, again, evidence that such practices are more effective may simply be waved aside. If something is enjoyable, that's reason enough to describe it as touchy-feely and deem it unworthy of consideration. Progressive educators may make a case for creating a more engaging curriculum or for bringing kids in on making decisions, only to be informed rather huffily that life isn't always going to be interesting (or responsive to kids' preferences), and students had better learn to deal with that fact, like it or not.

"Like it or not," in fact, is a favorite phrase of people who think this way. Another one begins "It's time they learned that . . . "—the implication being that children should be introduced to frustration and unhappiness without delay. There's work to be done! Life isn't supposed to be fun and games! Self-denial—whose adherents generally presume to deny others as well—is closely connected to fear of pleasure, redemption through suffering, and fury at anyone who coddles or indulges children. H. L. Mencken's definition of Puritanism seems apt here: "the haunting fear that someone, somewhere, may be happy."

Sometimes one suspects that the tacit message from such traditionalists is: "*I* don't get everything I want—why should they?" The educator John Holt once remarked that if people really felt that life was "nothing but drudgery, an endless list of dreary duties," one would hope they might "say, in effect, 'I have somehow missed the chance to put much joy and meaning into my own life; please educate my children so that they will do better.'"[23] Is our primary goal to help kids take delight in learning, or is it to train them to do what they're told, even if (or especially if) those things are unpleasant?

Perhaps the "take your medicine" (or mouthwash) stance is really a way of saying, "Oh, stop complaining, it's not that bad." Some adults may be eager to prescribe "character building" frustrations to children based on what they remember about, or generalize from, their own childhoods. "Hey, *I* got zeroes, *I* missed out on the trophy plenty of times—and I turned out just fine!" And that may be true. On the other hand, the speaker may be (1) incorrectly assuming that his or her own experiences set the boundary for how bad things can be, (2) remembering past events as somewhat more benign than they actually were, (3) underestimating the impact of those events by assessing his or her own psychological health a bit optimistically (since a defensive insistence that one "turned out just fine" can't always be taken at face value), or (4) misunderstanding causal connections. Even if someone really is flourishing in adulthood despite childhood challenges, luck may have played a prominent role in that outcome. In that case, it would be foolish, if not callous, to decree that all children should have to contend with similar challenges.

Regardless of the experiences that might be found among certain individuals, though, to endorse BGUTI is a way of saying to a child, "Your objections don't count. Your unhappiness doesn't matter. Suck it up." (This attitude is made strikingly explicit with posters and buttons that feature a diagonal red slash through the word *whining*.)[24] People who adopt this perspective are usually on top, issuing directives, not on the bottom being directed. "Learn to live with it because there's more coming later" can be rationalized as being in the best interests of those on the receiving end, but it may just mean "Do it because I said so." It functions as a tool to ensure compliance, which has the effect of cementing the power of those offering this advice.

Retention in Grade

One example of this attitude about deprivation involves literal failure— in a school setting. Over the last few decades, education researchers have discovered that just about the worst possible response when children are struggling academically is to flunk them and make them repeat a grade. Doing so has destructive effects on students' subsequent academic performance, on their self-confidence, and on the likelihood that they will eventually graduate. (The experience of having been held back a year is an even stronger predictor of dropping out than is socioeconomic status.[25])

Despite those disturbing findings, the practice of making children repeat a grade has grown in popularity "during the very time period that research has revealed its negative effects on those retained," as one scholar observed.[26] Retention is widely endorsed and employed not because it helps children—it clearly does not—but for ideological reasons. The argument seems to be that kids should be held back because they haven't earned the right to move on to the next grade level. If they haven't paid their dues, then allowing them to move on constitutes "social promotion." Traditionalists have successfully reframed the discussion so the question isn't "What's best for students?" (which often involves promotion with extra support) but "How can we make sure students don't get anything to which they're not entitled?"

In 2004, New York City mayor Michael Bloomberg decreed not only that underperforming third graders would be held back but also that their performance would be determined by a standardized test. (He did so after abruptly firing and replacing three members of the city's Panel for Educational Policy who disagreed with him on the issue.) "Bravo!" read one letter to the editor. "Eight years old is a perfect age to learn a rule of life: You have to earn your rewards, not count on free rides." And another: Social promotion "eats away at the moral fabric of our society by imbuing the young with a false sense of entitlement. Imagine their chagrin when on entering the work force, they realize that they must actually put nose to the grindstone to achieve success. That is, if achieving success is even a concept with which they have been made familiar after years of social promotion."[27]

PRESERVING THE STATUS QUO

When someone says that raising or educating children in a specific way will have a specific effect (for example, "If they don't have to struggle, they'll grow up feeling entitled"), it's sometimes possible to test that prediction with research. But *shoulds*—the subject of this chapter—are trickier to challenge than *wills*. The best we can do is press for clarification, shine a light on hidden assumptions, and tease out some of the moral and practical implications of a position. We can ask: Does it really make sense to demand that children earn everything they get, or is that an unnecessarily sour and stressful way to live? Should they have to strive *against* others, or is cooperation generally preferable (so that those they meet are more likely to be potential allies than rivals)? Is the prospect of a "feel-good" childhood really so worrisome that we need to contrive unpleasant and frustrating experiences for our kids?

In the introduction to this book, I mentioned George Lakoff's thesis that conservative views on a range of political issues are linked to what he calls a Strict Father model. That model emerges from a conviction that life is difficult and survival demands competition, self-reliance, and the enforcement of (and obedience to) strict rules. From this perspective, "nurturance is not unconditional," says Lakoff. "It must serve the function of authority, strength, and discipline." To get people to do what they would rather not, it's critical to offer rewards for obedience and punishment for disobedience, the hope being that this will strengthen people's willpower and self-reliance. Consistent with the last of these, "Mature children are on their own and parents are not to meddle." And consistent with the carrot-and-stick approach to socialization, "Rewards given to those who have not earned them through competition are immoral. They violate the entire system . . . and they remove the need for obedience to authority." Similarly, "If competition were removed, self-discipline would cease. . . . Competition therefore is moral."[28]

Lakoff's Strict Father model captures what I've been describing as a traditionalist worldview. It efficiently ties together the strong condemnation of permissiveness and helicopter parenting, the demands for stricter limits and punitive consequences for children, and the furious reaction to any arrangement that might soften the impact of competitive struggle or allow trophies, A's, or praise to be given out too readily. Lakoff shows how these positions are all facets of a single whole. And it is a *moral* whole, which explains why the attachment to these beliefs is not easily shaken by research concerning the practical effects of acting on them.

Whether this moral vision can be described as "conservative" is debatable. But that word does seem to apply in at least one respect: The *effect* of these positions is literally to conserve our current practices and institutions by discouraging us from critically analyzing them. Whether or not the premises of the argument are conservative, the implications surely are.

Consider: If the question is whether parents are too involved with their children's homework, then the question *isn't* whether the homework itself is worth doing—let alone why children should have to work what amounts to a second shift after having spent all day in school. If the question is whether we're praising kids too easily or often, then the question *isn't* whether praise, per se, is problematic because it functions as a way of controlling kids. If teachers are ridiculed for trying to correct students' assignments a little more gently, steering clear of large red X's,[29] then it's less likely that we'd ever examine the limitations of the bigger pedagogical picture: an approach to teaching and evaluation that consists of making kids cram forgettable facts into short-term memory and then spit out those facts on a test. Denunciations of grade inflation deflect our attention from the harm done by grading itself. Outrage over participation trophies means we're much less likely to explore the broader effects of competition. And so on.

What about BGUTI? Well, here's where conservatism is right out on the surface. "Better get used to it" assumes not only that life is unpleasant, but that nothing can be done about what makes it that way. It's just how things are. And because nothing can be done, nothing *should* be done. There's no point in working to improve our schools or workplaces; all kids can do is prepare to deal with reality. Our job is to get them ready. When an entire generation comes to regard rewards and punishments, or rating and ranking, as "just the way life works" rather than as practices that happen to define our society at this moment in history, their critical sensibilities are stillborn. Debatable policies are never debated. BGUTI becomes a self-fulfilling prophecy.

In Chapter 4, I suggested that people are better able to cope with challenging circumstances if they were nurtured and supported as children. It's success that prepares one to handle failure; it's unconditional acceptance that allows one to deal with subsequent rejection. But that doesn't mean children raised this way will just put up with disrespectful treatment, coercion, or competition. Indeed, they may be deeply disturbed by these things and committed to bringing about changes—a process in which we can and should support them, as I'll argue at the end of the book. But this is less likely to happen when children are treated more roughly, marinated in traditional values and practices, manipulated with bribes and threats from the beginning so it never occurs to them that *things could be otherwise*. BGUTI is a recipe for docility. It doesn't help kids deal with unpleasant stuff; it just makes it more likely that unpleasant stuff will be around indefinitely.

CHAPTER 6

The Attack on Self-Esteem

A new idea is hatched; it catches on; it begins to spread; it inspires a flurry of books and articles, conferences and seminars. And then it fades away. The cycle is common in many fields, but I'm most familiar with how it plays out in education, where the last couple of decades have witnessed a sudden (albeit fleeting) excitement about "outcome-based" and then "brain-based" schooling, about Total Quality Management, multiple intelligences, the "flipped" classroom, and several other hot developments, each of which cooled and was supplanted by the next big thing.

In the 1980s and '90s, self-esteem took its turn in the procession, with that phrase becoming a rallying cry for many American educators. Trying to improve children's perceptions of their own worth was described as a crucial contributor to how they fared academically and socially. The tipping point came in 1990 with the much-publicized release of a state-funded task force report in California. School-based programs to raise students' self-esteem began to sprout up across the country. State and local councils devoted to the cause were formed, newsletters circulated, and classroom curricula disseminated.

The quality of these efforts varied widely; they included carefully planned intervention programs as well as silly rituals in which kids were

surrounded by cheerfully reassuring posters and made to chant "I'm special!" Some proponents regarded self-esteem not merely as important but
as a cure-all—a "social vaccine" against crime and violence, substance
abuse, and other cultural diseases—even though a scholarly monograph
commissioned by the California task force failed, rather embarrassingly,
to find much data to justify this enthusiasm.[1]

At some point in the 1990s educators began drifting off to other projects. But the effort did leave one enduring legacy. It didn't have to do with
any of the publications or programs dedicated to supporting self-esteem,
though—it was the critical backlash that had sprung up. No sooner did
educators express an interest in trying to help kids feel better about themselves than the attacks began. A number of these articles, not surprisingly,
were written by conservative thinkers,[2] but, as with so many other aspects of parenting and education, their response was mirrored in mainstream media outlets. Hence "The Trouble with Self-Esteem" in *US News
& World Report* (1990), "Hey, I'm Terrific" in *Newsweek* (1992), "Down
from the Self-Esteem High" in the *New York Times* (1993), "A Full Head
of Esteem" in the *Washington Post* (1995), "Self-Esteem Self-Defeating?"
in the *Boston Globe* (1996), and many more along the same lines.

By now the councils and newsletters and classroom exercises devoted to boosting self-esteem are few and far between. Yet the furious
denunciations have continued: Another article called "The Trouble
with Self-Esteem," this one in the *New York Times Magazine*; "The Self-
Esteem Hoax" in the *Christian Science Monitor*; and "Self-Esteem: Why
We Need Less of It" in *Time* all appeared in 2002. Then, too, there are
the criticisms in books, from *The Myth of Self-Esteem* (1998) to *The Self-
Esteem Trap* (2009); in *Doonesbury*; in best sellers about children such as
NurtureShock; and in a steady stream of blog posts, newspaper columns,
and discipline manuals. Like someone still shrieking about the threat of
Communism, the attack continues long after its target has largely faded
away.

The idea that kids should be helped to regard themselves more favor-
ably continues to arouse such disproportionate contempt—the phrase
"using a howitzer to kill a butterfly" comes to mind—that one imagines a

psychoanalyst rubbing his chin thoughtfully and musing about the critics' unconscious motives. Having combed through major American newspapers, newsweeklies, and general-interest magazines, I've been unable to find a single article on the topic that doesn't take this negative view. Granted, there are plenty of self-help books about building self-esteem, but in mainstream periodicals, any time you see that phrase (at least in the context of kids), you can count on its being preceded by the adjective "inflated" or accompanied by a warning about "narcissism." Indeed, the arguments and rhetoric are so similar from one article or book to the next that you may find yourself wondering if a single person wrote all of them. And yet, just as with polemics about overparenting or the benefits of failure, many of these attacks on self-esteem are delivered in a tone of self-congratulation, as if it took extraordinary gumption to say pretty much what everyone else is saying.

SORTING TRUTH FROM FICTION

Critics of self-esteem have a tendency to slide into other familiar complaints: They also condemn excessive praise (as if self-esteem and praise were essentially the same thing),[3] our alleged reluctance to criticize children, the diminution of competition (and therefore excellence), the ease with which grades and trophies are acquired, and so on. Sometimes all these grievances are bundled together under the heading of "the self-esteem movement" in order to permit more efficient disparagement of everything that rankles traditionalists.

A fair amount of what's said in these articles and books consists of sweeping generalizations about lazy, entitled kids. The cumulative result of these attacks is that many parents and teachers are now embarrassed to point out that something is damaging to their children's self-esteem, even when that's an accurate description and a legitimate concern. Still, there are several questions about the concept that clearly need to be taken seriously. It's certainly reasonable, for example, to point out that raising someone's self-esteem isn't easy to do, and that, even if successful, such efforts aren't guaranteed to help children excel in school or become better people. So let's take a moment to review what we know about the subject.

Does self-esteem really matter?

Those who regard the whole concept as something unworthy of serious concern include some psychologists—Jean Twenge, Martin Seligman, and Roy Baumeister, to name three—who argue that it's merely a by-product of other qualities or that *high* self-esteem is not particularly beneficial and may even be pathological. However, they tend to make these arguments while rattling off various other complaints about children and parenting that are commonly heard from conservative social critics, suggesting that their views about self-esteem may reflect a larger worldview.[4]

It's fair to say there are difficulties with how the concept of self-esteem has been conceptualized and investigated, and cause and effect sometimes remain confused, as is true of many other topics in human behavior. Still, it's clear to the great majority of psychologists—theorists, researchers, and clinicians—that self-esteem does have predictive value. How people view themselves really does mean something.

Adolescents with low self-esteem, for example, have "poorer mental and physical health, worse economic prospects, and higher levels of criminal behavior during adulthood," even when other variables such as social class, gender, and depression are held constant. Preadolescents with low self-esteem are more likely to be aggressive a couple of years later and also to engage in "problem eating, suicidal ideation, and multiple health compromising behaviors." And low self-esteem apparently causes depression more than the other way around.[5]

People with high self-esteem, meanwhile, are apt to be more satisfied with life, less depressed, and more optimistic.[6] (There are other positive associations as well, but it's not always clear that they're *caused* by higher self-esteem.) What's more, researchers have documented a set of interesting connections to success and failure: First, people who hold a positive view of themselves are more likely to persist at a task even when it's difficult. At the same time, such people are more likely to recognize when persistence would be futile; they don't keep trying desperately in a way that proves self-defeating and irrational. Finally, higher self-esteem appears to create resilience so that the experience of failure isn't as discouraging.[7]

Does self-esteem promote higher achievement?

Here's a good example of where the concept was oversold. When you look at the research over the last few decades, the correlation between self-esteem and school achievement isn't all that impressive. To make matters worse, even when they are related, it's not clear that the former is responsible for the latter. Part of the problem, however, turns on how broadly or narrowly self-esteem has been defined. A lot of these studies focus "on the capacity of global measures of self-esteem to predict specific outcomes."[8] If you score kids on how they respond to prompts such as "I feel that I have a number of good qualities," the results aren't all that useful for predicting how well they'll do in math. But when you look at how children view their capability in a specific field, that *does* predict their performance. The effect isn't huge, but it's consistent, and it does seem to be causal according to two independent reviews of the research. "There is clear evidence . . . that prior levels of academic self-concept lead to higher levels of subsequent academic achievement beyond what can be explained by prior levels of academic achievement."[9]

Perhaps you've heard people say that "self-esteem isn't the cause of achievement; it's the result." This has become the mantra of traditionalists. Unfortunately, it represents an enormous oversimplification. I've already suggested that the first part of that statement is false, or at least greatly overstated: Some versions of self-esteem do contribute to achievement. But the evidence to support the second part, the proposition that doing well in school raises self-esteem, is "disappointingly weak."[10] Then, too, there's the question of whether "doing well in school" refers to accomplishments that are meaningful to students. (No "I Believe in Me!" self-esteem unit could possibly be more foolish than the expectation that students will feel good about themselves because they successfully filled out a worksheet or memorized a bunch of facts for a quiz. Ironically, many critics of self-esteem seem to prefer just this sort of schooling.)

People who insist that achievement produces self-esteem rather than the other way around are mostly telling us what they think *ought* to be the case. After all, even if there's reason to doubt that A causes B, that doesn't allow us to conclude that B causes A. It may be that something else altogether (C) causes both A and B, giving the appearance of a direct connection between the two.[11] Or it may be that A affects B, which, in turn, affects A. Indeed, there's good reason to believe that "gains in academic achievement that are facilitated by self-esteem, for example, may further enhance feelings of self-worth, thus setting the stage for additional achievement in school."[12]

A group of Australian researchers went a step further. They cautioned that it's actually counterproductive to ignore how kids feel about themselves (or about what they're doing) and focus only on how well they're doing it. "Interventions aimed at enhancing performance may unintentionally undermine self-concept in ways that will eventually undermine the short-term gains in performance," they pointed out. Their example was a study in which both competitive and cooperative strategies were introduced to improve physical fitness. Both produced temporary benefits, but cooperation improved—and competition undermined—the kids' *beliefs* about their physical ability.[13] It's shortsighted to concentrate only on skills and other outcomes. If children feel worse about themselves, which is a typical long-range effect of competition for both winners and losers, then any benefits that do show up aren't likely to last.[14] Thus, self-esteem really does play an important role—even if we're concerned only about achievement. And if we want to produce people who are also fully functioning, happy, and healthy, it matters even more.

Do programs to boost children's self-esteem actually work?

When I reviewed the research on this topic in the early 1990s, I didn't see much evidence of success. But there's now more reason to be hopeful that school-based interventions can make a difference—provided that (a) the focus is on improving the way children view their aptitude in specific areas, (b) the measure of success matches that focus rather than looking at global self-esteem, and (c) the program isn't ridiculous.[15] A 1998 review of 102 studies pronounced the results "encouraging. Programs seem able to enhance children's and adolescents' [self-esteem]." Eight years later, another group of researchers reanalyzed those evaluations—as well as an additional batch of studies—using different statistical techniques. They, too, found "promising" results regarding the "overall positive effectiveness of the interventions."[16]

Isn't it possible to have self-esteem that's too high?

The short answer: only if you've stacked the deck, rhetorically speaking, by *defining* high self-esteem as something bad. That's basically what Roy Baumeister did in a 1996 article whose subtitle was "The Dark Side of High Self-Esteem." His essay—which presented no new data, incidentally—was snapped up by the media and to this day is still triumphantly cited by critics of self-esteem: Aha! Dangerous criminals actually think too well of themselves, not too poorly! Self-esteem is the problem, not the solution. But Baumeister's conclusion was preordained by his premise. On his article's very first page, "high self-esteem" and "egotism" were used interchangeably. Since many violent people are egotistical, there must be a risk when self-esteem reaches a certain level. Q.E.D.

Complementing this and other examples of dubious and even offensive reasoning[17] was a remarkably simplistic understanding of human psychology. Baumeister basically assumed that we should take people's sweeping self-congratulatory statements about themselves—"I'm the greatest/smartest/strongest!"—at face value. Anyone who brags about how amazing he is must have very high self-esteem. This premise is also accepted by like-minded critics such as Jean Twenge ("As any parent of a two-year-old can tell you, most kids like themselves just fine—and make the demands to prove it"[18]), but it's unconvincing to anyone who realizes there's a world of difference between, on the one hand, genuinely positive self-regard and arrogant self-satisfaction.

Even people who have never read Freud or other depth psychologists understand that someone who feels compelled to swagger and boast, to flash his credentials or his bling, to tell you how much better he is than everyone else, may well be trying to compensate for the terrifying suspicion that, down deep, he's really not very impressive at all. Scratch a competitive person and you'll likely find persistent insecurity and self-doubt. So, too, for narcissists: They "report a grandiose sense of self . . . yet, covertly, they seem to experience symptoms of vulnerability; they are self-doubting."[19] The same is true of those who are aggressive. As the psychiatrist James Gilligan, an expert on criminal violence, has remarked, "I have yet to see a serious act of violence that was not provoked by the experience of feeling shamed and humiliated. . . . The most dangerous men on earth are those who are afraid that they are wimps."[20]

Grandiosity, narcissism, and perhaps competitiveness may be understood as strategies for dealing with underlying *low* self-esteem. But even if this isn't always true, people with those characteristics are clearly very different from those with high self-esteem. In the words of the late Morris Rosenberg, one of the pioneers in studying this topic, "With self-esteem we are asking whether the individual considers himself adequate—a person of worth—not whether he considers himself superior to others."[21] To that extent, the fact that grandiose people may become aggressive provides no reason to believe there's a "dark side" of high self-esteem.

Research confirms this. Whether or not high self-esteem and narcissism are positively correlated—and there's mixed evidence about that[22]— it's clear that "genuine self-esteem and narcissistic self-aggrandizement are distinct constructs."[23] Further, a series of studies with eleven-year-olds, fourteen-year-olds, and undergraduates found that aggression and delinquency were *negatively* related to self-esteem, meaning that we have more reason to worry when it's low than when it's high.[24] The same pattern showed up when other researchers looked at hypercompetitive individuals. They were "highly narcissistic. . . . At base, however, they were found to have low self-esteem."[25] And it showed up again when yet another group of investigators found that students with a sense of entitlement had lower self-esteem.[26]

Baumeister himself appeared to back-pedal a few years after publishing his much-quoted "dark side" article. In an essay with a different group of collaborators, he acknowledged that high self-esteem comes in different forms, that many people with high self-esteem aren't aggressive or narcissistic, and that "psychologists who wish to study or reduce aggression might be well advised to focus on factors other than self-esteem or, at least, to respect the heterogeneity of high self-esteem and therefore consider additional variables."[27] Unfortunately, his first paper had already done its damage: Many people continue to believe there's something unsavory about having high self-esteem, even though what's really problematic is (a) low self-esteem, (b) some aspect of self-esteem other than how high or low it is (which I'll discuss in a moment), or (c) something other than self-esteem.

But don't many young people have inflated self-esteem?

First of all, let's keep in mind that, on average, adolescents and young adults do not have higher self-esteem than older adults, nor is there good evidence to support the charge that young people today have higher self-esteem than young people had in years past.[28] Most important, though, if there's really nothing wrong with having high self-esteem, then what exactly is meant by saying that it's *inflated*? The answer is that young people feel better about themselves than critics believe they have a right to feel based on what they've accomplished.

This determination, of course, is grounded in value judgments, which need to be defended, about what level of achievement "justifies" a given level of self-esteem, and about the underlying belief that the two must be connected at all. But if the charge of inflated self-esteem also has an empirical basis, the claim seems to be that levels of achievement are low (or dropping) while levels of self-esteem are high (or rising). So let's take a look at that.

Even before the spike in popularity for school-based self-esteem programs, conservatives were already denouncing what they called the "self-esteem movement." "In the 1950s, before the Self-Esteem-Now theory was widely implemented in American schools," a writer named Barbara Lerner informed educators in 1985, "competence was widespread, and excellence was common enough to make American students equal to those of any nation. In the 1970s, that was no longer so." Students in fifth grade and above were "learning less," she said, at the same time that self-esteem had become "excessive."[29] This story soon became the conventional wisdom, often ungrammatically summarized as "Kids are doing bad and feeling good."[30]

The claim that children's self-esteem has risen over the decades, as I've already mentioned, lacks support. The corollary premise—that academic performance has dropped—is persuasive primarily to people whose knowledge of education is limited to what they read in the newspaper, which may help to explain its popularity among politicians. Lerner's nostalgia is just one more example of the Chicken Little school of thought— "The standards are falling! The standards are falling!"—which, as we saw in Chapter 1, has been on display in every generation.

Those who sound the identical alarms today tend to draw unfavorable comparisons between the current state of our schools and what they were thought to be like a few decades ago. The same is true of self-esteem: Twenge compared students' noxiously high levels of satisfaction with themselves in 2006 with the more decorous modesty of their counterparts in 1975.[31] In both cases, of course, what current curmudgeons see as the good old days (back when achievement was high and self-esteem was low) defined the very period that Lerner described as disgraceful— that is, the 1970s.

But regardless of one's point of comparison, the idea that students today are "doing bad[ly]" is difficult to support. Even if one looks at the results of standardized tests—a very poor indicator of meaningful learning[32]—the National Assessment of Educational Progress, commonly described as "the nation's report card," fails to support the commonly accepted story of decline. There hasn't been much change since NAEP testing began, and most of the change that has occurred has been for the better. In both reading and math, when the results for 2012 are compared to those for the early 1970s, some scores were approximately the same and some were markedly higher, depending on which age group and subject you look at.[33] But when critics who pound the lectern about declining scores are presented with statistics that show our schools are actually doing about as well as ever, they don't miss a beat. "Well, doing as well as we used to do just isn't good enough!" they declare—presumably in an attempt to distract us from the fact that their original claims were baseless.

Either that or they change the subject, switching from a comparison of now to then, to a comparison of us with them—"them" being students in other countries. But here, too, it turns out, the generally accepted story about poor performance on the part of US students is largely incorrect: They've held their own overall,[34] requiring critics to cherry-pick results to make the situation appear dire. In any case, it's frankly ridiculous to offer a summary statistic for all children at a given grade level in light of the enormous variation in scores *within* this country. Test results are largely a function of socioeconomic status. Our wealthier students per-form very well when compared to those in other countries; our poorer students do not. And the United States has a lot more child poverty than other industrialized nations.

American kids are sometimes compared to those in Asian countries, a particularly popular pastime after one survey showed that Asian stu-dents were critical of their own performance. This was supposed to rep-resent the ideal, and the opposite of our situation: They do well but feel badly anyway: the traditionalist's dream come true. Less commonly dis-cussed is the fact that many Asian leaders have become increasingly con-cerned about how their young people may be better at taking tests than at thinking, how they lack the impulse for creativity that's needed in their society.[35] As for that survey—now twenty-five years old—that compared math performance to kids' beliefs about their aptitude: It may say less about Americans' swelled heads than about the widely recognized Asian aversion to self-commendation.

But let's put all of these findings in perspective. Some of the talk about inflated self-esteem doesn't seem to be based on how well kids are actually doing. Rather, it reflects a way of looking at the world in which a sharp dichotomy is drawn between helping students to feel bet-ter about themselves, on the one hand, and spending time on academics, on the other. The former is depicted as a touchy-feely fad, the latter as old-fashioned honest toil. The former amounts to coddling students by pretending everything they do is fine, while the latter means facing up to hard truths and insisting that students measure up to tough standards. It's almost as if, regardless of the actual effects, attending to self-esteem is regarded as objectionable, a distraction from the unpleasant tasks that must be done, tasks that kids used to do uncomplainingly in the old days before we started worrying about how they *felt*.

In case it needs to be said, achievement is not undermined by paying attention to how kids feel about themselves—or about their teachers, the curriculum, and the whole experience of school. In fact, these things are closely related. Academic excellence is more likely to flourish when children enjoy what they're doing and when they do it in an atmosphere of exuberant discovery, in the kind of place where they plunge into their projects and can't wait to pick up where they left off yesterday. Success is often the result of kids' feeling confident about—yes, even pleased with—themselves for having figured things out.[36] No wonder the statistics belie the claim that a concern about children's feelings has displaced academic performance. Logic, meanwhile, challenges the charge that self-esteem is inflated.

"I LIKE MYSELF ONLY WHEN I . . . "

Peel back the criticism of self-esteem and you'll eventually uncover the same three values that fuel the attack on overparenting and indulgence. Part of the objection has to do with deprivation: Kids simply shouldn't be too pleased with themselves. Part of it is based on scarcity: Everyone can't be a winner, therefore everyone shouldn't feel good about him- or herself. And the primary dynamic at work here, the one I want to explore at length, is conditionality. To talk about "inflated" self-esteem is to assume that satisfaction with oneself must be justified by a certain level of accomplishment. Kids must earn the right to be happy with themselves by achieving something impressive. What really drives traditionalists to distraction isn't self-esteem itself or high self-esteem or even programs to raise self-esteem. It's the idea of unconditional self-esteem: allowing children to feel good about themselves "for no reason," as Twenge put it, or, in another writer's phrase, "just for *being*."[37] To these critics it seems self-evident that, just as praise ought to be offered only on a conditional basis,[38] so self-esteem should be thought of "as a reward rather than an entitlement" (Baumeister).[39] As important as it is to set stringent conditions for receiving stickers, A's, or trophies, it's even more vital to make sure that children feel valuable only on the basis of what they do, not for who they are.

We can begin, as usual, by asking whether this preference for conditional self-esteem rests on a belief that can be tested empirically. I can think of only one: a core assumption about motivation, which Twenge expressed as follows: "If a child feels great about himself even when he does nothing, why do anything? Self-esteem without basis encourages laziness rather than hard work." A columnist put it this way: "If people are perfect and lovable just the way they are, why should anyone need to change or strive?"[40]

If this is really supposed to be psychology (rather than theology), it is very bad psychology. There's absolutely no evidence to support the depressing premise that for things to get done, we need the anxious energy of perpetual self-doubt, the implication of which seems to be that productivity is inversely related to mental health. In reality, someone who has a core of faith in his or her own efficacy and an underlying conviction that he or she is a good person is no more likely than other people—and probably a good deal less likely—to opt for stagnation. As a rule, it's hard to *stop* happy, satisfied people from trying to learn or from trying to do a job of which they can be proud.

Why would anyone think that people who generally feel good about themselves will cease making an effort? If self-esteem must be earned in order to create motivation in people, then the underlying assumption is that "human nature is to do as little as necessary," as a writer named John Powers succinctly described it in an anti-self-esteem essay called "Feeling Good (for Nothing)."[41] Ultimately, this reflects the same bleak view that we encountered in Chapter 4: Without the artificial inducements of carrots and sticks, no one would try, learn, work, achieve, or grow because people respond only to extrinsic motivators. And that includes how you feel about yourself, which can be described as extrinsic even though it's internal.

A thorough refutation of this prejudice, beyond the brief description of *intrinsic* motivation that I offered earlier, would require a review of the entire fields of personality theory and the psychology of motivation. Numerous studies have confirmed that children are naturally inclined to try to figure things out, to push themselves to do things just beyond their current level. More broadly, the idea that it's natural to do as little as possible is a relic of "tension-reduction" or "homeostatic" theories, which hold that organisms always seek a state of rest. These theories are taught only in courses on the history of psychology; few beliefs in the social sciences have been so thoroughly repudiated. The desire to do as little as possible is not "human nature"; it is an aberration, a sign that something is amiss.[42]

The same people who warn that we won't bother to do anything if we're happy with ourselves, who believe that self-esteem should rise and fall with our accomplishments in order to goad us into getting off our butts, also tend to put their faith in the usefulness of screwing up and feeling bad. (Twenge: "Sometimes negative feelings can be a motivator." Powers: "Failure can be a terrific motivator."[43]) Of course it makes sense that these views would go hand-in-hand: Low self-esteem is a "negative feeling" about oneself, perhaps the result of a history of failure. But as I've noted, the data don't support claims for the benefits of failure. In fact, studies show that failure is *least* productive for people with low self-esteem (see pp. 122–23), which suggests that champions of perseverance and learning from one's mistakes should be defending rather than deriding the importance of self-esteem.

But of course they don't. And the feature of the whole "self-esteem movement" that elicits particularly withering criticism is loosened conditionality: the possibility that children may be getting something for nothing, or at least for less effort. "Something" includes that which is tangible (trophies), symbolic (grades), and verbal (praise); now, in the case of self-esteem, it extends to the psychological.

The fact is that *no research has ever shown that unconditionality has adverse consequences*. It may offend the sensibilities of those with what Lakoff calls a Strict Father morality, but to the best of my knowledge not a single article or book has ever cited evidence showing it to be disadvantageous in terms of future achievement, psychological health, or anything else. In fact, the research reveals exactly the opposite to be true, particularly where self-esteem is concerned.

To understand this, we need to take a step back. I've been arguing that self-esteem is a reasonably important variable and that higher self-esteem is generally better than lower. But over the last few years a number of psychologists have suggested that what matters most about self-esteem isn't how much of it one has. Just as there are different ways of thinking about motivation (for example, whether it's intrinsic or extrinsic) instead of seeing it as a single entity that can go up or down, the same is true here. In particular, self-esteem varies in terms of *stability*. If it's unstable or fragile, even more than if it's predictably low, the result may be anger or depression. Conversely, even someone whose self-esteem is generally high may struggle with self-doubt and become defensive if that positive view isn't secure. As one group of researchers put it, "Individuals with fragile high self-esteem are willing to go to great lengths to defend their positive, yet vulnerable, feelings of self-worth. . . . [They] often overreact to perceived threats to their self-worth by becoming angry and either criticizing or attacking the source of the threat."[44]

Interestingly, one indication that someone has unstable self-esteem is "a greater tendency to invoke one's feelings of self-worth in everyday activities."[45] The more variation there is in how you feel about yourself from one situation to the next, the more likely you are to be preoccupied with the whole issue of self-esteem. People with a steady, even if not completely positive, view of their own competence or value don't have to spend time thinking about how good they are or deliberately trying to feel better about themselves.

But what *makes* self-esteem unstable? All of us receive feedback that is sometimes positive and sometime negative; all of us do some things we're proud of and some things we regret. Yet the stability of one person's self-esteem may be quite different from someone else's. What accounts for that? The crucial determinant of stability, it seems, is unconditionality. It's a solid core of belief in yourself, an abiding sense that you're competent and worthwhile—*even when you screw up or fall short*—that creates a more stable form of self-esteem, which, in turn, carries a range of psychological and social advantages.

The flip side is that, where self-esteem is concerned, fragility is really a symptom of conditionality.[46] If you think well of yourself only under certain conditions—if you regard self-esteem as something that must always be earned and therefore is forever in doubt—then you're in for trouble, psychologically speaking. Low self-esteem ("I don't feel very good about myself") is bad enough; self-esteem that's contingent ("I feel good about myself only when . . . ") is even more worrisome.

Contingent on what, though? Some bases for feeling good about oneself may be worse than others. Jennifer Crocker, a psychologist at Ohio State University, and her colleagues have shown that the prognosis is particularly bad when self-esteem hinges on outdoing others (competitive success), approval by others, physical appearance, or academic achievement.[47] Consider the last of those. When children's self-esteem rises or falls with how well they do at school, achievement can resemble an addiction, "requiring ever greater success to avoid feelings of worthlessness." And if it looks as though success is unlikely, kids may "disengage from the task, deciding it doesn't matter, rather than suffer the loss of self-esteem that accompanies failure."

That, you may remember, is what's known as self-handicapping (pp. 96–97): If I need to do well in order to feel good about myself, that may sometimes light a fire under me so I will avoid embarrassing myself. But if I face something really hard, I'll create an excuse for not having succeeded. Either way, my real goal isn't to learn; it's to rescue my shaky belief in my own competence. If I can do that by figuring out a reason why it makes sense that I fell short, then that's what I'll choose. The bottom line is that "contingent self-worth is an ineffective source of motivation."[48] People who *don't* think their value hinges on their performance, meanwhile, are more likely to see failure as just a temporary set-back, a problem to be solved.

The danger here isn't limited to *achievement*-based self-esteem, however. In fact, it may not matter what exactly one has to do or be in order to feel good about oneself. The problem is inherent to the idea of conditionality, which is "associated with anxiety, hostility, defensiveness, and the risk of depression."[49] And that's not all. Studies have found that contingent self-esteem is related to feelings of helplessness and also to "maladaptive perfectionism." Teenagers whose acceptance of themselves depends on external factors suffer more intensely if they're bullied. College students with conditional self-esteem are more likely to drink "as a means of gaining social approval or avoiding social rejection."[50] Some psychologists have suggested that it can also contribute to narcissism and materialistic values. And when people with conditional self-esteem have children of their own, they may base how they feel about themselves on how successful those children are. That not only impairs their own emotional functioning but also leads to a controlling style of parenting. Which may start the cycle all over again in the next generation.[51]

Even before researchers began collecting all these data, many psychotherapists had figured it out. Alice Miller wrote that one is free from depression "only when self-esteem is based on the authenticity of one's own feelings and not on the possession of certain qualities."[52] Carl Rogers traced any number of problems to our having been taught to place "conditions of worth" on ourselves; psychotherapists attempt to supply the "unconditional positive regard" that we may have been missing. Experimental evidence seems to confirm that people who have that unconditional faith in themselves are less likely to be anxious or depressed.[53]

This is powerful stuff. The very unconditionality that is ridiculed by conservatives—indeed, that seems to account for their penchant for vilifying the whole "self-esteem movement"—turns out to be a defining feature of psychological health! It's precisely what we should be helping our children to acquire. That doesn't mean harboring unrealistic or grandiose beliefs about one's own competence. Quite the contrary: It means being sufficiently secure about oneself so as to be able to acknowledge one's failings and try to improve.

Neither does unconditional or stable self-esteem imply that our feelings about ourselves never vary. It's natural to be happier (in general, and with oneself) when we're successful and to be disappointed when we aren't. But underlying those temporary fluctuations is a permanent reservoir of respect for oneself, a fundamental acceptance of one's own worth.[54] In one of my favorite movies, *Harold and Maude*, the almost-eighty-year-old Maude admits that, even though she's impatient with people who are too attached to their possessions, she, too, enjoys "collecting things." But she immediately qualifies this by describing those things as "incidental, not integral, if you know what I mean." That's an apt way of thinking about our successes and failures with respect to self-esteem: Their impact isn't *integral* to how we see ourselves.

HOW DOES SELF-ESTEEM
BECOME CONDITIONAL?

So what determines whether people place conditions on the way they regard themselves? There are no hard-and-fast answers here; no one has ever conducted a study that can settle the matter once and for all. In fact, there may not *be* a single answer for everyone. But the best guess is that conditional self-esteem results from having been esteemed conditionally by others. When children feel as though they must fulfill certain conditions to be loved by their parents—a feeling typically evoked by the use of psychological control (see pp. 62–64)—it's not easy for them to accept themselves unconditionally. And everything goes downhill from there.

Susan Harter, a developmental psychologist at the University of Denver, points out that "level of support and conditionality of support are correlated with one another." In other words, the kind of parents who are not especially warm and loving also tend to be the kind who put conditions on the affection they do provide. But even when you hold the level of support constant, the degree of conditionality counts. "At relatively high as well as relatively low levels of support," she explains, "*the more conditional the support, the lower one's self-esteem*"[55]—and the more likely it is that one's self-esteem will also be conditional.[56]

That's not really surprising, is it? Children don't just need to be loved; they need to know that nothing they do will change the fact that they're loved. They require reassurance that their "lovability" isn't in question, which is another way of talking about self-esteem. By contrast, one conservative critic of self-esteem not only complains about "unearned praise" for children but expresses distaste for how "today's parents" are likely to express "enthusiasm for their children's very existence."[57]

Would that it were true! The eminent psychoanalyst and social critic Erich Fromm put it this way:

> Unconditional love corresponds to one of the deepest longings, not only of the child, but of every human being; on the other hand, to be loved because of one's merit, because one deserves it, always leaves doubt; maybe

I did not please the person I want to love me, maybe this, or that—there is always a fear that love could disappear. Furthermore, "deserved" love easily leaves a bitter feeling that one is not loved for oneself, that one is loved *only* because one pleases, that one is, in the last analysis, not loved at all but used.[58]

Beginning in 2004, two Israeli researchers, Avi Assor and Guy Roth, and their colleagues have been conducting experiments to examine this issue scientifically. They started by asking college students whether the love they had received from their parents seemed to depend on whether they had succeeded in school, practiced hard for sports, been considerate toward others, or suppressed emotions such as anger and fear. The answer: Yes, that was indeed true for many of them. (Their parents probably would have been dismayed to hear they felt that way. But what determines a psychological outcome isn't what parents think they're doing; it's how the children experience it.) It turned out that kids who received what they interpreted as conditional approval were indeed somewhat more likely to act the way the parent wanted. But that compliance came at a steep price. First, these children tended to resent and dislike their parents. Second, they were more likely to attribute their behavior to "strong internal pressure" than to "a real sense of choice." Moreover, their satisfaction after succeeding at something was usually short-lived, and they often felt guilty or ashamed.

The researchers then interviewed a group of mothers of grown children. With this generation, too, conditional parenting had proved damaging. Those mothers who, when they were young, sensed they were loved only when they lived up to their parents' expectations now felt less worthy as adults. Yet despite the negative effects, these mothers were more likely to use conditional affection with their own children.[59] Apart from being profoundly depressing, that finding can serve as a metaphorical Rorschach test, revealing something about one's way of thinking about such issues. Is it mysterious and counterintuitive? (Why on earth would someone do to her children exactly what damaged *her*?) Or is it perfectly predictable? (How could someone love her children unconditionally if she never received that kind of love herself?)

Assor, Roth, and their collaborators have gone on to publish a variety of replications and extensions of these original studies. In one of them, their subjects were ninth graders, and this time giving more attention and affection when children did what parents wanted was carefully distinguished from giving less when they didn't. The studies showed that both positive and negative versions of conditional parenting were harmful, but in slightly different ways. The positive kind—praise for success—sometimes succeeded in getting children to work harder on academic tasks, but, again, at the cost of unhealthy feelings of "internal compulsion." Negative conditional parenting, meanwhile, didn't even work in the short run; it just increased the teenagers' resentment toward their parents.[60]

In their other studies, which were conducted with children from age five to twenty-three, conditional parenting had consistently disturbing effects on their emotional and social well-being:

- If young children got the idea that their parents valued them more when they were happy, that interfered with their ability to recognize and respond to sadness in other people.
- If young adults had perceived that their parents' affection varied with the extent to which they were helpful and considerate, that affected the way these grown children thought about helping: It seemed less a matter of choice than something they felt they had to do to try to feel better about themselves.
- If teenagers got the idea that their parents' approval of them depended on how well they did in school, they were apt to be self-aggrandizing when they succeeded and ashamed when they failed. "Conditional positive regard promote[d] the development of a fragile, contingent . . . and unstable sense of self."[61]

Regardless of the child's age, regardless of what behavior is required as a condition of the parent's love, and regardless of whether love is offered for engaging in that behavior or withheld for *not* engaging in it, the outcomes are troubling. (In fact, they're troubling even when a teacher rather than a parent seems to accept children only conditionally.[62]) One way of making sense of these findings, I've argued, is to consider the creation of conditional *self*-acceptance. The adult's "My care for you depends on your doing *x*" becomes the child's "I'm worthwhile only if I do *x*." Research confirms that conditionality is a recipe for dysfunction.

But our objections may go beyond what the data say. In a scholarly article entitled "Contingencies of Self-Worth," Jennifer Crocker and Connie Wolfe took two dozen pages to review empirical findings on the topic. Then, at the very end, they took the unusual step of adding a personal note:

> We are alarmed at the suggestion that schools should be teaching or creating self-esteem that is justified by achievements or "warranted" (Baumeister, 1999; Seligman, 1998). Such recommendations are equally lacking in empirical support. Furthermore, and perhaps more seriously, the logical implication of this approach is that some children's low self-esteem is warranted and that children who do not achieve in socially desirable ways, such as getting good grades, being attractive and popular, or being good at sports, rightly believe that they are not worthy human beings. It is a slippery slope from the view that self-esteem can be warranted or unwarranted to the view that some people are unworthy and justifiably devalued.[63]

The attack on "empty" or "excessive" praise, or on "unearned" grades or trophies, is not just about what adults offer to kids; it's ultimately about how kids view themselves. There's no evidence to support the idea that self-esteem is "inflated" or that children do better when their view of themselves varies with their performance (or with anything else). But once again, this critique is based less on evidence than on the value judgment that feeling good about oneself is something one *ought* to have to earn. Crocker and Wolfe confronted that value judgment head-on, saying, in effect, that this is an appalling way to raise and educate children. How well you do things should be incidental, not integral, to the way you regard yourself.

CHAPTER 7

Why Self-Discipline Is Overrated

A Closer Look at Grit, Marshmallows, and Control from Within

There's not much mystery about the purpose of punishments and rewards: They're generally intended to elicit compliance. Any adult who regards that as a priority will be tempted to make children suffer in some way if they fail to do what they're told, if they slack off or talk back. Alternatively, he or she may offer praise or some other goodie when they follow directions. But the problem with both of these strategies, even for someone who finds them morally unobjectionable, is that they require continuous monitoring. An authority figure has to be available to hand out rewards or punishments as the child's behavior merits, and that's just not very practical. Thus, those who place a premium on obedience may dream of somehow "equipping the child with a built-in supervisor"[1] so he'll keep following the rules, even when no adult is around.

Think for a moment about the word *disciplined*. It can refer to making a concerted effort at a task ("She's so disciplined that she spent more than an hour weeding the garden") or to having been trained to obey authority ("They've been disciplined, so they shouldn't give the baby-sitter any trouble"). If the goal is to induce children to work hard or to behave in a particular way on their own, then the most expedient arrangement for parents and teachers is to get the children to *discipline themselves*. Or, as we prefer to say, to be self-disciplined.

This basic concept actually includes a constellation of specific ideas. "Self-discipline" might be defined as marshaling one's willpower to accomplish things that are regarded as desirable, whereas "self-control" means applying that same sort of willpower to prevent oneself from doing what is seen to be *un*desirable. In practice, these often function as two aspects of the same machinery of self-regulation—the point being to override one's "natural" tendencies—so I'll use the two terms more or less interchangeably. There are also two specific applications of self-discipline: perseverance (or "grit"); and the practice of deferring gratification, in which kids are transformed from lazy grasshoppers into hard-working ants by convincing them to put off doing what they enjoy.

Search for these terms in indexes of published books, scholarly articles, or Internet sites, and you'll quickly discover how rare it is to find a discouraging word, or even a penetrating question, about their value. That may be because all of them fit naturally with the traditionalist sensibility I've been exploring throughout this book. Anyone who believes that children are spoiled, disobedient, and self-satisfied, that they don't do enough to earn the praise they get or the esteem they have for themselves, would probably see these as promising strategies to make kids act in such a way as to become more deserving.

Which brings us to the marshmallow meme.

S'MORE MISREPRESENTATION OF RESEARCH

Back in the 1960s, at the Stanford University laboratory of a psychologist named Walter Mischel, preschool-age children were left alone in a room after having been told they could get a small treat (say, a marshmallow or pretzel) by ringing a bell at any time to summon the experimenter—or, if they held out until he returned on his own, they could have a bigger treat (two marshmallows or pretzels). More than four decades later,

Mischel's studies have resurfaced, perhaps reflecting a fresh wave of interest in the broader issue of self-discipline. The way his results are typically summarized, however, turns out to be rather different from what the research actually found.

Let's back up a step. Mischel had made a name for himself among psychologists with a subversive argument that threatened to turn the field of personality theory upside down. His contention was that we're too quick to assume that each of us has a stable personality that manifests itself across different situations and can be identified by psychological tests. We may *think* of ourselves as having generalized traits, but how we act turns out, for the most part, to be a function of the various environments in which we find ourselves. What's attributed to your "personality" is really just a bunch of cognitive strategies that you devise to deal with what happens to you. Mischel was curious about how each of us comes up with those strategies, but he doubted they added up to a distinctive and invariant profile.[2]

That's the context in which his marshmallow experiments should be understood, but it's not the context in which they're normally presented. Usually, we're just told that the children who were able to wait for an extra treat scored better on measures of cognitive and social skills many years later and that they had higher SAT scores. Teach kids to put off the payoff as long as possible and they'll end up more successful.

But the marshmallow studies actually don't support that conclusion at all. Here's why:

1. What mattered was the setting, not the individual's self-control. What mostly interested Mischel, as a student of cognitive strategies, wasn't *whether* children could wait for a bigger treat—which, by the way, most of them could.[3] It wasn't even whether waiters fared better in life than non-waiters. Rather, the central question was *how* children go about trying to wait and which strategies help. It turned out that kids waited longer when they were distracted by a toy. What worked best wasn't (in his words) "self-denial and grim determination" but doing something enjoyable while waiting *so that self-control wasn't needed at all.*[4]

Mischel and his colleagues systematically varied the details of the situation to see if children's willingness to wait was different under each condition. These included telling them about the marshmallow as opposed to showing it to them, encouraging them to think about its shape rather than its taste, and suggesting a distraction strategy instead of having the kids come up with their own. Sure enough, such factors made a big difference. In fact, they were more important for predicting the outcome than any trait the child possessed.[5]

Of course that's exactly the conclusion we'd expect from Walter Mischel in light of his theoretical views. But it's precisely the opposite of the usual message that (a) self-control is a matter of individual character, which (b) we ought to be helping children to develop.[6] In fact, when these children were tracked down ten years later, those who had been more likely to wait for a bigger snack didn't have any more self-control or willpower than the others.[7]

This is hardly the only psychology study whose central finding was changed in the telling. (Another example is the famous Milgram experiments.[8]) But Mischel's work provides a classic illustration of how research can be distorted in the service of an ideological agenda. Consider, for example, this passage from an article about the marshmallow studies that appeared in the *New Yorker* in 2009:

> Mischel argues that intelligence is largely at the mercy of self-control: even the smartest kids still need to do their homework. "What we're really measuring with the marshmallows isn't will power or self-control," Mischel says. "It's much more important than that. This task forces kids to find a way to make the situation work for them."[9]

The writer, Jonah Lehrer, sticks in a curious non sequitur about homework. (Even if self-control did turn out to be a valuable attribute, it's neither necessary for, nor enhanced by, making students do more academic assignments when they get home from school.) More important, though, Mischel emphasizes that his experiments weren't about self-control at all, yet Lehrer introduces that direct quote by asserting exactly the opposite—that self-control is even more important than intelligence. Usually you have to dig up the original study to determine whether (and how) the press coverage has misrepresented it. In this case the inaccurate conclusion is right there for any reasonably careful reader to spot—as if Lehrer weren't even aware of what he'd done.

2. Deferral of gratification may be an effect, not a cause. Just because some children were more effective than others at distracting themselves from the snack doesn't mean this capacity was *responsible* for the impressive results found ten years later. Instead, both of these things may have been due to something about their home environment.[10] If that's true, there's no reason to believe that enhancing children's ability to defer gratification would be beneficial: It was just a marker, not a cause. By way of analogy, teenagers who visit ski resorts over winter break probably have a superior record of being admitted to the Ivy League. Should we therefore hire consultants to teach low-income children how to ski in order to improve the odds that colleges will accept them?

3. What counts is just the capacity to distract oneself. Even to the extent that Mischel looked at characteristics of individual children in addition to the details of the situation, he was primarily concerned with "cognitive competencies"—strategies for how to think about (or stop thinking about) something attractive—and how those competencies may be related to other skills that will be assessed years later. In fact, those outcomes were not associated with the ability to defer gratification, per se, but only with the ability to distract oneself when distractions weren't provided by the experimenters.[11]

What's more, that facility for creating a distraction turned out to be significantly correlated with plain old intelligence[12]—a very interesting finding because other writers have argued that self-discipline and intelligence are two entirely different things and that we ought to train children to acquire the former.[13] It isn't really so surprising, then, that kids' capacity to come up with a way to think about something other than the food was associated with their SAT scores. This doesn't mean willpower makes kids successful; it means the same loose cluster of mental proficiencies that helped them with distraction when they were young also helped them score well on a test of reasoning when they were older. (In fact, when the researchers held those scores constant, most, though not all, of the *other* long-term benefits associated with their marshmallow-related behavior evaporated.)[14]

4. Holding out for more isn't necessarily the smarter choice. Finally, most people who cite these experiments take for granted that it's always better to wait for two marshmallows—that is, to defer gratification. But is that really true? Mischel, for one, didn't think so. "The decision to delay or not to delay hinges, in part, on the individual's values and expectations with regard to the specific contingencies," he and his colleagues wrote. "In a given situation, therefore, postponing gratification may or may not be a wise or adaptive choice."[15] Sometimes a marshmallow in the hand is better than two in the bush.

It's true, for example, that if you spend too much of your money when you're young, you may regret it when you're old. But how much should you deprive yourself—and perhaps your children—in order to accumulate savings for retirement? For one thing, a group of economists argued that as our health declines we derive less pleasure from what we're able to buy.[16] More generally, as John Maynard Keynes famously pointed out, "In the long run, we are all dead."

To take what you can while you can may be a rational choice, depending on what you happen to be doing. Some tasks favor that strategy; others favor waiting. In one experiment, researchers fiddled with the algorithm that determined how points were earned in a simulation game and then watched how that change interacted with the personalities of the people who were playing. "Impulsivity," they concluded, "is not a purely maladaptive trait but one whose consequences hinge on the structure of the decision-making environment."[17]

What's more, someone's inclination to take now rather than wait can depend on what that person has experienced in the past. "For a child accustomed to stolen possessions and broken promises, the only guaranteed treats are the ones you have already swallowed," remarked a group of social scientists at the University of Rochester. In 2013 they set up their own version of Mischel's experiment for preschool-age children. But before any marshmallows made an appearance, they introduced a couple of art projects. During this period, the kids were encouraged to wait for "a brand-new set of exciting art supplies" rather than using the well-worn crayons and dinky little stickers that were already available. After a few minutes, the adult returned. Half the kids received the promised, far-superior materials. But the other half got only an apology: "I'm sorry, but I made a mistake. We don't have any other art supplies after all."

Then it was time for the marshmallow challenge. And how long did the children wait for two to appear before they gave up and ate the one sitting in front of them? Well, it depended on their earlier experience. Those for whom the adult had proved unreliable (by failing to deliver the promised art supplies) waited only about three minutes. But those who had learned that good things do come to those who wait were willing to hold off, on average, for a remarkable twelve minutes.

The researchers' point, which they described in an article called "Rational Snacking," was twofold. The decision about whether to defer gratification may tell us what the child has already learned about whether waiting is likely to be worth it. If her experience is that it isn't, then taking whatever is available at the moment is a perfectly reasonable choice. But that possibility also blasts a marshmallow-sized hole in the conclusion that the capacity to defer gratification produces various later-life benefits. "It is premature to conclude that most of the observed variance—and the longitudinal correlation between wait-times and later life outcomes—is due to differences in individuals' self-control capacities. Rather, an unreliable worldview, in addition to self-control, may be causally related to later life outcomes." Success may reflect one's earlier experiences, in which case self-restraint would be just another *result* of those experiences, not the *explanation* for how well one fares later.[18]

"Rational Snacking" helps to clarify what may have been going on in Mischel's original experiments, where there was no effort to learn about the children's lives before they walked into his lab. But even on their own, those experiments simply don't support the case for willpower and self-denial that traditionalists have tried to make. Waiting for a bigger treat doesn't always make sense. And when it does, the question is, "What changes in the environment can facilitate that choice?" In other words: How can distractions make self-discipline irrelevant?

SELF-CONTROLLED TO A FAULT

Much might be made of the mainstream media's many misinterpretations of Mischel's marshmallows. Those misreadings are likely related to the value the writer places on having children defer gratification, which, in turn, reflects widely shared and largely uncritical support for the idea of self-discipline in general. So let's turn our attention to that concept.

The party line—from therapists, journalists, educators, and parenting advisers—is that discipline should give way to self-discipline, that control from within is better than control from without, that kids should internalize a desire to succeed and (what we regard as) good values. But there's much more to the story here, psychologically, philosophically, and even politically. If we're interested in what's healthiest for kids rather than just in getting them to follow directions, then we will likely see the situation as more complicated. Is it useful to be able to persevere at worthwhile tasks? Undoubtedly. Do some children seem less able than others to do so? Again, yes. But it's not at all clear that self-discipline should enjoy a privileged status compared to other attributes. In some contexts, it may not be desirable at all.

If that proposition seems surprising, it may be because self-discipline (or deferral of gratification) is usually described as an "ability" or "skill." The question is how proficient you are at making yourself get to work, or at resisting temptation. Some abilities and skills are more useful than others, but we don't tend to think of any of them as bad things to have, or something of which you could have too much.

Several decades ago, however, the late Jack Block, an eminent research psychologist, offered a different perspective. Self-regulation may not be a skill, like having a good sense of direction, so much as "an orientation toward motivational expression"—a psychological tendency, if you will—like being introverted or extroverted. He proposed that people can be described in terms of their level of "ego control," which means the extent to which impulses and feelings are either expressed or suppressed. Those who are undercontrolled are impulsive and distractible, and children who fit that profile are somewhat more likely to suffer from health problems and financial difficulties when they grow up, as well as to have committed a crime.[19] But other individuals are *over*controlled. Their actions seem to be compelled rather than freely chosen, and they often seem joyless.

Block made two complementary points. First, a lack of self-control isn't always a bad thing because it may "provide the basis for spontaneity, flexibility, expressions of interpersonal warmth, openness to experience, and creativ[ity]." Second, too much self-control is as worrisome as too little, even though parents and teachers tend to be more irritated by undercontrol in children and thus more likely to define the latter as a problem. "The idea of self-control is generally praised," Block observed, but we should be careful not to endorse "the replacement of unbridled impulsivity with categorical, pervasive, rigid impulse control." As long as you get your work done and don't make trouble, people in positions of authority don't care if you're "rigid, unexpressive, routinized, and flattened in affect." But that's just not an ideal way to live.[20]

When Block said that self-control is "generally praised" in our society, he was putting it mildly. Those who write on the subject rarely if ever consider the possibility that it can be overdone. In addition to Lehrer's article about Mischel's experiments, we might add a popular book called *How Children Succeed* by journalist Paul Tough (who argued in an earlier essay that adults should organize and plan children's play for them in an effort to help them acquire more self-control). Two neuroscientists, meanwhile, declared in the *New York Times*, "All [children] can benefit from building self-control." And a typical discussion of the topic in an education journal included the assertion that "the promotion of self-discipline is an important goal for all schools."[21] Given this consensus, we shouldn't be shocked to learn that there is now a self-help program called *Self-Discipline in 10 Days* for those who lack the, um, self-discipline to develop this attribute on their own (or the ability to defer gratification for more than a week and a half).[22]

A dose of skepticism would seem to be called for here, if only because this enthusiasm seems every bit as intemperate as those declarations a couple of decades ago that self-esteem can serve as a social vaccine. (Of course the latter claims were scorned by some of the same people who now gush about the wonders of self-control.) But the problem isn't just a one-sided picture of self-discipline—it's a failure to appreciate the relevance of the circumstances in which we find ourselves. "Disciplined and directed behavior, which can be advantageous in some situations," said Block and his colleagues, "is likely to be detrimental" in others.[23]

That's similar to a point Mischel made about delaying gratification, years after his experiments were concluded. We've already heard him say that whether it's smart to wait for a larger reward depends on the context. But he also pointed out that some people tend to be overly inclined to wait. While the inability to delay may be a problem, he said, "the other extreme—excessive delay of gratification—also has its personal costs and can be disadvantageous. . . . Whether one should or should not delay gratification or 'exercise the will' in any particular choice is often anything but self-evident."[24]

This may sound obvious: Naturally one can go too far in either direction—with deferral of gratification or self-discipline in general. Yet some social scientists have explicitly disputed this claim. Martin Seligman and a colleague wrote, "Our belief [is] that there is no true disadvantage of having too much self-control."[25] And a group of researchers that included Roy Baumeister professed to have data demonstrating that self-control is "beneficial and adaptive in a linear fashion. We found no evidence that any psychological problems are linked to high self-control."[26]

That assertion turns out to be rather misleading for two reasons. First, it's based on the researchers' having found an inverse relationship between self-control and negative emotions (among undergraduates who filled out a questionnaire). Other research, however, has found a similar inverse relationship between self-control and *positive* emotions.[27] Even if highly self-controlled people aren't always unhappy, they're also not particularly happy; their emotional life tends to be muted.

Second, Block and his associates noticed that there was something fishy about the questionnaire used by this group of researchers. It included questions "reflective of an appropriate level of control and [of] undercontrol, but not overcontrol. It is therefore not surprising that the

correlates of the scale do not indicate maladaptive consequences associated with very high levels of control." In other words, the clean bill of
health they awarded to self-control was virtually predetermined by the
design of their study.[28]

Overall, the data do indeed support Block's balanced view that "although it may be psychologically undesirable to be extremely impulsive,
it is also psychologically undesirable to be extremely controlled":[29]

- A high degree of self-control tends to be associated with less spontaneity and a blander emotional life.
- Preschool children who seemed overcontrolled were likely to be
  conventional, moralistic, and uncomfortable with uncertainty
  when they were young adults.
- Highly self-controlled teenagers were likely never to have used
  drugs, but they were also less well-adjusted overall than those who
  had "lower ego control and may have experimented briefly with
  drugs."
- "A tendency toward overcontrol puts young women (but not young
  men) at risk for the development of depression."
- A preoccupation with self-control is a key feature of anorexia.
- When there's plenty of time, impulsive people don't perform as
  well as self-controlled people on certain tasks, but those results are
  reversed when decisions must be made quickly.[30]

The more you explore the dynamics of self-discipline, the more you
come to understand why it isn't always productive or healthy. Consider
a student who always starts her homework the moment she walks in the
door. Is this an admirable display of "effortful self-control"[31]—of what
can be achieved by force of will given that there are other things this girl
would rather be doing? Or might it reflect her acute discomfort with
having anything unfinished? It's possible that she wants—or, more accurately, *needs*—to get the assignment out of the way in order to stave off
anxiety.[32]

Self-discipline can be less a sign of health than of vulnerability. It may
suggest a fear of being overwhelmed by external forces, or by one's own

desires, that must be suppressed through continual effort. One might say that such individuals suffer from a fear of being *out* of control. Half a century ago, the psychologist David Shapiro described how someone can function as "his own overseer, issuing commands, directives, reminders, warnings, and admonitions concerning not only what is to be done and what is not to be done, but also what is to be wanted, felt, and even thought." Secure, healthy people can be playful, flexible, open to new experiences and self-discovery, deriving satisfaction from the process rather than always being focused on the product. An extremely self-disciplined individual, by contrast, may not "feel comfortable with any activity that lacks an aim or a purpose beyond its own pleasure, and usually . . . [does] not recognize the possibility of finding life satisfying without a continuous sense of purpose and effort."[33]

A couple of interesting paradoxes follow from this analysis. One is that while self-discipline implies an exercise of the will, and therefore a free choice, many such people are actually not free at all, psychologically speaking. It's not that they've decided to discipline themselves so much as that they can't allow themselves to be undisciplined. The same is true of deferral of gratification: When Block and a colleague conducted an experiment in which teenagers had to choose between getting paid a certain amount now or more money later, those who waited "were not just 'better' at self-control, but in a sense . . . seemed to be unable to avoid it."[34]

A second paradox is that impressive self-discipline may contain the seeds of its own undoing: an explosive failure of control, which psychologists call "disinhibition." From one unhealthy extreme (even if it's not always recognized as such), people may suddenly find themselves at the other: The compliant citizen abruptly acts out in appalling fashion; the pious teetotaler goes on a dangerous drinking binge; absolute abstinence gives way to reckless, unprotected sex.[35] Moreover, making an effort to inhibit potentially undesirable behaviors can have other negative effects. A detailed review of research concerning all sorts of attempts to suppress one's feelings and behaviors concludes that the results of self-control often include "discomfort or distress" and "cognitive disruption (including distractibility and intrusive, obsessive thoughts about the proscribed behavior)."[36]

In short, we shouldn't always be reassured to learn that children are remarkably self-disciplined. The same caution is appropriate regarding those who are inclined to delay gratification: Delayers "tend to be somewhat overcontrolled and unnecessarily inhibited."[37] Likewise for those who always persist at a task, even when they're unsuccessful. (I'll have more to say about the last of these tendencies, commonly romanticized as tenacity or "grit.") On the other hand, self-discipline obviously isn't always pathological. So what distinguishes the healthy and adaptive kind? Moderation, perhaps, but also flexibility. What counts is the capacity to decide whether and when to persevere—or to control oneself, delay pleasure, or follow the rules—rather than the simple tendency to do these things. It's this capacity, rather than self-discipline or self-control itself, that children would benefit from acquiring.[38]

CONTROLLED FROM WITHIN

What passes for discussions of self-discipline tends to resemble unreflective cheerleading for the concept. The result is that we may not even stop to consider that too much of it can be as unhealthy as too little. But I'd like to push beyond this point, and in the process provide a fuller answer to that question about distinguishing the good kind from the bad. What we really need to ask about self-discipline, just as with love or self-esteem, is not merely "How much?" but "What kind?"

One of the most fruitful ways of thinking about this issue emerges from the work of psychologists Edward Deci and Richard Ryan. I've already drawn from their theory and research in reconsidering the casual way people tend to treat motivation as if it were a single substance that's possessed in a certain quantity. We want kids to have more of it, so we try to "motivate" them. In fact, though, as I explained in Chapter 4, we'd do better to think in terms of different types of motivation—intrinsic and extrinsic. And the type matters more than the amount. *Intrinsic* motivation, you'll recall, means wanting to do something for its own sake, whereas *extrinsic* motivation concerns a reward or punishment that a behavior may elicit. Furthermore, these two varieties aren't just different; they're often inversely related. The more that people are led to focus on an extrinsic reason for doing something, the more likely that their interest in the task itself will diminish.

Here's the puzzle, though: Children do some things that aren't intrinsically appealing, and they sometimes do them in the absence of rewards. Why? We might say they've *internalized* a commitment to doing them. This, of course, brings us right back to the idea of self-discipline, which is where many parents and educators have placed their bets. As I noted at the beginning of this chapter, they want kids to comply with their expectations without having to stand next to them, carrots and sticks at the ready. They want kids to follow the straight and narrow, even when no one is watching.

Deci and Ryan, however, are not finished complicating our lives. Having shown that there are different kinds of motivation (which are not equally desirable), they go on to suggest that there are also different kinds of internalization (where exactly the same thing may be true). This is a possibility that few people, including researchers, seem to have considered. Even someone who's aware of the difference between intrinsic and extrinsic may just insist that children should be helped to "internalize good values (or behaviors)" and leave it at that.

But what exactly does that internalization look like? On the one hand, someone else's rule or standard can be swallowed whole, or "introjected," so it controls children from the inside: "Behaviors are performed because one 'should' do them, or because not doing so might engender anxiety, guilt, or loss of esteem." On the other hand, internalization can take place more authentically, so the behavior is experienced as "volitional or self-determined." It has been accepted—fully integrated into one's value structure—and feels chosen.[39] A child, for example, may study because she knows she's supposed to do so and will feel lousy about herself if she doesn't. Or she may understand the benefits of doing so and want to follow through, even if it's not always pleasurable.

Controlling adults end up promoting the former (introjected) approach, and that often results in a style of learning that's rigid, superficial, narrow, and ultimately less successful (if the assignment involves anything more ambitious than rote memorization).[40] This same basic distinction between types of internalization has proved relevant not

only to academics, but to sports, romantic love, generosity, political involvement, and religion—with research in each case, much of it done by
Deci, Ryan, and their associates, demonstrating that the integrated kind
of internalization (in terms of the way one pursues any of those activities) leads to better outcomes than the introjected kind.[41]

The upshot is that *just because motivation is internal doesn't mean it's
intrinsic or integrated or ideal.* If a child feels controlled, he's still at the
mercy of rewards and punishments. It's just that now they live inside
him. To do one thing is to be rewarded (temporarily) with good feelings
about himself; to do another thing is to feel lousy. What drives this form
of internalization, in other words, is a concept we've already encountered: conditional self-esteem. And the result is that such children are
likely to be conflicted, unhappy, and typically less likely to succeed—at
least by meaningful criteria—at whatever they're doing.[42] Their reason
for acting is inside them, and yet it doesn't feel as though it's coming
from them. They may be suffering from what the psychoanalyst Karen
Horney called the "tyranny of the should"—to the point that they no
longer even know what they really want or who they really are.

Many older children have internalized just such a compulsion to do
well in school. They look like every parent's dream of a dedicated student, but in reality they may have mortgaged their present lives to the
future: noses to the grindstone, perseverant to a fault, stressed to the
max. High school is just preparation for college, and college consists of
collecting credentials for whatever comes next—year after year of holding out for the possibility of more marshmallows. Nothing right now
has any value, or provides any gratification, in itself. These students may
be skilled test-takers and grade grubbers and gratification delayers, but
they are often motivated by a perpetual need to feel better about themselves rather than by anything resembling curiosity.

By the same token, children who have introjected commands to be
polite or dutiful or helpful are not really moral agents in any meaningful
sense. They haven't chosen to do good because they don't experience
themselves as choosing. After all, ensuring that children internalize our
values isn't the same thing as helping them to develop their own. Moreover, that sense of *having* to act in a certain way plays havoc with their

emotions, which they either can't control (the result being that feelings bubble up dangerously of their own accord) or feel they must suppress.[43] Again, notice how this brings us a step beyond Block's work: It's not just that some kids regulate themselves *too much*; it's that the *way* they've been taught to regulate themselves is unhealthy. It has negative effects on their intellectual, moral, and emotional development.

So what does all this mean in terms of how we regard "self-discipline"? Our answer will depend on how we decide to define the term. If we're using it to include something autonomous or integrated, then it can be beneficial, at least in moderation: A twelve-year-old tears himself away from Facebook to help his parent clean the house. It's not his favorite activity, but he understands and fully embraces the value of pitching in and therefore does so willingly.

But that scenario may be the exception in our culture. As the education scholar Nel Noddings observed, "Most self-discipline is an internalization of the stern and watchful other"[44]—a controlling and not very healthy affair. My sense is that most people who use the term have never really thought about this distinction. Even those who are well meaning may therefore find themselves endorsing introjection because they assume that self-discipline is a good thing, period.

The failure to distinguish between different versions also confuses certain claims made about the topic. Here's one example: A number of researchers, most prominently Roy Baumeister, have maintained that self-control is like a muscle. It requires energy and is therefore subject to being depleted. If you use it for one thing, you'll have, at least temporarily, less capacity to use it for another. At first it appears that there's a fair amount of evidence in support of this "strength" model. In different experiments, people who had been told to avoid thinking about a white bear, or to stop themselves from eating sweets, or to suppress their emotional responses to a movie, seemed to have less self-control later (for example, to stifle laughter or limit their alcohol consumption) or simply less inclination to persevere at physically or mentally taxing tasks.[45]

Does that mean self-control is something that can be used up? Apparently so, if we assume it comes in only one flavor. But our analysis changes once we realize that people exert self-control in different ways and for different reasons. Depletion may well take place when people introject a demand to do something, but it doesn't seem to happen under autonomy-supportive conditions that promote integrated self-regulation. Then, self-control doesn't run out, and it's possible to keep going at a subsequent task without apparent fatigue. In fact, when people experience their motivation as autonomous, they may have more vitality than when they started.[46]

Incidentally, this isn't the only reason to be skeptical of the strength model of self-control. Its accuracy also seems to depend on whether people *believe* it's accurate—that is, whether they assume self-control is a limited resource.[47] But my larger point is that we should question not only how self-control or self-discipline works but also whether all versions of it are desirable. If we overlook the differences in how we (and our children) internalize a commitment to do something, or if we deny that it's possible to be overly controlled, we end up endorsing the idea too quickly and too broadly. And we lose sight of the fact that control from within isn't inherently more humane, or otherwise preferable, than control from without.

GRIT

It's long been known that cognitive ability isn't the only factor that determines how children will fare in school and in life. That recognition got a big boost in 1996 with science writer Dan Goleman's book *Emotional Intelligence*, in which he discusses the importance of self-awareness, altruism, personal motivation, empathy, and the ability to love and be loved. But a funny thing has happened to the message since then. When you hear about the limits of IQ these days, it's usually in the context of a conservative narrative that emphasizes not altruism or empathy but something that sounds very much like the Protestant work ethic. More than smarts, we're told, what kids need to succeed is old-fashioned *grit* and *perseverance, self-discipline* and *willpower.* The goal is to make sure they'll be able to resist temptation, override their unconstructive impulses, put off doing what they enjoy in order to grind through whatever they've been told to do—and keep at it for as long as it takes.[48]

The term "grit" was popularized by Angela Duckworth, a former student of Martin Seligman's at the University of Pennsylvania. She uses the term to denote the sort of self-discipline that's required to make people persist at something over a long period of time. There is no pretense of objectivity in her work: Duckworth is *selling* grit rather than dispassionately investigating its effects. "As educators and parents," she and her colleagues wrote in her first paper on the topic, "we should encourage children to work not only with intensity but also with stamina."[49] This is essentially the same message that's been drummed into us from Aesop's fables, Benjamin Franklin's aphorisms, Christian denunciations of sloth, and of course the nineteenth-century chant invented to make children do their homework: "If at first you don't succeed, try, try again."

"Grittier individuals, by staying the course, may sometimes miss out on new opportunities," Duckworth acknowledges. But she doesn't see this as a problem. In fact, grit, as she defines and defends it, *means* doing "a particular thing in life and choos[ing] to give up a lot of other things in order to do it."[50] For example, she has no use for children who experiment with several musical instruments. "The kid who sticks with one instrument is demonstrating grit," she says. "Maybe it's more fun to try something new, but high levels of achievement require a certain single-mindedness."[51]

This comment is revealing for a couple of reasons. First, while Duckworth has conducted research on the subject, her recommendations ultimately emerge not from evidence but from the fact that she personally thinks people should spend all their time trying to improve at one thing rather than exploring, and becoming reasonably competent at, several things. This may facilitate improvement at the single activity one pursues, but if you happen to favor breadth and variety, Duckworth offers no reason why you should accept her preference for a life of specialization—or, by extension, why you should endorse the idea of grit, which is rooted in that preference.

Second, the phrase "maybe it's more fun to try something new, but . . . " may well be at the core of this way of thinking. One suspects that sticking with one thing has been commended to us not in spite of the fact that it's less fun but *because* it's less fun. Grit seems closely connected to the value of deprivation. Hard, unpleasant labor isn't just thought to be necessary for reaching a goal; it's regarded as a virtue in itself. Conversely, doing what you enjoy is seen as less admirable and perhaps morally deficient. (More about this later.)

When you read them carefully, Duckworth's experiments don't offer much in the way of independent support for those familiar exhortations to work hard and never quit. What's most striking about her publications, in fact, are their problematic premises and the critical distinctions they ignore.

1. Not everything is worth doing, let alone doing for extended periods.

At what activities are we encouraged to display grit? The question is never posed and, indeed, what's celebrated (by Duckworth as well as others who have eagerly grabbed hold of the concept[52]) is the very fact of persisting—apparently at anything. This is reminiscent of platitudes about "following your dream," as if a dream to become famous were equivalent to a dream to end child malnutrition. The amorality of the concept enables the immorality of some individuals who exemplify it.[53] Most tyrants, after all, have grit to spare. To put it differently, glorifying the idea of grit gets things backward. We, as well as our children, should first decide what one ought to do, and why. *Then* we can talk about what's helpful for doing it effectively: careful planning, a capacity for working with others, courage, a balance between self-confidence and humility, and, yes, persistence—among many other qualities. But there's nothing admirable about grit, per se. In fact, this would be a better world if people who were up to no good had less of it.

2. Persistence can be counterproductive and unhealthy.

Sometimes it pays to stick with something over the long haul, and few of us want to see our kids throw in the towel at the first sign of difficulty. But, as with self-control more generally, grit can sometimes be inappropriate and unhealthy, even if the activity isn't morally objectionable. On certain occasions it just doesn't make sense to persist with a problem that resists solution, to keep working toward a goal that's almost certainly unattainable, to continue at a task that no longer provides any satisfaction. When people *do* keep going under these conditions, they may be displaying a "refusal to disengage" that's both counterproductive (in terms of outcome) and pathological (in terms of motivation). Let's look at each of these in turn.

Anyone who talks about grit as an unalloyed good may need to be reminded of the proverbial Law of Holes: When you're in one, stop digging. Gritty people sometimes exhibit "nonproductive persistence"; they try and try again, even though the result may be either unremitting failure or "a costly or inefficient success that could have been surpassed easily by alternative courses of action," as one group of psychologists explained. The latter category includes certain strategies in warfare, certain methodologies in science, and certain decisions in investing.[54] Even if you don't crash and burn by staying the course, you may not fare nearly as well as if you had stopped, reassessed, and tried something else. As the authors of a book called *Mastering the Art of Quitting* point out, "A culture that only trumpets the virtue of staying the course . . . prevents us from moving on and setting new goals." We benefit from the "freedom to explore an activity and to abandon it when it turn[s] out not to be a good fit."[55]

Moreover, the advantages of knowing when *not* to persist extend not only to the outcomes of a decision but to the effects on the individual who made it. One line of research shows that "people who can disengage from unattainable goals enjoy better well-being, have more normative patterns of cortisol secretion, and experience fewer symptoms of everyday illness than do people who have difficulty disengaging from unattainable goals."[56] That's a powerful qualification to all those simple claims that persistence is desirable.

Just as the *effects* of displaying unqualified grit may not always be optimal, the *motives* for doing so raise important psychological questions. What matters isn't just how long one persists, or at what, but *why* one does so. Do I remain at a soul-sucking job because of a realistic concern that I won't be hired anywhere else? Or is it because I'm loath to admit defeat or afraid of being thought a failure? Do I continue trying to master French cooking or golf (in the absence of evidence that I have any gift for it) because I have a passion for the activity? Or does my persistence reflect an inability to change course, a compulsive conviction that one must always finish anything one starts? (The fear that I'll be labeled a quitter may not be unrealistic if a strong social norm supports persisting no matter what. An accumulation of declarations that "grit is good" may help to create and reinforce just such a norm, thereby contributing to unhealthy reasons for persisting.)

Interestingly, those who stick with something out of genuine enjoyment may experience less need for self-discipline. They don't have to grit their teeth to keep doing it, and it doesn't matter if they're not the sort of person who scores high on Duckworth's "grit scale." The essayist Annie Dillard, discussing the commitment to being a writer, commented, "You don't do it from willpower; you do it from an abiding passion." In fact, it's not unlike being a parent, she added. "If you have a little baby crying in the middle of the night, and if you depend only on willpower to get you out of bed to feed the baby, that baby will starve. You do it out of love."[57]

Quality of life is affected not only by what we do (that is, our behavior) but also by why we do it. That truth keeps surfacing throughout this book, proving relevant to issues ranging from overparenting to internalization. Theorists who stay at the surface, focused only on what can be seen and measured, will just want to know how much grit someone tends to display. They won't bother to ask whether she does so because of her love of what she's doing or because of a desperate (and anxiety-provoking) need to prove her competence. As long as kids are pushing themselves, we're supposed to nod our approval.

Thus, as the epigraph to one of her articles, Duckworth chose this quote from the actor Will Smith: "I'm not afraid to die on a treadmill. I will not be outworked, period. You might have more talent than me . . . but if we get on the treadmill together, there are two things: You're getting off first, or I'm going to die. It's really that simple."[58] This declaration will strike many of us as frankly disturbing—an example of the dark side of persistence. It seems to illustrate a pathological fear of losing, a compulsive need to triumph over others, the rigid overcompensation that so often underlies macho boasting.[59] To Duckworth, however, Smith won't get off the damn treadmill and is therefore a model to be celebrated.

To know when to pull the plug requires not only wisdom and a capacity to adopt a long-term perspective but also a measure of gumption. Because continuing to do what one has been doing often represents the path of least resistance, it can take guts to cut one's losses and say ¡Basta! And that's as important a message to teach one's children as is the usefulness of perseverance. Most of us want to encourage our kids to find something they love doing—and to help to *spark* that love (of writing, perhaps, to take Dillard's example). That's very different from telling them they ought to finish whatever they start, no matter how miserable it makes them.

3. There's less to the benefits of grit than meets the eye.

Duckworth's primary rationale for promoting grit is that it will produce "high levels of achievement." That may sound commendable, but take a moment to reflect on other possible goals one might have—for example, helping children to lead a life that's happy and fulfilling, morally admirable, creative, or characterized by psychological health. Any of those objectives would almost certainly lead to prescriptions quite different from "Do one thing and never give up."

Moreover, if you look closely at Duckworth's research, the benefits of grit she claims to have demonstrated turn out to be either circular or simply dubious. In one of her studies, she found that freshman cadets at West Point who scored high on her grit questionnaire ("I finish whatever I begin") were less likely to quit during the grueling summer training program.[60] This experiment does serve the narrow purpose of establishing the validity of the items on her questionnaire but otherwise seems to prove only that people who are persistent persist.

Another pair of studies looked at an elite group of middle schoolers who qualified for the National Spelling Bee. Duckworth reported that they performed better in that competition if they were higher in grit, "whereas spellers higher in openness to experience—defined as preferring using their imagination, playing with ideas, and otherwise enjoying a complex mental life—perform[ed] worse." She also found that the most effective preparation strategy was "solitary deliberate practice activities" rather than, say, reading books.[61]

What's striking here aren't the findings themselves but the lesson Duckworth seems to derive from them. If enjoying a complex mental life (or reading for pleasure) interferes with performance in a one-shot contest to see who can spell more obscure words correctly—and if sufficient grittiness to spend time alone memorizing lists of words helps to achieve that goal—this is regarded as an argument in favor of grit. Presumably it also argues against having a complex mental life or engaging in "leisure reading."

(Ironically, if we were interested in how well kids can spell—by which I mean (a) most kids, not just champion spellers, and (b) as judged by their actual writing rather than in the contrived format of a spelling bee—other research has found that reading, apart from its other benefits, is actually more effective than drill and practice.[62] But to a proponent of grit, reading is less onerous, demands less self-discipline, and is therefore less admirable.)

The relevant issue, just as with the choice between learning how to play one musical instrument versus several of them, is more about ends than means. How important is it that kids who are exceptionally good spellers win more championships? Should we favor any strategy or personality feature that contributes to that objective (or to anything that could be described as "higher achievement") regardless of what it involves and what it displaces?

The outcome measure that Duckworth uses most often as a marker for achievement is school performance. Her argument is that self-discipline, and grit in particular, result in better grades. Her first experiment, which attracted considerable media attention, found that, among eighth graders at one magnet school with competitive admissions, self-discipline was a stronger predictor of academic success than IQ scores were, and that this attribute explained why girls, at least at that particular school, got better grades than boys did.[63] Teachers gave more A's to students who reported, for example, that they tended to put off doing what they enjoy until they finished their homework.

Again, though, what exactly should we conclude from that fact? Suppose it had been discovered that the students with the best grades were those who nodded and smiled at everything their teacher said. Would that argue for encouraging kids to become better at brown-nosing? Or might it instead call into question the usefulness of grades as a variable? What if it had been discovered that self-discipline on the part of adults was associated with more positive evaluations from their supervisors at work? We'd have to conclude that employees who did what their bosses wanted, regardless of whether it was satisfying or sensible, elicited a favorable verdict from those same bosses. But so what?

Good grades, in other words, are often just a sign of approval by the person with the power in a classroom. But even when they serve other functions, grades suffer from low levels of validity and reliability.[64] Moreover, students who pursue higher grades—in many cases, perhaps, with an impressive show of grit—tend to be less interested in what they're learning, more likely to think in a superficial fashion (and less likely to retain information), and inclined to prefer the easiest possible task whenever they have a choice—because the goal isn't to explore ideas but to do whatever is necessary to snag the A (see p. 85).

Moreover, students with high grades seem, on average, to be overly conformist and not particularly creative. For evidence of that, we need look no further than two studies that Duckworth herself cited to prove that self-discipline predicts academic performance. One of the studies found that such performance "seemed as much a function of attention to details and the rules of the academic game as it was of intellectual talent." High-achieving students "were not particularly interested in ideas or in cultural or aesthetic pursuits. Additionally, they were not particularly tolerant or empathic; however, they did seem stable, pragmatic, and task-oriented, and lived in harmony with the rules and conventions of society. Finally, relative to students in general, these superior achievers seemed somewhat stodgy and unoriginal."[65] The other study she mentioned also found that self-control was significantly correlated with students' grades—but so was conformity and an aversion to risk-taking.[66]

Do more self-disciplined or persistent students—which may include a disproportionate number of girls[67]—get higher grades? Perhaps. But that doesn't make a case for grit so much as it points up the limitations of grades as an outcome measure. More generally, the only people likely to be persuaded by studies dealing with persistence are those who already approved of that quality—without regard for the widely varying reasons one might have for refusing to give up or the widely varying results of doing so.

SELF-DISCIPLINE AS A MORAL IMPERATIVE

If control over the self can sometimes be unhealthy, if waiting for more marshmallows or refusing to give up doesn't always make sense, then why do so many people offer an unqualified endorsement of self-discipline, deferral of gratification, and grit? At various points in this book, I've suggested that a traditionalist perspective is based not only on assumptions about how things are but on beliefs about how things should be. Ideology, not just evidence, often accounts for stern condemnations of permissiveness, helicopter parenting, and the self-esteem movement—as well as enthusiasm about rewards, competition, and the alleged benefits of failure. The same is true here. The uniformly good press that self-discipline gets is a matter of conviction as much as prediction, so the fact that it doesn't always produce good results may not dim the ardor of those who insist our children need to learn to control themselves.

Self-discipline is at the heart of George Lakoff's Strict Father model of conservatism. That model's emphasis on "Moral Strength" makes self-discipline "a primary moral requirement," whereas "the lack of it [is] immoral"—a sign of self-indulgence and therefore moral weakness. Whether it offers practical benefits, psychological or otherwise, is beside the point.[68] To put it another way, the *difficulty* of making oneself do what one would rather not—or restraining oneself from doing what affords pleasure—is valued for its own sake. Suffering and deprivation (see pp. 113–15) are the requirements for, and perhaps the manifestations of, that "moral strength" Lakoff mentions. And as usual, a deeply conservative worldview has been adopted and accepted widely. Paul Tough, for example, declared in the pages of the *New York Times Magazine* that "what kids need more than anything is a little hardship: some challenge, some deprivation that they can overcome."[69]

One thinks of the credo so beloved by those who aspire to a culture of machismo: "What does not kill me makes me stronger,"[70] which Nietzsche introduced with the phrase "From the military school of life." This sensibility has echoes in Eastern cultures—*gambaru* (tough it out, suck it up) in Japan and *chi ku* ("eating bitterness") in China—as well as in Western religions. Angela Duckworth has observed that "every major religious tradition advocates forsaking pleasure in the moment to realize greater, deferred rewards."[71] Indeed, the case for self-control may be primarily theological. The ultimate in putting off gratification, after all, is a call to wait until after one is dead to collect one's prize for sacrificing and suffering. Nor is this a purely theoretical connection. People who identify themselves as religious—and their children—tend to exercise more self-control than others.[72]

To more fully understand what lies behind attempts to rein in the self, let's ask a different question: What must be true about children—or people in general—if self-discipline is required to make them do valuable things? Consider this reflection by conservative columnist David Brooks:

> In Lincoln's day, to achieve maturity was to succeed in the conquest of the self. Human beings were born with sin, inflected with dark passions and satanic temptations. The transition to adulthood consisted of achieving mastery over them. You can read commencement addresses from the 19th and early 20th centuries in which the speakers would talk about the beast within and the need for iron character to subdue it. Schoolhouse readers emphasized self-discipline. The whole character-building model was sin-centric.[73]

The implication here seems to be that self-discipline is a historical relic, which is far from the truth. Today we may be spared the florid, exhortatory rhetoric of yesteryear, but an Internet search for "self-discipline" or "self-control" offers ample evidence of how these concepts are still very much in fashion. Nevertheless, Brooks offers a useful, if disconcerting, reminder of the sin-centric assumptions on which the gospel of self-discipline (still) rests. It's because our preferences are regarded as unworthy, our desires as shameful, that we must strive to overcome them. Taken to its logical conclusion, human life is seen as a constant struggle to stifle and transcend ourselves. Morality consists of the triumph of mind over body, reason over desire, will over want.

This sensibility shows up not only among preachers and right-wing cultural commentators but also in the work of researchers who don't just study self-discipline (or perseverance) but vigorously defend its importance. Baumeister, for example, has said more than once that his "advice is to forget about self-esteem and concentrate on teaching your children self-control."[74] Here he manages to combine two prescriptions in one sentence: Don't think too well of yourself . . . and get to work! His academic articles—and those of certain other social scientists—clearly reflect this worldview.

One educator contends that we need to teach self-discipline because of "our natural egoism [that threatens to] lead us into 'a condition of warre one against another.'" His approving allusion to Thomas Hobbes's dismal view of our species is followed by the remarkable assertion that "social class differences appear to be largely a function of the ability to defer gratification." Thus, our obligation is to "connect the lower social classes to the middle classes who may provide role models for self-discipline."[75] While few people admit to this sort of thinking nowadays, its impact can still be witnessed—for example, in many charter schools that serve predominantly low-income African American and Latino students. It's not uncommon to find a system of almost militaristic behavior control, with public humiliation for noncompliance and an array of rewards for obedience that calls to mind the token economy programs developed in prisons and psychiatric hospitals. Such authoritarian discipline is blithely justified in the name of "teaching self-control" to poor kids of color.[76]

Another feature of conservatism that's sometimes reflected in the call to impart self-discipline is the familiar complaint that our society—or at least its youth—has forgotten the value of hard work, the importance of duty, the need to accept personal responsibility, and so on. Of course, as with accusations of permissiveness, we sometimes forget that "the older generation has complained about the lack of self-control among the younger generation for decades, if not centuries," says C. Peter Herman, a researcher at the University of Toronto. "The older generation of Vikings no doubt complained that the younger generation were getting soft and did not rape and pillage with the same dedication as in years gone by."[77]

Interestingly, many secular institutions and liberal individuals—who would strenuously object to the notion that children are self-centered little beasts that need to be tamed—uncritically embrace the concept of self-discipline, which ultimately can be traced back to this very premise. It's admirable to reject coercion and punishment in favor of gentler methods, but if self-discipline amounts to installing a policeman inside each child, then it's worth thinking about the worldview from which that concept emerges.

As I've said, that doesn't mean there's no value at all to the *capacity* to exercise self-discipline (or persistence) on those occasions when it's useful for reaching goals we regard as worthwhile. The trick is to steer between the extremes of inadequate and excessive self-control, and to engage in a healthy kind of regulation that helps us to lead productive and satisfying lives. Similarly, we want our children to be able to strike a balance between the present and the future, between what feels good now and what's likely to yield enduring satisfaction. But my point is that the case against a simplistic embrace of self-discipline or grit isn't based only on what we know about its psychological dynamics. There's also reason for concern about its philosophical premises. The case for self-control is based on assumptions and beliefs that many of us will find troubling on close inspection.

IT'S NOT JUST YOU

When you hear someone insist, "Children need more than intelligence to succeed," the traits they're encouraged to acquire, as I've mentioned, are more likely to include self-discipline than empathy. But let's pause to consider the significance of thinking about *any* list of individual qualities—the attributes a particular child possesses (or lacks). When we encounter a behavior we don't like, we assume the child needs to develop certain characteristics like grit or self-control. The implication is that it's the kid who needs to be fixed.

But what if it turned out that persistence or an inclination to delay gratification was mostly predicted by the situations in which people find themselves and the nature of the tasks they're asked to perform? That possibility is consistent with Walter Mischel's theory of personality. Indeed, it matches what he discovered about waiting for an extra marshmallow: Whether children did so was largely determined by the way the experiment was conducted (pp. 143–44). What we should be talking about, he and his colleagues emphasized, is not

> the *ability* to defer immediate gratification. This ability has been viewed as an enduring trait of "ego strength" on which individuals differed stably and consistently in many situations. In fact, as the present data indicate, under appropriate . . . conditions, virtually all subjects, even young children, could manage to delay for lengthy time periods.[78]

Similarly, other experts have argued that it may make more sense to think of self-control in general as "a situational concept, not an individual trait" in light of the fact that any individual "will display different degrees of self-control in different situations."[79]

This critical shift in thinking fits perfectly with a large body of evidence from the field of social psychology that shows how we act and who we are reflect the circumstances in which we find ourselves. The most famous social psych studies are variations on this theme: Set up ordinary children in an extended team competition at summer camp, and you'll elicit unprecedented levels of hostility, even if the kids had never seemed particularly aggressive. Randomly assign adults—chosen for their psychological normality—to the role of inmate or guard in a mock prison, and they will start to become their roles, to frightening effect. Make slight changes to an academic environment and a significant number of students will cheat—or, under other conditions, will refrain from doing so. (Cheating "is as much a function of the particular situation in which [the student] is placed as it is of his . . . general ideas and ideals."[80])

The notion that each of us isn't entirely the master of his own fate can be awfully hard to accept. It's quite common to attribute to an individual's personality or character what is actually a function of the social environment—so common, in fact, that psychologists have dubbed this the Fundamental Attribution Error. It's a bias that may be particularly prevalent in *our* society, where individualism is both a descriptive reality and a cherished ideal. We Americans stubbornly resist the possibility that what we do is profoundly shaped by policies, norms, systems, and other structural realities. We prefer to believe that people who commit crimes are morally deficient, that the have-nots in our midst are lazy (or at least insufficiently resourceful), that overweight people simply lack the willpower to stop eating, and so on.[81] If only all those folks would just exercise a little personal responsibility, a bit more self-control!

The Fundamental Attribution Error is painfully pervasive when the conversation turns to academic failure. Driving Duckworth and Seligman's study of student performance was their belief that underachievement *isn't* explained by structural factors—social, economic, or even educational. Rather, they insisted, it should be attributed to the students themselves, and specifically to their "failure to exercise self-discipline." The entire conceptual edifice of grit is constructed on that individualistic premise, one that remains popular for ideological reasons even though it's been repeatedly debunked by research.

When students are tripped up by challenges, they may respond by tuning out, acting out, or dropping out. Often, however, they do so not because of a defect in their makeup (lack of stick-to-itiveness) but because of structural factors. For one, those challenges—what they were asked to do—may not have been particularly engaging or relevant. Finger-wagging adults who exhort children to "do their best" sometimes don't offer a persuasive reason for why a given task should be done at all, let alone done well. And when students throw up their hands after failing at something they were asked to do, it may be less because they lack grit than because they weren't really "asked" to do it—they were *told* to do it.

They had nothing to say about the content or context of the curriculum. People of all ages are more likely to persevere when they have a chance to make decisions about the things that affect them. Thus, if students *don't* persist, it may be because they were excluded from any decision-making role rather than because their attitude, motivation, or character needs to be corrected.

There are, of course, many other systemic factors that can make learning go awry, but within the field of education, says researcher Val Gillies, "policy-makers' attentions have shifted away from structures and processes [and] towards a focus on personal skills and self-efficacy." Even relatively benign strategies designed to enhance social and emotional learning are sometimes motivated less by a desire to foster kids' well-being than by a hope that teaching them to regulate (rather than express) their feelings will make it easier for adults to manage them and keep them "on task." After all, Gillies points out, "Emotions are subversive in school."[82] And so is attention to structures and processes.

WHO BENEFITS?

Nothing I've said here should be taken to mean that personal responsibility doesn't matter, or that differences in people's attitudes and temperaments don't play a role in determining their actions. But if we minimize the importance of the environments in which those individuals function, we're less able to understand what's going on. Not only that, but the more we fault people for lacking self-discipline or the ability to control their impulses, the less likely we'll be to question the structures that shape what they do. There's no reason to challenge, let alone change, the way things have been set up if we assume people just need to buckle down and try harder.

To put it differently, the attention paid to self-discipline is not only philosophically conservative in its premises (as I've been arguing) but also politically conservative in its consequences:

- If consumers are drowning in debt, the effect of framing the problem as a lack of self-control is to deflect attention from the concerted efforts of the credit industry to get people hooked on borrowing money as early in life as possible.[83]

- The "Keep America Beautiful" campaign launched in the 1950s that urged us to stop being litterbugs was financed by the American Can Company and other corporations. The effect was to blame individuals and discourage questions about who profits from the production of disposable merchandise and its packaging.[84]

- Conservative criminologists have claimed that crime is due to a lack of self-control on the part of criminals, which, in turn, can be blamed on bad parenting. If that's true, then there's no need to address systemic factors such as poverty and unemployment. Indeed, the most prominent proponents of this theory have explicitly called for an approach to crime control "that would reduce the role of the state."[85]

- Mischel's marshmallow experiments have been used—for example, by David Brooks—to justify focusing less on "structural reforms" to improve education or reduce poverty. Instead, we're advised to look at traits possessed by individuals—specifically, the ability to exercise good old-fashioned self-control.[86] Similarly, Paul Tough has declared, "There is no antipoverty tool we can provide for disadvantaged young people that will be more valuable than the character strengths . . . [such as] conscientiousness, grit, resilience, perseverance, and optimism."[87]

All of this brings to mind the Latin question "*Cui bono?*" which means "Who benefits?" Whose interests are served by the astonishing proposition that no antipoverty tool (presumably including food stamps, Medicaid, and public housing) is more valuable than an effort to train poor kids to persist at whatever they're told to do? The implication is that if people find themselves struggling to earn a living or pay off their debts, the fault doesn't lie with the structure of our economic system (in which the net wealth of the richest 1 percent of the population is triple that of the bottom *80* percent).[88] Rather, those people have only their own lack of "character strengths" to blame.

Consider the locker room bromides (about how a quitter never wins and a winner never quits) that are barked at athletes before they attempt to defeat another group of athletes whose coach has told them the same thing. Or the speeches at expensive business luncheons that remind us there's no such thing as a free lunch—and sermonize about the virtue of initiative and self-sufficiency. Or the posters in which inspirational slogans, superimposed on photos of sunsets and mountains, exhort workers or students to "Reach for the stars" and assure them "You can if you think you can!"

Some of us regard all of this with a mixture of queasiness, dismay, and amusement. (This reaction is sometimes expressed satirically, with examples ranging from Sinclair Lewis's *Babbitt* a century ago to a recent series of parody posters called Demotivators.[89]) We read yet another paean to grit, or hear children being pushed to work hard no matter how dull or difficult the task, and our first reaction is to wonder who the hell benefits from this. We may notice that inspirational posters and training in the deferral of gratification seem to be employed with particular intensity in inner-city schools.[90] Jonathan Kozol pointed out the political implications of making poor African American students chant, "Yes, I can! I know I can!" or "If it is to be, it's up to me." Such slogans are very popular with affluent white people, he noticed, maybe because "if it's up to 'them' . . . it isn't up to 'us,' which appears to sweep the deck of many pressing and potentially disruptive and expensive obligations we may otherwise believe our nation needs to contemplate."[91]

Matthew Lieberman, a neuroscientist at UCLA, speculates that "self-control may support society's interests more than our own."[92] That divergence is worth taking a moment to consider. If "society" meant "other people," then we might infer a moral obligation to regulate our impulses in the hope that everyone else would benefit. But what if the advantages flow not so much out as up, less to others in general than to those in positions of power? Overcontrolled individuals may lead lives of quiet desperation, but they probably won't make trouble. That's why the social scientists who came up with the creepy phrase that opened this chapter—"equipping the child with a built-in supervisor"—went on to point out that this arrangement is useful for creating "a self-controlled—not just controlled—citizenry and work force."[93] That doesn't help your neighbor or your colleague any more than it helps you, but it's extremely convenient for whoever owns your company.

The priority given to conformity is easy to observe when the morning bell rings for school. To an empathic educator like the late Ted Sizer, the routine to which kids are subjected is damn near intolerable. Try following a high school student around for a full day, he urged, in case you've forgotten what it's like

> to change subjects abruptly every hour, to be talked at incessantly, to be asked to sit still for long periods, to be endlessly tested and measured against others, to be moved around in cohorts by people who really do not know who you are, to be denied any civility like a coffee break and asked to eat lunch in twenty-three minutes, to be rarely trusted, and to repeat the same regimen with virtually no variation for week after week, year after year.[94]

His understanding of how things look from the students' point of view informed Sizer's lifelong efforts to change the structure of American education. Now compare that perspective to those of experts whose first, and often only, question about the status quo is: How do we get kids to put up with it? For Duckworth, the challenge is how to make students pay "attention to a teacher rather than daydreaming," persist "on long-term assignments despite boredom and frustration," choose "homework over TV," and "behav[e] properly in class"?[95] In her more recent research, she created a task that is deliberately boring, the point being to come up with strategies that will lead students to resist the temptation to do something more interesting instead.[96] Again, *cui bono*?

Given these priorities, it makes perfect sense that Duckworth would turn to grades as evidence that grit is beneficial—not only because she assumes grades offer an accurate summary of learning but because "grades can motivate students to comply with teacher directives."[97] They are, in other words, useful as rewards or threats. Are the teacher's directives reasonable or constructive? Same answer as to the question of whether the homework assignments are worth doing: It doesn't matter. The point is to produce obedience—ideally, *habitual* obedience.[98] This is the mindset that underlies all the enthusiasm about grit and self-discipline, even if it's rarely spelled out.

Along the same lines, in an article called "Can Teachers Increase Students' Self-Control?" (as usual, the question is "can" not "should"), a cognitive psychologist named Daniel Willingham offers as a role model a hypothetical child who looks through his classroom window and sees "construction workers pour[ing] cement for a sidewalk" but "manages to ignore this interesting scene and focus on his work."[99] Again, the question of whether his "work" has any value is never raised. It may be a fill-in-the-blank waste of the time, but the teacher has assigned it, and that means an exemplary student is one who ignores a fascinating real-life lesson in how a sidewalk is created, who refrains from asking the teacher why that lesson can't be incorporated into the curriculum. He stifles his curiosity, exercises his self-control, and does what he's told.

To identify a lack of self-discipline as the central problem with children is to make them conform to a status quo that is left unexamined and therefore probably won't change. This is conservatism in the word's purest sense. But it doesn't describe only those who are trying to sell us grit. It also applies to those who worry about the possibility that children will be spoiled or feel too pleased with themselves. In fact, every chapter of this book could have been subtitled "*Cui Bono?*" What's the effect, and who's the beneficiary, of framing the problem with parenting in terms of lax discipline and insufficient conditionality? BGUTI, meanwhile, is by definition a way of teaching children that the status quo cannot be questioned, only prepared for. Obviously it's important to ask whether our assumptions about children—what they're like and how they're raised—are true, and whether the underlying values are defensible. But it's also worth asking whose interests they serve. Too often, it's not those of the kids themselves.

If we accept the timeworn complaints that parents are too permissive, we'll be inclined to crack down on kids by imposing tougher punishments, tighter regulations, stricter limits, less trust. If we're persuaded by accusations of overparenting, we may be tempted to provide less support than children need (in the name of promoting self-sufficiency). If we accept the claim that kids need to experience more failure, more competition, more frustration, more conditions attached to a sense of self-worth—well, none of what follows from this advice is likely to do kids much good. Neither will a regimen of making them discipline themselves to do whatever they're told and then keep at it.

What's more likely to benefit our children—and to improve the society in which they (and we) live—is to turn the traditionalists' approach on its head. How to do so is the subject of our final chapter.

CHAPTER 8

Raising Rebels

Complaints that kids today are lazy, entitled, and self-centered tend to be accompanied by a pile of prescriptions for how to improve them: Impose clear expectations and firm limits, then hold children "accountable" (in other words, punish them if they disobey); push them toward self-sufficiency; insist that self-worth and positive comments from others must be earned; provide plenty of experiences with competition and failure; promote self-discipline and grit. In essence, children should be well behaved and hard working. They should accommodate themselves to the unforgiving demands of the real world, follow the rules, and *do what they're told*.

Throughout this book I've rejected these recommendations, along with the unflattering descriptions of children with which they're associated. Now, I'd like to question the connection. Why is it so widely assumed that these beliefs about children, even if they were accurate, lead naturally to those recommendations? Imagine for a moment that there really was good reason to conclude that most young people think too much of themselves or think only *about* themselves. Why should that prompt calls for a renewed focus on getting them to toe the line? Why, in short, would obedience be the cure for self-absorption or self-centeredness?

I'd like to propose a different response: Encourage young people to focus on the needs and rights of others, to examine the practices and institutions that get in the way of making everyone's lives better, to summon the courage to question what one is told and be willing to *break* the rules sometimes.

I'm not talking about a knee-jerk opposition to everything, the kind of reactive sensibility that was captured by the Marx Brothers' lyric "Whatever it is, I'm against it." Rather, I have in mind a thoughtful skepticism, a reflective rebelliousness, a selective defiance based on principle.[1] One should be "critical" in both senses of that word: willing to find fault but also dependent on careful analysis. It's not "If you say yes, I'll say no," but rather "If you say or do something that doesn't make sense, I'll ask why—then, if necessary, say no (and suggest that other people do the same)."

I'm not talking about rudeness: Resistance should be not only reasoned but also respectful. Nor am I talking about arrogance: One should turn a skeptical eye not only on what others are doing but also on one's own beliefs and actions. Someone with a strong core of unconditional self-esteem has sufficient security to challenge him- or herself and admit mistakes. To be critical only of other people's ideas is to risk hubris and stagnation; to be critical only of one's own ideas is to risk timidity and indecision.

Finally, I'm not talking about cynicism. Instead, I want to promote skepticism, which means one doesn't automatically accept whatever people in authority say. A willingness to question the way things are paradoxically affirms a vision of the way things ought to be. One may well be offended by the violation of important values (such as honesty, compassion, or fairness) and, as a result, moved to acts of resistance. The cynic, by contrast, remains passive and apolitical, dismissing activism as pointless and believing in nothing but self-interest.[2]

It's been said that the personal is political, and there's no doubt that parenting is intensely personal. To argue against traditional ways of raising children, or to suggest that we can help children stand up for what they think is right, doesn't *introduce* politics into parenting. It's always been there. If we've failed to notice the political implications of child rearing, it may be because most advice on the subject has the effect of perpetuating the status quo. Hence the need to keep asking, "*Cui bono?*"

When, for example, a researcher such as Diana Baumrind defends the idea of "moral internalization," which she defines as "the process by which children come to espouse and conform to society's rules, even when they are free of external surveillance or the expectation of external inducement," that's intensely political.[3] The cornerstone of her notion of "authoritative" discipline is the creation of built-in supervisors to ensure conformity. But too many people respond by asking, "What's the most efficient way to achieve such internalization?" and skirting the question of the *value* of those rules they're being asked to internalize. In fact, we should invite our children to join us in asking which rules are worth following, and why.

Whether we decide to do so will depend on our answer to a different sort of question: What kind of people do we want our children to become? Do we hope they'll be willing to question the existing order, to be outraged by outrageous things, to demand changes in unfair schools and workplaces? Or is the primary point to get them to conform to whatever exists?

Almost half a century ago, conservatives blamed a surge in college campus unrest on permissive parenting. My first response (in Chapter 1) was to question the accuracy of that causal link. Another response to their claim, however, might be: "*Blamed*?!" If there really were a connection, it would constitute a powerful argument in *favor* of such parenting.[4] The political and cultural activism of the 1960s, after all, was defined by efforts to challenge oppressive institutions and restrictive assumptions, to demand equal rights for women and people of color, to oppose war and promote awareness about the environmental costs of economic growth. If a certain approach to parenting really could produce people who devoted themselves to those democratizing struggles, we should be sharing the good news with parents today.

My argument, in sum, is that the real alternative to narcissistic self-absorption is not mindless obedience but reflective rebelliousness. And even though there is no credible evidence that narcissistic self-absorption is more common in today's youth than it was in those of previous generations, promoting reflective rebelliousness still seems like a pretty good idea.

AN EPIDEMIC OF ACQUIESCENCE

Suppose that a teenager somewhere in Ohio showed up at school yesterday morning in a bathing suit, announcing that he should be free to wear anything he finds comfortable and telling the principal defiantly, "My parents agree with me, and my dad is a lawyer." It's safe to predict that this episode would become an instant media sensation. Within hours, bloggers and cable TV pundits would be citing it as an example of what *kids these days* are like. The primary debate in online forums would pit those who blamed the out-of-control kids against those who blamed their spineless, overindulgent parents.

But a couple of million students in Ohio didn't do anything like that yesterday. They dressed in a way that adults deemed acceptable, showed up on time, grew silent on command, sat passively as their teachers lectured at them, obediently pulled out their textbooks and worksheets, and in the evening did pretty much whatever their parents told them to do. True, some kids may have misbehaved or complied only reluctantly and sullenly. But by and large the student in the bathing suit, who will be cited as evidence for a familiar array of generalizations, is an aberration.

That much is unsurprising. But this hypothetical scenario raises an important question: Is it possible that not everything all those obedient kids were told to do (and did) was really worth doing, that many of the rules they followed weren't entirely justified? Could it be, in other words, that the proper cause for concern is not our underdressed outlier but all those "good" children who failed to question, think critically, and respond with the appropriate measure of independent thought?

Most children seem eager, even desperate, to please those in authority, reluctant to rock the boat even when the boat clearly needs rocking. In a way, an occasional roll-your-eyes story of excess in the other direction marks the exception that proves the rule. And the rule is a silent epidemic of obedience. For every kid who is slapped with the label "Oppositional Defiant Disorder," hundreds suffer from what one educator has mischievously called Compliance Acquiescent Disorder. The symptoms of CAD, he explained, include the following: "defers to authority," "actively obeys rules," "fails to argue back," "knuckles under instead of mobilizing others in support," and "stays restrained when outrage is warranted."[5]

The joke here, of course, is that these symptoms are widely celebrated as proof of successful socialization. Perhaps that's because adults, who can think of no higher honorific to bestow on a child than "well behaved," are themselves reluctant to question and speak out. All around us we find people who sound like Robert Frost's neighbor, the man who "will not go beyond his father's saying." When questioned about one of their habits or beliefs, they're apt to reply, "Well, that's just the way I was raised," as if this ended the conversation, as if it were impossible to critically examine the values to which one has become accustomed.

This failure to question would be disturbing even if our only goal were to understand the world more accurately. Intellectual progress demands that we refuse to take things at face value or accept everything we've been told. It requires us always to entertain the possibility that the conventional wisdom may be mistaken. Science, as Richard Feynman remarked, might be defined as "the belief in the ignorance of authority"—a statement that could be dismissed as hyperbolic were it not for Feynman's eminence as a scientist. Incidentally, a key objective J. K. Rowling said she had in mind while writing the Harry Potter series was to encourage her young readers to "question authority."[6]

Of course, that stance is especially crucial if our objective is not only to understand the world but to improve it, if we want not only to find out what is true but to do what is right. Just outside your front door there are social and political realities that fail to meet the most elementary standard of moral acceptability. How, then, can we in good conscience teach our children that things should be accepted as they are—"accepted" in the sense of regarding them as either inevitable or desirable? Rather, we should invite children to analyze the status quo and decide which institutions and traditions may need to be changed. We ought to help them talk back to the world.

In my experience, most parents sincerely want their children to be assertive, independent thinkers who are unafraid to stand their ground . . . with their peers. When a child demonstrates the identical sort of courage in interactions with *them*, it's a different story: At best, it's a troublesome phase that kids go through; at worst, it's an example of uncooperative, disrespectful, disobedient, defiant behavior that must be stamped out. The truth is that if we want children to be able to resist peer pressure and grow into principled and brave adults, we have to actively welcome their questioning and being assertive with *us*. We have to move beyond our need to win arguments and impose our will, beyond our fear that we'll be seen as weak or permissive if our kids are given leave to challenge us.

Children and adults in less-powerful groups are sometimes actively discouraged from asking why (let alone saying no), regardless of how legitimate such a response may be. The consequences of being perceived as a troublemaker may be more dire for those already at a disadvantage by virtue of their race or social status. They are therefore urged to keep their heads down and hope to join the ranks of the privileged rather than impertinently questioning the moral justification of a system of privilege. (Of course, discouraging children's dissent makes it more likely that an unfair system will continue.)

At the same time, though, it sometimes seems that affluent, successful, college-bound students are particularly careful to avoid doing anything that might alienate those in a position of authority. The question "'Why do we have to learn this?' . . . came largely from students in the lower tracks," a math teacher reported. "Those who were succeeding in school, the 'best students,' didn't seem to be as concerned with 'Why?'" Or if they did doubt the value of what they were being told to do, they weren't about to say so. As one graduate explained to a journalist, "We didn't get [to college] by rocking the boat."[7]

So who is left to rock it if no one will play that role? Who will take his cue from Bartleby in Melville's short story, the character who created an uproar when "in a singularly mild, firm voice, [he] replied, 'I would prefer not to'"? After three conservative members of a church in Fulton, Missouri, criticized the fact that the local high school had staged *Grease*—despite the fact that the script had been carefully edited by the drama teacher to omit possibly offensive content—the superintendent, without any public discussion, canceled the next play that was scheduled to be performed. It was, if you can bear the irony, Arthur Miller's *The Crucible*, which concerns the terrible consequences of religious zealotry and conformity. Neither the drama teacher nor the students, who had already begun preparing for their auditions, could figure out what was supposed to be objectionable about the play. But one student said, "It's over. We can't do anything about it. We just have to obey."[8]

The novelist and critic Mark Slouka shakes his head at this sort of passivity, and particularly at the widespread tendency to confuse it with maturity. "What we require most in America today are bad soldiers: stubborn, independent-minded men and women, reluctant to give orders and loath to receive them, loyal not to authority, nor to any specific company or team, but to the ideals of open debate, equality, honesty, and fairness."[9]

Such men and women start life as boys and girls in whom we nourish the characteristics of persistent questioners and reflective rebels.

As a rule, researchers in developmental psychology and, for that matter, parenting advisers, tend to mirror the norms of the culture in which they work. Few spend much time examining the goals and assumptions that underlie their studies (or, in the case of advisers, their advice). The question of what constitutes *healthy* development or a desirable outcome— and what makes it so—is likely to be passed over quickly or ignored altogether. What's healthy may simply be equated with what's normal. If a certain style of parenting is associated with socially acceptable behavior on the child's part—"appropriate" deference to the parent and fidelity to what's considered proper conduct—then this is judged to be a successful intervention. By declining to ask whether the society's norms are defensible, whether a parent's actions (that may have elicited a child's "misbehavior") were reasonable, it's possible to avoid what a professor of mine, a psychiatrist, once dismissed as "the whole value muddle."

But there are exceptions. Rather than just defining it as a positive outcome, a few researchers have asked whether compliance is always and necessarily a good thing. And those who have asked that question have discovered that the answer is often no. I summarized some of their results in a previous book: explorations of "compulsive compliance" and studies that found resistance to parental authority is often associated with a healthier sense of psychological autonomy.[10] More recent research has confirmed this, showing that "high-defiant toddlers . . . are likely to develop better on average than their low-defiant peers."[11]

Of course much depends on the extent and type of the defiance—or compliance. Moreover, we'd need to consider the context: What sort of demand, request, or situation prompted the child's response? (As usual, behaviors are too often thought to reflect only the individual's personality rather than the interaction between the individual and a particular environment.) What's undeniable, though, is that it's possible for children to be too well behaved. And that's true in terms of psychological outcomes, whether or not our basic values make us uneasy about people who shrug their shoulders and say, like that frustrated young actor in Missouri, "We just have to obey."

Shrugging wasn't an option for Katelyn Campbell, who was outraged by an assembly to promote sexual abstinence in her public high school. The speaker, sponsored by a religious group, told students that condoms were unsafe, urged them to "embrace God's plan for sexual purity," and reduced some students to tears with statements such as "If you are on birth control, your mother probably hates you." Katelyn didn't just complain to a friend; she spoke out to the local newspaper and enlisted the help of the American Civil Liberties Union. As a result, she reports, the principal threatened to inform Wellesley College, which had just awarded her a scholarship, that she was a troublemaker. Graduation plans at the high school were changed so that Katelyn and several other seniors were no longer permitted to speak. And she was shunned and spit on by other students.[12]

The notion that children should be "critics of other people's ideas, analyzers of evidence, and makers of their own personal marks on this most complex world" is, according to educator Deborah Meier, "an idea with revolutionary implications. If we take it seriously." Meier, for one, did take it seriously, not only as a theorist but also as the founder of several remarkable schools. A junior high school principal in the same neighborhood as one of Meier's schools remarked, "You can always tell the kids" who attended it. "They don't accept anything you tell them at face value. They're always asking, 'Why?'"[13]

As Katelyn discovered—or may have known already—not every-one welcomes this proclivity. Aside from those who aren't happy about having their authority questioned, bystanders who didn't speak out sometimes resent someone who did.[14] In the long run, however, the con-sequences are bleak for all of us, and for our democracy, when people remain silent. A society in which no one is willing to risk being called a troublemaker is a place where power is certain to be abused.

A RECIPE FOR REFLECTIVE REBELLIOUSNESS

No parent wants his or her child to be spit on or threatened, but every parent should—and I think many parents would—be proud to raise a child who's willing to take a risk to do what's right. Sometimes, though, we may need a reality check, an invitation to reconsider our priorities. Not long ago I came across a blog post in which a father (and executive) described what a friend of his had to say over lunch about her two teen-age children. This woman's fifteen-year-old son regularly resisted doing his homework, she complained, despite the fact that he was taking med-ication for ADHD and seeing a "coach for his executive functioning is-sues." By contrast, her thirteen-year-old daughter "does exactly what she is supposed to do and gets all A's and B's." At this point, the writer had an interesting response. He asked which of her children was likely to "do great things" in life. She unhesitatingly replied, "My son, for sure. . . . He's very motivated to work on whatever he finds interesting, he's highly creative, and he has many interests. My daughter just focuses on what she's supposed to do at the moment." In that case, the writer wondered, why was she "spending all of her time, resources, and emotional energy trying to fix her son rather than trying to inspire her daughter?"[15]

His question was probably rhetorical, but if we treat it as real—and consider its relevance more generally—we'd have to acknowledge that almost all of us are subject to powerful social pressures to make our children conform, play it safe, and get ahead (or at least avoid falling behind). It takes courage on our part to encourage our children to be courageous. Perhaps the kid who objects to spending his after-school hours filling out more worksheets and slogging through textbooks will grow up to do great things, but if he doesn't do what he's told right now we may worry about his grades or the possibility of receiving stern missives from the school. Some of us may even find noncompliance irksome in its own right. ("You're the child; you don't get to decide.") When we pause to take the long view, yes, this kid may be more impressive than his sibling who passively follows directions, but on a given Thursday evening, it's the sibling who makes our lives easier.

I think our challenge as parents is to rise above that preference for the child of least resistance and to think beyond short-term success as a criterion—particularly if success is defined by conventional and insipid standards. Don't we want our kids to be inspiring rather than spend their lives just collecting tokens (grades, money, approval)? Don't we want them to think in the plural rather than focusing only on what will benefit them personally? Don't we want them to appraise traditions with fresh eyes and raise questions about what seems silly or self-defeating or oppressive, rather than doing what has always been done just because it's always been done?

There are three fundamental components of this more ambitious agenda. The first is to support kids' inclination to *care* and develop a "prosocial" orientation. The second is to support their *self-confidence* and assertiveness. And the third is to help them embrace the value of *skepticism* and nonconformity.

Psychologists use the word *prosocial* to refer to actions intended to benefit someone else as well as a general concern about the welfare of others: an inclination to see the world from perspectives other than one's own, to feel the emotions of other people along with them, and to care about others and help those who need it. These varied elements involve the head as well as the heart, reflecting a commitment to moral principles as well as a connection to real human beings (including people to whom we're not related and whom we may not even know). Elsewhere, I've drawn from a large published literature to describe various strategies, programs, and resources for how one can raise a prosocial child.[16]

It is possible, however, to have sympathy or empathy to spare yet not to act on what one feels. In some situations it can require a fair measure of self-confidence to come to someone's aid. To be sure, it's also possible to be assertive (and to demonstrate grit) only in the service of one's own needs. We meet people every day who are bold and persistent but entirely motivated by self-interest. My point here, though, is that concern about other people doesn't always translate into action unless there's some gumption mixed in with the care. The good news is that both characteristics can result from the same approach to child rearing, one characterized by a warm, empathic style that facilitates secure attachment. This tends to promote self-confidence and autonomy as well as a concern about others.[17]

But even individuals who are both confident and caring may be unwilling to swim against the tide. The last component is a proclivity for asking "Why?" and, when necessary, saying "No." Because more has been written about promoting assertiveness and care, it's this third factor on which I'd like to focus.

THE GRASS MOMENT

Here's another hypothetical school scenario. A principal announces that, because of a recent outbreak of graffiti in the bathrooms (involving spray-painted assertions regarding certain features of the principal's own anatomy), no student will be permitted to use the bathroom unless accompanied by a teacher. What interests me is figuring out how we can raise children whose first and last response to this directive isn't likely to be "Well, like it or not, that's the rule now, so there's nothing we can do."

The alternative involves two discrete steps. First, the student must question the inevitability and desirability of the decree, at least within his or her own mind: Was that a reasonable thing for the principal to do? Is the point really to "protect student safety"? How else might he have dealt with the graffiti problem? What are the implications of requiring students to be escorted to the bathroom? Any of these questions may lead the student to decide the new policy is unacceptable—even if other people appear to be accepting it (or at least not doing anything about it). That decision can prompt, or be prompted by, the recognition that certain things aren't just "a part of life"; they can and should be called into question. I call this the Grass Moment, based on a *Far Side* cartoon in which several cows in a pasture are grazing contentedly until one of them suddenly lifts its head and says, "Hey, wait a minute! This is grass! We've been eating *grass!*"

The second step is for the student—ideally after conversations with others—to consider what sort of action to take. What can we do besides grumble? Well, we could find a sympathetic teacher, organize a larger group of kids, or rally the parents. We could start a petition, meet with the principal, complain to the school board, or write a letter to the newspaper. We could amend the existing graffiti ("and he doesn't just have one; he *is* one"), arrange a pee-in at the principal's office, or show up outside his house at night with loud music and a megaphone ("No privacy for us, no peace for you"). The possibilities are limited only by one's imagination. And, well, by the law.

We may approve of some of these responses more than others, but all of them, as well as the process of choosing among them, reflect a disposition for skepticism and critical thinking, a disinclination to take things at face value, a tendency to ask why things are the way they are. Self-assertion may be necessary to organize resistance, but clearly it isn't sufficient. Again, not all assertiveness is about standing up for a principle (or against a principal), nor is it necessarily even rebellious.

Now consider a second case: A group of friends decides to pull a cruel prank, perhaps involving online harassment, on someone in their class who doesn't quite fit in. What does it take, beyond simple courage or compassion, for one member of that group to say, "I'm sorry, guys, but that's just a rotten thing to do, and I don't want any part of it"? Notice that the same kind of responses are required as in the first case: seeing the idea as something that can be challenged, and then speaking out and perhaps taking some other kind of action to stop it. Notice, too, that the same personality characteristics may be required here as in that first example. The difference is that just about all of us grown-ups admire the kid who stands up to a bullying peer group, whereas we get nervous when he or she rebels against a school administrator (let alone against *us*).

If we're willing to get over that nervousness, our task is not just to teach a set of skills but to cultivate a disposition.[18] That disposition— particularly the inclination to be bold rather than reticent—is obviously influenced by one's inborn temperament. But parenting plays a role, too. In a study conducted during the 1960s, researchers asked more than a thousand undergraduates about their childhoods. It turned out that those who were involved in social service activities (community volunteer work) and political activism (protesting in behalf of a cause) were less likely to have been raised in homes characterized by a traditional, punitive approach to discipline. Their parents, more than those of other students, seemed generally respectful of them and had expected them to be responsible and mature.[19]

Nonpunitive guidance and a trusting relationship with one's children—relying on love and reason more than on power—define what I've called a "working with" approach to parenting. That approach is also associated with a focus on ambitious long-term goals, such as wanting kids to grow up as happy, ethical, compassionate, creative, independent thinkers. (All of this can be contrasted with more controlling methods as well as with a predominant focus on compliance.) The idea is to support children's autonomy in a way that complements their concern about others. Autonomy support, remember, is not the same as pressure to become more independent.[20] The point is to "work with," not to say, "Figure it out by yourself." It's an active and interactive process in which we provide guidance, assist kids in becoming more skilled and confident at deciding, and let them know we're there to help when they need it (not when we need them to need us).

This support helps to create a sense of safety for children. They're more willing to venture out, take a stand, accept that they'll sometimes make mistakes, and question authority. We have to make it clear that we really do welcome offbeat responses and won't become defensive when they challenge what we've said. In fact, we may want to help them figure out how to frame their arguments against us as convincingly as possible, even when we don't agree with their position. Our goal isn't to win a debate but to encourage them to think for themselves and teach them to become more skilled at doing so.[21]

The bottom line is that kids learn to make good decisions by making decisions, not by following directions. If we want them to take responsibility for making the world a better place, then we need to *give* them responsibilities. That means dialing back our control, whether of the flagrant or subtle variety. (An example of the latter is praise for pleasing us, which tends to promote insecurity and dependence on authority. The more we praise, the more they need to hear it.) This approach to parenting shows them on a daily basis how cooperation and respect can inform the way we deal with others. And if they see *us* questioning authority and taking a stand for a principle—in our work lives and as citizens—that, too, sets a powerful example.

TALKING IT OUT

To this point I've been describing a general approach to parenting that might be expected to promote reflective rebelliousness. I'd like to conclude with a few words about how we can talk with our children directly about this way of living one's life.

Just as we want them to be able to decide when it's appropriate to exercise self-discipline (rather than simply "being self-disciplined"), so we want them to be flexible in thinking about when, as well as how, one ought to question and object. In one offensive situation, it will make more sense to hold one's nose and bite one's tongue; in a second case, it may be possible to find a compromise; in a third, speaking out will seem the only defensible response despite the risks it entails—and adults must help children fully understand those risks. Many considerations—practical and moral, short-term and long-term—may have to be weighed in deciding on a response to a disturbing situation. But notice how this balanced way of framing the role for parents differs from more conventional advice, which emphasizes the importance of following directions and being polite no matter what the situation, or teaches children to think exclusively in terms of self-interest.

From about the age of five, kids tend to latch onto the concept of fairness, denouncing with genuine outrage whatever seems to violate that ideal. Sometimes they react that way about matters that seem trivial to us, but with our help they may soon begin to apply the concept to broader issues. Similarly, kids may insist it's not fair that *they* were denied something they'd been promised (or something a sibling received), but here, too, we can help them understand that other people have comparable concerns—and, in fact, fairness by definition extends beyond their personal claims. Thus, we can build on children's instinct to complain that something is unfair so that eventually they notice larger injustices. At that point, we help them develop and refine their sense of moral outrage—the insight needed to recognize wrongs and the courage needed to oppose them.

By our own reactions to unfairness, we model for children, showing them what it means to notice, to care, to take responsibility. But modeling, when you think about it, just tries to get someone to behave in a particular way; it doesn't necessarily promote a dedication to, or an understanding of, that behavior. Because imitation falls short of these more ambitious goals, we need to supplement showing with telling—or, more accurately, with conversation. In fact, the two can be combined into what might be called "deep modeling." Here, we not only set an example for children but try to be explicit about what we're doing and why we're doing it.

Consider the challenge of real-world ethical conundrums. It's fine for us to model honesty and compassion for our kids, but what happens when those two values seem to pull in opposite directions—for example, when telling the truth may hurt someone's feelings? Similarly, it's easy to say we should look out for other people's interests, but to what extent must we give up something we enjoy so someone else will benefit?

We can let children know how *we* think (and feel) our way through similar dilemmas by describing to them the factors we consider in making decisions: our previous experiences, the principles from which we're operating, and all the thoughts and emotions we take into account. From watching and listening to us, kids not only learn more about how we try to live a moral life; they also figure out that morality is rarely cut-and-dried. It's less often a choice between good and bad than between two goods or two bads.

Deep modeling might be thought of as a way of taking children "backstage," in the way that terrific teachers actually write, or solve problems, in front of students, freely making mistakes and thinking aloud about how to correct them. Kids are thereby able to experience what happens before (or behind or beneath) the ethical decisions that adults make, the essays they publish, and the scientific principles they discover—rather than being presented with these things as so many *faits accomplis*. This not only helps them learn about how a moral individual, writer, or scientist acts; it has a refreshing way of debunking authority, showing the decider behind the decision, someone who is imperfect and often uncertain, struggling to figure stuff out—or do the right thing and make his or her way in the world. It shows them how to question and it encourages them to do so.

Since many—too many—of our children's values and attitudes are formed by the mass media, every parent ought to offer an informal multiyear course in media literacy. Even if we were inclined to do so, most of us outside the Amish community will find it difficult to shield kids from movies, reality shows, sitcoms, and video games—and the smorgasbord of violence, competition, sexism, and consumerism they beam into our homes. We may not be able to say, "Don't watch," but we can watch *with* them and show them how to view critically, how to recognize propaganda tricks used to sell them stuff they don't need, how to identify hidden values and defuse attempts to manipulate them.

> You see how they tried to make you feel there's something wrong with you unless you buy their product? Did you notice how all these reality shows are contests? (Pretty soon you get the idea that it's natural for people to try to beat each other rather than work together.) Why do you think almost all the women—but not most of the men—who tell us about the news or the weather are young and attractive? How did the writer of this show manage to make us feel as if that character was justified in punching the other guy? (In real life, what else could someone in his situation have done if he was treated badly?) Did you pick up on the stereotypes in that comedy about fat people / smart people / old people / gays / Arabs? Did you know that the more TV someone watches, the more they likely he or she is to believe that most people are just out for themselves and would take advantage of you if given a chance?[22] Can you see why people might come to believe that?

This has to be done artfully, perhaps sparingly, lest we turn the living room into a classroom (in the worst sense of that word) with the result that our "students" understandably just want to be left alone to enjoy whatever they're watching. In any case, such questions and observations from us may eventually become unnecessary as kids make it clear from their observations that they've acquired a skeptical sensibility. They proudly spot the Madison Avenue trickery and the dubious values just below the surface of so many Hollywood productions.

Other results of our effort to help kids become reflective rebels may not be obvious right away, however. They may adopt a critical stance, but only later, when they're older and ready. Even then, they may decide not to respond to a given situation the same way we would, and that's something we have to respect. Any list of long-term goals for our children we formulate should include a meta-goal: We want them to be thoughtful enough to formulate meaningful goals for themselves. And whatever they come up with ultimately must supersede our goals for them.

I began this book by examining complaints about permissive parenting: accusations that we let kids get away with too much, accompanied by demands that we clamp down. I conclude now by pointing out that it's actually powerful adults and their institutions that get away with too much, which is why we need to raise a generation of kids who will push back. The same conservatism on display in our culture's attitudes about children and parenting reveals itself again in the willingness to allow those institutions to continue unchallenged and unquestioned. Let's ask whether widely accepted beliefs about narcissistic young people and helicopter parenting, conditional self-esteem and competition, really make sense. And then let's take the commitment to rethink the conventional wisdom that's reflected in this question—and pass it on to our kids.

Notes

1. Lakoff, p. xv.

2. All I've been able to find is a pair of studies in which a sample of devout Christians was asked to talk about their lives. Those who identified themselves as political conservatives (which doesn't mean they necessarily held specific positions on the public policy issues Lakoff talks about) were more likely to emphasize the importance of respect for authority, strict rules, self-discipline, and personal responsibility (see McAdams et al.).

3. Many conservatives support vouchers, in which public money is used to pay for private schools, whereas liberals are more likely to support subtler forms of privatization, such as diverting scarce public funds to privately managed, but still nominally public, charter schools.

4. In 2009, I listed several excerpts from Bush's and Obama's speeches about education and invited readers to try to match each passage with the correct president. See http://bit.ly/WmZsf.

5. Three examples of this: Frank Bruni of the *New York Times,* Scot Lehigh of the *Boston Globe*, and the late William Raspberry of the *Washington Post*. Of course many other columnists take a conservative view of raising children; I'm focusing here on those whose views about this issue seem to contrast with their position on other matters.

6. Here is just a sampling in this genre that have been published relatively recently: *The Myth of Self-Esteem, The Self-Esteem Trap, The Feel-Good*

Curriculum, The Epidemic, Overindulged Children, Spoiling Childhood, The Narcissism Epidemic, Generation Me, and *Pampered Child Syndrome.* If you go back another decade or two (or ten), you'll find many more along the same lines, as we'll see in Chapter 1.

7. For examples, see Bernstein and Triger, Gibbs 2009, Gosman, Hays, Kolbert, Mamen, Marano, Nelson, Rutherford, Stearns, Stein, Twenge 2006, Vinson, Warner, and Young-Eisendrath, among others.

8. One perceptive writer (Dries) noticed two articles that appeared during the same month in 2012, one in *Forbes* titled "Why Millennials Are Spending More Than They Earn, and Parents Are Footing the Bill," which painted young adults as materialistic spendthrifts; and the other in the *Boston Globe* titled "Generation Broke," which described the same generation as cheapskates whose underconsumption is bad for the economy. Another observer, meanwhile, pointed out that "the same people who say [young people] have no attention span [also] say they spend all their time playing video games, in which they show sustained attention" (researcher Michael Posner, quoted in Glassman).

CHAPTER 1

1. Hersey, p. 136. The author adds, "Nor will reading problems be solved by any single, simple panacea, such as 'going back to phonetics'" (p. 137)—a caution just as relevant, and just as frequently ignored, today. Eight years earlier, in 1946, a professor at Princeton complained, "I know of no college or university in the country that doesn't have to offer most or all of its freshmen courses in remedial English, beginning mathematics, beginning science, and beginning foreign languages. Consequently, we give two or three years of college and the rest in high school work." (Theodore M. Greene's essay in the *Los Angeles Times* is quoted by education writer Susan Ohanian on her website, www.susan ohanian.org.)

2. For details about the misleading claims and tendentious use of data on which the report is based, see Berliner and Biddle; and Bracey.

3. Rothstein, Chapter 1. Quotation appears on p. 20. After producing a similar list of complaints in reverse chronological order, an historian observes, "Each probe resolutely refused to cite its predecessors, creating a sense of novel failure [in] every generation" (Stearns, p. 85). The idea that schools are worse today than in the past has also been forcefully rebutted in Berliner and Biddle, and in many writings by the late Gerald Bracey.

4. The 1911 quotation is from Comer, who also complained that "the rising generation cannot spell . . . its English is slipshod." She traced this disgraceful state of affairs to the fact that students were "victims of a good many haphazard

educational experiments. New ideas in pedagogy have run amuck for the last twenty-five years." The 1917 quotation is from a study published that year in the *Journal of Educational Psychology*, cited in a September 2007 post on www.blog 4history.com.

5. Mansfield. For more on this topic, see my discussion on pp. 110–13.

6. Briggs et al. I acquired a copy of the original report from the Harvard University archives after seeing a reference to it in Lewis.

7. Shaw, p. 18.

8. Bird and Bird, pp. 60, 77, 160, 154.

9. Gibbs 2001.

10. Ehrensaft, p. 183.

11. Wyden, p. 127.

12. Lear, pp. 11, 14.

13. Beecher, p. 3.

14. "Not strict enough" poll cited by Mintz, p. 292; *Parents* article cited by Hulbert, p. 213.

15. Ricker, p. 25.

16. Spock 1946, p. 265. And a few pages later: "Some gentle, unselfish parents devote so much effort to being tactful and generous to a child that they give him the feeling that he's the crown prince, or rather the king" (p. 268).

17. The 1948 speech is quoted in Hulbert, p. 245. The magazine article: Spock 1971. A biographer contends that "the idea of permissiveness seemed foreign to his very soul. He had not been raised in a permissive home, nor had he tolerated such in his own house" (Maier, p. 325). For more of his response to the permissiveness charge, see the 1985 edition of *Baby and Child Care*, pp. 8–14, 398–99.

18. Cross, p. 195.

19. Quoted in Hulbert, p. 99. Hulbert argues that the pendulum has long been swinging between child- and parent-centered models of child rearing. So, too, the author Christina Hardyment: "Regardless of the time at which they are writing, [child-care experts] can be classified as cuddly or astringent—lap theorists or iron men (or maidens). The latter claim that things are now disgracefully lax, the former that fifty years ago child-care was appallingly strict" (p. xiv).

20. Comer, pp. 31, 34, 37.

21. Boas, p. 3.

22. Trollope, p. 173.

23. Quoted in Mintz, p. 19.

24. The last two quotations can readily be found floating around the Internet— along with expressions of doubt about their authenticity.

25. Mamen, p. 9.

26. See the 1997 and 1999 surveys entitled "Kids These Days" conducted by Public Agenda, a public opinion firm. Details about the latter report are available on Public Agenda's website; the former report was summarized in Applebome.

27. Anderson is quoted in Cable, p. 190. The Young-Bruehl quotation appears on p. 4 of her book. Also see Holt 1974.

28. See Zelizer; and Alwin 1996.

29. Reverend Benjamin Wadsworth is quoted in Mintz, p. 11. Mintz summarizes his history of American childhood as follows: "There has never been a time when the overwhelming majority of American children were well cared for and their experiences idyllic. Nor has childhood ever been an age of innocence, at least not for most children" (p. vii).

30. DeMause, pp. 285–86. So, too, the Australian writer Robin Grille: "Child abuse and neglect [have] only recently become a minority occurrence, and only in some of the world's societies. . . . We should view much of human history as a holocaust against children" (p. 92).

31. Alwin 1989, p. 195.

32. Hays, p. 45.

33. Ehrenreich, p. 87.

34. See Hulbert; and Mintz.

35. "Full-blown permissiveness, even as an ideal, lasted for less than a decade. By the early fifties, most experts were renouncing 'overpermissiveness' and stressing 'the importance of setting limits.' . . . So, long before permissiveness became a political slur, it had fallen out of favor and come to be seen as a mistake, an overcorrection perhaps, but still a pitfall for the unwary parent" (Ehrenreich, p. 89). "Although the childrearing techniques of the postwar era are commonly labeled 'permissive,' childrearing was not nearly as indulgent as later commentators assumed. For one thing, no generation in American history was less likely to be breastfed. . . . Nor were parents especially permissive in terms of infantile sexuality or toilet training. The overwhelming majority of parents regarded masturbation as undesirable and attempted to stop it, while nearly half of all children began toilet training before they were nine months old [in the postwar years]" (Mintz, p. 281).

36. See, for example, Baumrind 1966, p. 889.

37. Goodlad. His subsequent investigations, as well as those of most other observers, suggest that, outside of a few oases of progressive education, his conclusion mostly remains true. In fact, the impact of corporate-styled school "reform," which I described briefly in the introduction, has made schools even more traditional.

38. As research psychologist Laurence Steinberg points out (personal communication, July 2008), parenting styles in most studies are assessed in relative terms—how one subject compares to everyone else in the sample—so it's not clear where one would set the cut-off on various scales for determining that a response meets the criteria for being deemed permissive in an absolute sense.

39. Not all researchers solicit children's perspectives along with the parents', so the latter are simply taken at face value. But when both are included, they often don't tell the same story. In one study, "parents rated the family's cohesion and communication more highly than their children did" (Givertz and Segrin, 11). In another, "parents generally reported that they included their children more in family decision making than the children perceived to be true" (Eccles et al., pp. 62–63). In a third, there were "significant perception differences between children and their parents on all but one of the family functioning scales and on all scales measuring child-rearing practices" (Stevens et al., p. 423). In a fourth, children were less likely to categorize their parents as supportive and more likely to see them as harsh, when compared to the parents' self-reports (Kim et al., p. 16).

40. When it's possible to confirm what actually happened, children's perceptions of their parents' behaviors prove to be at least as accurate as the parents' reports of their own behaviors. (Three studies are cited to support this claim in Kernis et al. 2000, p. 30.) Even when it's impossible to know the truth, child reports of parenting are often "more strongly related to developmental outcomes than [are] parent reports" (Kins et al., p. 1106). In other words, it's the child's experience that determines the impact.

41. Alwin 1988, 1989.

42. I began to suspect a pattern when I subsequently came across this sentence in one of Twenge's articles (2013b, p. 23): "For example, social networking sites such as Facebook increase users' narcissism and materialism (Wilcox and Stephen, in press)"—only to discover that Wilcox and Stephen's study contained no discussion of either narcissism or materialism.

43. Penn. This passage and the quotations that follow appear on pages 113–17.

44. One could raise questions about whether the poll respondents are truly representative of the general population and also about the accuracy of people's self-reports, but these questions also apply to many studies published in scholarly journals. What distinguishes the latter is a reliance on measurement instruments whose validity and reliability have been established. A fair amount of thought would go into constructing a definition of permissiveness, which might be based on whether respondents strongly agree with, agree with, are undecided about, disagree with, or strongly disagree with a series of statements (overall summaries of their parenting practices as well as examples of how they tend to deal

with specific challenges that arise). The relationships among those individual responses would be carefully measured. Ideally, the responses would be compared to those provided by the children in some of the same households or even to samples of actual parent-child interaction as observed and coded by the experimenters. Now compare that methodical validation process to a poll that includes a single question: "Would you describe your parenting as strict or permissive?"

45. The single exception is his reference to a 1968 poll finding about attitudes toward spanking. See below.

46. For example, a classic study, which has been confirmed by more recent research, found that the babies most likely to fuss and cry were those whose parents *hadn't* responded promptly to their cries earlier. Parents who held back for fear of spoiling often set a vicious circle into motion: Ignoring the baby's cries led to more crying as the baby grew, which further discouraged the parent from responding, which made the baby even more irritable, and so on (Bell and Ainsworth). More generally, research has confirmed that mothers who were most worried about spoiling their babies were least likely to provide a warm, caring, emotionally supportive environment (Luster et al.).

47. For a more detailed examination of time-out, a technique sometimes classified in the psychological literature as "love withdrawal," see Kohn 2005a.

48. Another national poll, taken in 2005, reported that 72 percent of American adults think it's "OK to spank a kid." See http://www.surveyusa.com/50 StateDisciplineChild0805SortedbySpank.htm.

49. "Even as the percentage of Americans who approve of spanking has fallen dramatically in the last half century, the actual incidence of it has barely budged" (Burnett, p. 18). For example, "data from a nationally representative longitudinal study of over 21,000 children . . . found that by the time these children reached the fifth grade in 2003, 80% had been corporally punished by their parents" (Gershoff and Bitensky, p. 232).

50. For examples, see Kohn 1999b.

51. E. Shapiro.

52. For example, Gentile et al.; Twenge 2013a; Twenge and Campbell 2008; Twenge and Foster.

53. Twenge 2006; Twenge and Campbell 2010.

54. One might be able to devise a psychological scenario in which these two characteristics are theoretically compatible, but empirically there is a significant negative correlation between them (Trzesniewski and Donnellan 2010, p. 59). Also, Twenge is extremely critical of how young people today are ostensibly too concerned with being happy, yet she then criticizes them (or their priorities) on the grounds that they're less happy than earlier generations—a claim that other researchers have failed to replicate, incidentally (see below).

55. For more on the hazards of generalizing from such "cross-temporal meta-analytic" studies, see Trzesniewski and Donnellan 2010.

56. "Adaptive narcissism is characterized by healthy ambitions, energy, creativity, and empathy, supported by an underlying sense of self that is firm and cohesive" (Cramer, p. 19). This isn't just a theoretical interpretation; some of the dimensions listed on the Narcissistic Personality Inventory are empirically correlated with healthy adjustment (Watson et al.), particularly for younger adults (Hill and Roberts). Twenge's assertion that "narcissism is one of the few personality traits that psychologists agree is almost completely negative" (2006, p. 68) is patently false.

57. Ramsey et al., p. 232, found a negative relationship between them. For a list of several studies that found them to be positively correlated—albeit modestly—see Foster et al., p. 471. But again, a positive correlation between self-esteem and overall narcissism scores may be misleading because the strength and direction of that relationships depend on which subscales—that is, which components of narcissism—one chooses to look at. See Ackerman et al.

58. Whereas the prevalence of narcissism apparently decreases with age (see note 66 below), "Self-esteem increases during young and middle adulthood, reaches a peak at about age 60 years, and declines in old age" (Orth et al. 2010, p. 652; also see Erol and Orth—and Wagner et al. for data showing that any decline in old age is minimal). On pages 125–26, I discuss the conceptual differences between self-esteem and narcissism or grandiosity.

59. "It is not altogether clear what this would mean because the NPI measures a multifaceted construct and the individual facets are not always strongly intercorrelated" (Trzesniewski et al. 2008b, p. 910).

60. Donnellan and Trzesniewski, pp. 7–8.

61. Brent Roberts, personal communication, January 2013.

62. Donnellan et al.

63. Trzesniewski et al. 2008a, p. 184; Trzesniewski and Donnellan 2010; Donnellan and Trzesniewski, pp. 4–6.

64. Erol and Orth; Orth et al. 2010. Quotation from the former study, p. 614.

65. Liberman 2013.

66. Roberts et al. Quotations appear on pp. 100–1. Even Twenge and her collaborators, in a different study that collected self-reports from thousands of people at once on the Internet, found that older people were less narcissistic than younger people (Foster et al.).

67. Konrath et al. The change "is admittedly minor (i.e., about one third of a scale point) . . . and still leaves today's college student around the midpoint in these traits" (p. 187). Even assuming this finding is replicated by other studies, which remains to be seen, it's not clear what significance to attach to the timing

of this decline, which doesn't correspond to Twenge's, or anyone else's, claims about when young people were supposed to have begun exhibiting more narcissistic tendencies. In any case, a lower score on these measures may not have much significance. As Dan Batson, a leading authority on altruism and empathy, commented about this study, "The idea that [students are] less capable of caring than they were 20 years ago—that just seems unlikely. I don't think we change like that. But our situation may have changed. One may feel pressure to pull back on the scope of one's concern . . . and say, 'I've got to deal with the needs that are pressing right here'" (quoted in O'Brien). One further concern: Are self-reported levels of empathy meaningful, or is it possible that "what we're measuring is not changes in what they really feel, but rather changes in what they think that they should want us to think that they feel?" (Liberman 2012).

68. Pryor et al., p. 26; Astin et al., p. 45. Of course this surge may reflect students' perception that volunteer work will enhance their chances of being admitted to a selective college.

69. This was the finding of a 2012 Pew Research survey. See www.pewsocial trends.org/2012/02/09/young-underemployed-and-optimistic/5/.

70. This conclusion is offered by researcher Keith Macky and his colleagues, quoted in Donnellan and Trzesniewski, p. 8. Emphasis added.

71. On these last two points, see Arnett 2007 and 2010.

72. Jencks, p. 89.

73. All societies require a certain degree of conformity, he said, but when "skepticism and resistance to established authority ceases, democracy becomes a mere façade for preserving the status quo" (Jencks, p. 76).

74. Agnew is quoted in a book by journalist Jules Witcover, which is cited in Ehrenreich, p. 71. Presumably these rhetorical flourishes were created by one of Agnew's two speechwriters, Patrick Buchanan and William Safire.

75. Ehrenreich, pp. 71–72.

76. Flacks, pp. 142–43. Like Jencks, Flacks points out that the characterization of these parents as permissive is mistaken to begin with: "The humanist values of activist parents leads . . . toward an emphasis on encouraging the autonomy of the child and a skepticism about conventional moral standards. But such child-rearing practices do not seem to be characterized by indulgence, or by a failure by the parents to assert standards. As a matter of fact, activists' parents typically had high expectations and standards—for instance . . . they strongly and directly influenced their children to maintain interest in intellectual and creative activity, in academic work, and in socially useful activity." Flacks also found that student activism "is strongly related to the political interests and attitudes of their parents" (p. 142). But that doesn't mean that parenting style is completely unrelated to children's activism, as I'll explain in chapter 8.

77. This assertion was made by Kevin Ryan, founder of the Center for Character and Social Responsibility at Boston University. It's contained in an undated list entitled "Ten Tips for Raising Children of Character," which appears on a number of websites.

78. For an argument that, "without corroborating evidence, we cannot trust people's memories about early childhood," see Halverson. Quotation appears on p. 436.

79. Givertz and Segrin; Otway and Vignoles; Ramsey et al.; Watson et al. 1992. Another researcher looked at "pampering" (which he divided into four subcategories) and compared them to overall scores on the NPI as well as to seven of its scales. Of forty comparisons, only eight reached conventional levels of statistical significance and those were all fairly small. There was no relation between overall pampering in childhood and the summary narcissism score (Capron).

80. Cramer, p. 26. This was one of the rare studies that followed a sample from early childhood to early adulthood. It included assessments by the children's parents.

81. Taylor et al. As the authors succinctly explained the result, "The child learns to be aggressive by being treated directly with aggression" (p. 1063).

82. I cite a series of studies in Kohn 1992, esp. pp. 138–43, 238. Ironically, some of the same people who criticize young people for being self-centered are also enthusiastic proponents of setting children against one another in contests and are critical of parents and teachers who look for alternatives to competition (e.g., Twenge 2006). For more about competition, see pp. 34, 81–84, 107–10.

CHAPTER 2

1. *Unconditional Parenting* (Kohn 2005a).

2. For a list of examples, see Kohn 2005a, p. 4.

3. Gosman, p. 180; Shaw, p. 115; Mogel, pp. 72, 124.

4. Hart et al.

5. Undoubtedly the relationship is reciprocal, but developmental experts have established conclusively that parenting styles, which reflect stable patterns and attitudes, affect children's behavior above and beyond the extent to which they're affected by that behavior.

6. Statistics Canada.

7. Rhee et al.

8. For a comprehensive review of the research, see Gershoff. For examples of studies conducted since that review, see Taylor et al.; Gromoske and Maguire-Jack; and MacKenzie et al.

9. Both styles were related to what are called internalizing symptoms (anxiety, depression), but even here the association to authoritarian parenting was stronger than the relation to permissive parenting (Cohen et al.)

10. Givertz and Segrin.

11. Baumrind is strikingly conservative in her beliefs about children, parenting, and human nature. She strongly supports the use of extrinsic motivators and "contingent reinforcement," which she assumes are required in the service of family "structure." She approves of spanking, dismisses criticisms of punishment as "utopian," and declares that parents who don't use power to compel obedience will be seen as "indecisive" (Baumrind 1996). Elsewhere, she has written, "The parent who expresses love unconditionally is encouraging the child to be selfish and demanding" (Baumrind 1972, p. 278). These values are baked into the notion of "authoritative" parenting, which, she acknowledges, is "no less power-assertive than the disciplinary style of authoritarian parents" (Baumrind 2012, p. 41), despite the fact that it is positioned as—and derives its appeal from appearing to be—a moderate alternative to the two extremes.

12. This begins with Baumrind's original investigations. When a researcher named Catherine Lewis looked carefully at the data Baumrind had provided, she found that positive outcomes for authoritative parenting weren't at all a function of the use of firm enforcement. Children whose parents were high in warmth but low in "demandingness" did just as well as children whose parents were high in both—probably, Lewis suggested, because control in the traditional sense isn't actually required to create structure and predictability as Baumrind and many others assumed (Lewis 1981).

By the same token, Baumrind originally blurred the important differences between "permissive" parents who were neglectful and those who were deliberately democratic. Children in the latter group were not at risk, and that suggests, as another psychologist put it, that "a close look at Baumrind's actual data may reveal significant support for child-centered parenting" (Crain, p. 18) even though she personally opposes that style. (Eventually Baumrind did introduce these and other distinctions by adding several new categories, including "democratic" parenting, to her original three.)

Subsequent research supports the view that child-centered parenting, rather than the kind Baumrind prefers, has positive effects. A huge study of teenagers (Lamborn et al. 1991) found benefits from what was described as "authoritative" parenting, but that term had been defined to mean that parents were aware of, and involved with, their children's lives, not that they were even the least bit punitive or controlling. Another study (Strage and Brandt) similarly cited Baumrind by way of suggesting that parents need to be both supportive and demanding, but it turned out that being demanding when their children were young was unrelated, or even negatively related, to various desirable out-comes. By contrast, the extent to which the parents had been supportive, and also the extent to which they had encouraged their children's independence, had a strong positive relationship to those same outcomes. A third study (Weiss and Schwarz) used college students as subjects and classified them according to six parenting styles. Those raised by permissive ("nondirective") parents fared quite well overall, their outcomes closely resembling those from "authoritative" families. That fact was clear only because the investigators distinguished per-missiveness from a more detrimental "unengaged" approach in which parents weren't just neglecting but rejecting. In all, the "distinguishing factor in late-adolescent outcome" wasn't control or firmness but "parental supportiveness" (quotation on p. 2111).

13. All of these ideas are described at some length in Kohn 2005a.

14. The three studies: Kochanska et al.; Joussemet et al. 2005; and Garber et al. Also, a review of research over more than four decades and across cultures finds that the extent to which people experienced their parents as accepting rather than rejecting is strongly associated with the quality of their psychological ad-justment (Rohner). For an overview of research on the benefits of autonomy-supportive parenting, see Joussemet et al. 2008.

15. Many studies have found this to be true. For three recent examples, see Zhou et al., Knafo and Plomin; Mikulincer et al.

16. See Hoffman and Saltzstein; and Krevans and Gibbs. Strayer and Roberts found that "fathers who were authoritarian and mothers who used anxiety and guilt control" had children who were more likely to be angry. That anger, in turn, was negatively related to empathy (p. 246).

17. I made this point in a book called *The Brighter Side of Human Nature* (Kohn 1990), drawing from the work of Martin Hoffman, Ervin Staub, and others. It was empirically confirmed by a group of researchers in 2005, who explained that people who felt securely attached as children are more likely to "perceive others not only as sources of security and support, but also as suffer-ing human beings who have important needs and therefore deserve support.... Thus, if we wish to help children and adults develop their natural potential for compassion and altruism, one way to do so would be to help them achieve at-tachment security" (Mikulincer et al., pp. 818, 837).

18. Trzesniewski and Donnellan (2010, p. 70) invoke this bias to explain con-clusions about "Generation Me." They credit identification of the bias itself to Amos Tversky and Daniel Kahneman.

19. Eibach et al.; and Eibach and Libby. The first quotation is from the for-mer, p. 918; the second is from the latter, p. 419. Such beliefs may be reversible. These researchers discovered that, while many people think adolescents today

are less moral than adolescents in earlier times, adults who were specifically asked (by the experimenters) to reflect on how their own moral perspectives had changed became less likely to make that assumption.

20. Mogel, p. 62.

21. Ibid., p. 79.

22. Okay, *our* position.

23. Shaw, p. 131.

24. For example, see Bird and Bird; Gosman.

25. Zuk.

26. Psychologist: Arnett 2008, p. 677. Essayist: Hoagland, p. 34.

27. Luster et al.

28. I offer a number of examples pertaining to classroom management and character education in Kohn 1996, chapter 1; and Kohn 1997a, respectively.

29. Mamen, pp. 24, 29. Mogel's book is replete with similar examples.

30. Brooks 2010.

CHAPTER 3

1. Orenstein and Goldstein, respectively.

2. *Atlantic* blog: Lahey. Australian study: Locke et al.

3. Blog post: Belkin 2010. Column: Belkin 2009. Law review article: Bernstein and Triger.

4. This may have been the import of a *New Yorker* cartoon in which a mother standing next to her son confides to his teacher, "It's a lot of pressure on me not to pressure him." Indeed, one small study—featuring in-depth interviews of fifty-six elementary school students and their parents—found that middle-class parents "did not—as commonly thought—swoop in to 'save' the student from problems in school" (Sparks, p. 11). In fact, these parents seemed "very conscious of the helicopter parent stereotype, saying things like 'I'm not one of those helicopter moms.' . . . They recognized that they could not (and possibly should not) always be there to do for their children, and understood that schools expect children to take responsibility for their own learning needs." (The latter quotation is from a personal communication from the study's author, Jessica McCrory Calarco, in August 2012.)

5. Academic article: Vinson. *Time* cover story: Gibbs 2009.

6. The article: Roosevelt. The study: Greenberger et al. Academic entitlement didn't seem particularly common among students in this study, but even the amount that did turn up was probably overstated because of how the concept was measured. The most frequently endorsed item on the questionnaire—the only item, in fact, with which a majority of students agreed—read as follows:

"If I have explained to my professor that I am trying hard, I think he/she should give me some consideration with respect to my course grade." (Not an automatic A, mind you—just "some consideration.") The second most-endorsed item, by 41 percent of the students, was this: "I feel I have been poorly treated if a professor cancels an appointment with me on the same day as we were supposed to meet." Does such a reaction really constitute "entitlement"?

7. Most writers expressed incredulity or disgust at today's entitled students, or offered their own explanations for this phenomenon (whose reality they took for granted). Should we be satisfied with a heart surgeon lacking talent just because he worked really hard? asked one. Would a professional athlete get signed merely because he made an effort? another wanted to know. It's all because when these students competed as children, everyone got a trophy, declared a third.

8. For example, see Day and Padilla-Walker and the research they cited before describing their own findings.

9. Marilyn Watson, personal communication, March 2013.

10. Ungar, p. 262.

11. Segrin et al., especially pp. 238–40. Another pair of researchers defines it as "intrusive and unnecessary micromanagement of a child's independent activities, and strong affection in the absence of child distress or need for comforting" (Padilla-Walker and Nelson, p. 1178). "The term 'helicopter parent' was coined by Charles Fay and Foster Cline (authors of the Love and Logic parenting series) and was popularized by a [1991] *Newsweek* article" (Somers and Settle, p. 19).

12. Munich and Munich, p. 228.

13. Rosenfeld and Wise, p. xviii.

14. Levine.

15. For repeated examples of such misleading citations, see Bernstein and Triger. This article is also the source of the assertion that this generation of young people is "the first . . . raised by intensive parents."

16. Segrin et al. When I say "weak," I mean a correlation of .11, which means that, even if we accept that those two ideas were validly defined and measured in the study, each explains only about 1 percent of the variation in the other.

17. See Lessard et al.; quotations on pp. 528, 522. Arnett (2007) has challenged the tendency to classify as entitlement (in the purely negative sense of the word) what might better be described as high aspirations on the part of adolescents and young adults. A "sense of entitlement" is also central to sociologist Annette Lareau's account of how middle-class children are prepared for success: They're encouraged to have opinions and speak up, to believe they have "a right to pursue their individual preferences and to actively manage interactions in institutional settings"—as opposed to a "sense of constraint" that's more characteristic of working-class and poor children (Lareau, p. 6).

18. The studies: Wood; Hudson and Dodd; and McLeod et al., respectively.

19. Jennifer Hudson of Macquarie University is quoted in Sullivan.

20. In reality, there is often a reciprocal relationship rather than a neat cause-and-effect relationship between two variables. One affects the other, which then affects the first. Thus, even if a parent is hovering because of the child's apparent unhappiness or neediness, those characteristics may have been amplified by a parenting style that cultivates or encourages the child's dependence.

21. Several studies observed parent-child interactions during assigned tasks and noted the extent to which the parent took over for the child—a pretty clear example of control. The meta-analysis of anxiety (McLeod et al.) explicitly tallied examples of controlling parenting. And it was "higher parental control" that "was associated with significantly higher psychological entitlement" in another study (Givertz and Segrin).

22. Grolnick, p. 150. Also see a review of relevant research in Joussemet et al. 2008.

23. See Wendy Grolnick's work; Pomerantz et al., esp. pp. 381–84; and Wuyts et al.

24. Soenens and Vansteenkiste, pp. 92–93; Grolnick, p. 30. Also, "in a study of parenting in emerging adulthood . . . mothers and fathers [who] scored high on indices of control—both behavioral and psychological control . . . had children with the most negative child outcomes" (Padilla-Walker and Nelson, p. 1179).

25. Wang et al.; Soenens and Vansteenkiste, pp. 94–95; Grolnick, pp. 71–79; Ng et al. It's sometimes assumed that control is less destructive, and autonomy support is less beneficial, in more collectivist societies. This misapprehension may be based on a confusion of autonomy with individualism. An autonomous person, psychologically speaking, experiences his or her actions as "authentic," "integrated," "willingly enacted"—but doesn't necessarily see him- or herself as separate from others, independent, or in opposition to the larger culture (Chirkov et al.). Thus, "because of its pressuring and manipulative character, psychological control frustrates individuals' universal need for volitional functioning" (Soenens and Vansteenkiste, p. 95)—including in Asian societies.

26. Kim et al.

27. See in particular the work of Brian Barber, including the collection of essays he edited in 2002.

28. I discussed the contrast between conditional and unconditional parenting in a previous book (Kohn 2005a) and will have more to say about the relevance of that distinction to self-esteem in chapter 6.

29. Barber 1996, p. 3299. Citations within this sentence have been omitted.

30. Soenens et al. 2005; Soenens et al. 2008.

31. Soenens and Vansteenkiste, p. 89.

32. Aunola and Nurmi.

33. Kins et al., p. 1107. Some children "go back and forth between feelings of excessive loyalty [to their parents] and feelings of resentment for not being accepted for who they are" (Soenens and Vansteenkiste, p. 82). Elsewhere, these theorists suggest that there may actually be two versions of psychological control: the kind whose primary purpose is "to make children emotionally and psychologically dependent on the parent" and the kind used to enforce impossibly high standards of achievement (Soenens et al. 2010).

34. Givertz and Segrin; Assor and Tal, p. 257 (emphasis added).

35. Baldwin and Sinclair, p. 1138.

36. Slater, pp. 22, 57; Bowles and Gintis, p. 145 (emphasis added). One implication is that "internal motivation" is not necessarily a good thing and is quite different from *intrinsic* motivation. I'll say more about this in chapter 7.

37. I offered some thoughts on this question in Kohn 2005a, chapter 6. Grolnick divides possible explanations into pressures that parents experience from *below* (that is, from their children, who may be experienced as challenging as a result of their temperaments), from *above* or *without* (social and economic factors that induce parents to socialize children in certain ways), and from *within* (having to do with the parent's own needs and background).

38. Conditional parenting "originates, at least in part, from parents' own experience of being subjected to the practice of [conditional parenting] as children, and from parents' contingent self-esteem and competitive world view" (Assor et al., in press).

39. Grolnick et al.; and Wuyts et al. Also see Soenens and Vansteenkiste, pp. 90–91.

40. Soenins, Vansteenkiste, and Luyten, pp. 246, 248.

41. For more on this point, see chapter 4.

42. Fingerman et al., p. 880.

43. According to one national study in 2007, nearly 40 percent of college freshmen had some kind of contact with their parents every day (Liu et al., p. 16). And the National Survey of Student Engagement, conducted that same year with freshmen and seniors, found that about seven of ten students communicated "very often" with at least one of their parents (NSSE, p. 24).

44. When students' ethnic backgrounds were examined, amount of parental contact and amount of parental involvement didn't always rise and fall together. See Wolf et al.

45. NSSE, p. 25.

46. The first comment is a direct quotation from Marjorie Savage, director of the parent-liaison program the University of Minnesota; the second is a paraphrase. Both appeared in Hoover.

47. First study: Rettner. Second study: Padilla-Walker and Nelson, p. 1188.

48. Gardner. Sure enough, National Public Radio broadcast a segment on the topic in early 2012 and declared that "one-quarter of employers reported hearing from parents urging the employer to hire their son or daughter"—instead of noting that, despite the common belief that such behavior was widespread, more than three-quarters of employers had never encountered it.

49. Fingerman et al. "Intense" support was defined as offering several types—emotional, practical, financial, etc.—several times a week. The one-in-five statistic was based on interviews with the children; it dropped to one in six if the estimate was based on the parents' reports. And the researchers noted that, because of the sample they used, the results probably overstated the prevalence of intense support compared to the general population.

50. Rettner.

51. LeMoyne and Buchanan. Having a helicopter parent, based on the student's report, explained less than 9 percent of the variation in well-being.

52. Schiffrin et al.

53. Padilla-Walker and Nelson emphasize that HP can be distinguished from other forms of control because it also includes parental support for children and involvement in their lives. They point to a factor analysis as empirical confirmation of this distinction, but of course the relationships they found among those attributes are just a function of the items they included in their questionnaire as examples of HP—which is to say, how they chose to define the concept in the first place. Interestingly, reports of parental "warmth" were not correlated with other aspects of HP, raising the possibility that parents' concern "for their children's well-being . . . may also be driven by concern for how their children's behavior will reflect on them"—a motive consistent with the use of psychological control.

54. LeMoyne and Buchanan, p. 414 (emphasis added); and Schiffrin et al.

55. Personal communication with Neil Montgomery, July 2010.

56. Kins et al., pp. 1106.

57. Padilla-Walker and Nelson.

58. Adams 2012a, 2012b. The latter article reported that 33 percent of the population now graduates from college, as compared with 12 percent in the 1970s, with "record levels of college completion among all groups: men and women; blacks, whites, and Hispanics; and foreign- and native-born Americans."

59. NSSE, p. 25.

60. Kinzie quoted in Aucoin; Kuh quoted in Mathews.

61. Personal communication with Neil Montgomery, July 2010.

62. Small et al.

63. Coontz quoted in Aucoin.

64. Fingerman et al., pp. 890, 888. As if to confirm the researchers' point about uninformed statements in the popular media, a *Time* cover story the following year asserted that the trend of young adults' living with their parents means "their development is stunted" (Stein, p. 28).

65. Nor is this necessarily a bad thing. As Arnett and Fishel point out, people in their late twenties are probably more likely to make better decisions about marriage partners and careers than people in their early twenties (p. 15).

66. Silva.

67. Stein, p. 28. The writer plucks this statistic from a national poll sponsored by Clark University but fails to report the broader array of results, which fails to support his attack on Millennials. For one thing, only 30 percent lived with their parents. For another thing, when the cohort is broken down by age, only 15 percent of twenty-six- to twenty-nine-year-olds still lived with their parents, as compared with 38 percent who lived with their husband or wife. Also, interestingly, 69 percent of the total sample received little or no financial support from their parents (Arnett and Schwab).

68. Settersten. Likewise Arnett and Fishel: "Research strongly indicates that when parents are able and willing to provide financial and emotional support during their grown-up kids' twenties, the kids are more likely to emerge successfully into a stable and self-sufficient adulthood in their thirties" (pp. 278–80).

69. One college professor recalls that she once opined airily about the benefits of independence and the need for parents to back off. "Before I became a college parent, it was easy to come up with rules of disengagement for my students' mothers and fathers. Now that I am one myself, I finally know what it is parents are going through" (Boylan).

70. The *Time* cover is cited by Arnett 2008, who offers a lucid analysis of the resentment of emerging adults on the part of those who are older.

71. Wolf et al., p. 332. On the general shift away from a simplistic equation of individuation with healthy development, see Samuolis et al.

72. Soenens et al. 2007. This, of course, is related to the confusion between autonomy support and individualism discussed in note 25, above.

73. Schiffrin et al.

74. Wolf et al., pp. 330, 332.

75. See Stephens et al.

76. Wolf et al., p. 350.

77. How much they want: Higher Education Research Institute. How much they get: Wolf et al.; Hoover. There is also a gender difference in the frequency of contact with parents: Wolf et al., p. 331.

78. Stephens et al., pp. 1193, 1192.

79. Arnett and Fishel, p. 92.

80. Depending on which issues they were asked about (e.g., applying to college, choosing courses, choosing activities, dealing with college officials), the range of students saying they thought their parents had the right amount of involvement was 72 to 84 percent, and the proportion saying their parents weren't involved enough was 6 to 24 percent. "Students of color were more likely than white students to indicate that their parents were involved too little in all areas . . . [especially in] decisions made after college admission" (Higher Education Research Institute).

81. For an example, see Nelson.

82. Fingerman et al., p. 882.

CHAPTER 4

1. Neil Williams, quoted in Gehring. An educator at California State University at Sacramento adds, "In this day and age, when school violence is so prevalent, why would any physical educator or recreator want to promote a game that involves throwing objects at people? . . . Professionals dumped traditional dodge ball in physical education classes years ago" (Reese).

2. Steven Pinker, for example, in the middle of a careful analysis of the historical decline of violence, abruptly becomes unhinged over the fact that "in school district after school district, *dodge ball has been banned*" (indignant italics his). He quotes a statement by the National Association for Sport and Physical Education that points out the activity is not particularly popular among children who get "hit hard in the stomach, head, or groin. And it is not appropriate to teach our children that you win by hurting others"—only to deride these concerns by claiming that the comment "must have been written by someone who was never a boy, and quite possibly has never met one" (Pinker, p. 379).

3. "Hopscotch? Well, Maybe."

4. Marrero. Something similar happened in San Diego in the early 1990s. The school board accepted a proposal (by a community task force on dropout prevention) in which high school juniors and seniors who failed a course would be able to retake it without penalty, with their record indicating "no credit" rather than an "F." The move "triggered an avalanche of phone calls and letters" opposed to the idea (Smollar), and it was shelved before it could take effect.

5. Phelps.

6. For example, educational psychologist Harold Stevenson decried the awarding of unmerited trophies, along with "indiscriminate praise" and "lenient grading systems," in a *New York Times* op-ed in 1994.

7. Merryman.

8. Kohn 1999a.

9. Studies of what the psychologist Mihaly Csikszentmihalyi calls "flow"—which consists of feeling active, challenged, and fully engaged by what one is doing—have shown that people report more of these pleasurable experiences while at work than anywhere else. (This is true of workers on assembly lines, too.) In fact, "flowlike situations occurred more than three times as often in work as in leisure" (Csikszentmihalyi and LeFevre, p. 818). Another researcher independently found that when participants were asked to rate the enjoyment they derived from more than two dozen common activities, it turned out that "the intrinsic rewards from work are, on average, higher than the intrinsic rewards from leisure" (Juster, p. 340).

10. It shouldn't be surprising that competition, which is about proving one's superiority over others, has the effect of retarding the development of empathy and helping. (For evidence, see Kohn 1992.) In light of that fact, it's ironic that many writers who are critical of efforts to boost children's self-esteem—warning that we're promoting a narcissistic preoccupation with the self—are also dismissive of attempts to rein in competition. (For an example, see Twenge 2006).

11. The latest data confirm that people generally do not perform better on straightforward tasks when they're competing than when they're not. (See a new meta-analysis by Murayama and Elliot.) But again, competition's effect is likely to be detrimental, not merely neutral, on more complex tasks. And competition also comes up short when compared to cooperation rather than just to the absence of competition. For evidence related to these points as well as to its negative impact on self-esteem, relationships, and intrinsic motivation, see Kohn 1992.

12. See Kohn 1992, chapter 4; Orlick; and games listed on websites such as cooperativegames.com and familypastimes.com.

13. Goldstein.

14. Samuelson. In this column he equates the elimination of class rank with excessive praise and, of course, participation trophies.

15. See "Class Rank." Says William Fitzsimmons, Harvard's longtime dean of undergraduate admissions, "In recent years we have gotten away from [class rank]. . . . Oftentimes there are no meaningful differences whatsoever between someone who is number one and someone who is number 81" (quoted in Pappano).

16. "Class rank can also be manipulated. As early as ninth grade, top students figure out the selection procedures and find ways to improve their standing in comparison to classmates. They'll take, for instance, an 'easier' Advanced Placement course—AP Biology instead of AP Chemistry. Others don't take certain

required classes—namely courses that don't carry bonus points—until the latter half of their senior year, after class rankings are tabulated and sent out in college applications. More worrisome is the practice of teenagers who won't pursue an interest in, say, photography for fear of lowering their average. Those classes normally do not carry bonus points. 'A client of mine told me that taking music or journalism was out of the question because she couldn't justify what it would do to her GPA,' [education consultant David] Altshuler recalls. 'I can tell you there was a lot less joy in her curriculum'" (Suarez).

17. Kohn 1999a, 1999b, 2011b.

18. George.

19. Fogarty, p. 27.

20. For evidence against these practices, see Kohn 2000 and 2011, respectively. For examples of BGUTI justifications for them, see Kohn 2005b.

21. See Kohn 2006.

22. Bauerlein.

23. Sengupta, p. B4.

24. For example, see Bensman; Gray and Chanoff; and Posner. Admittedly, such upbeat accounts are more suggestive than definitive—first, because the writers are obviously sympathetic to these alternative schools; and second, because of the possibility of a selection effect: The outcomes may be due to the kinds of children who attend such schools in the first place rather than to the effect of attending these schools. (It would be impractical and unethical to randomly assign a large group of children to different kinds of schools.) Still, there doesn't appear to be any evidence pointing to the opposite conclusion.

25. Reynolds and Baird conducted the first study and cited the second (by Jeylan T. Mortimer and colleagues).

26. Gosman, p. 106.

27. Blog post: Lahey. Education columnist: Hoerr 2012. Tough interview: Wente. Like so many other commentators, Tough contrasts the practice of making sure kids fail so they will develop self-discipline (good) with praising them too much to raise their self-esteem (bad). I'll have more to say later about self-discipline, praise, and self-esteem.

28. Also, we should be careful to define what we mean by successful. To be rich or famous is not necessarily to be an admirable or psychologically healthy human being. Plenty of corporate titans and politicians who point to their humble origins and repeated defeats on the way to victory have ended up "successful" only in a narrow and ultimately not very important sense of the word.

29. That a bad grade often leads to misbehavior—not just the other way around—was recently confirmed by researchers who followed students over several years: Zimmermann et al.

30. Combs, p. 123.

31. Too much emphasis on success *or* failure—that is, on results—can be a problem. This is a fascinating revelation in its own right, but one that would take us too far afield here. Suffice it to say that when we get kids thinking about their achievement or performance rather than focusing on the learning itself, the outcomes are often disappointing. The simple-minded emphasis on results and "rigor" that characterizes demands for accountability in education often creates an approach to teaching that interferes with intellectual discovery and exploration. The problem isn't just that achievement is typically defined only as scores on standardized tests; it's that most education reformers are unfamiliar with the distinction between performance and learning. For more on this, see the research cited in Kohn 1999b, Chapter 2.

32. For two examples, see Allen and Wuensch; and Boggiano et al. More generally, see the work of Andrew Elliot on performance-approach versus performance-avoidance orientations—for example, Elliot and Harackiewicz.

33. Stipek, pp. 130–31.

34. By contrast, kids who succeed are more likely to explain what happens by citing the effort they made, which creates an auspicious (rather than vicious) circle. See, for example, the results of a study with elementary school students of different ages by Wigfield. The work of Bernard Weiner and Carol Dweck is also relevant here.

35. Covington, p. 78.

36. For example, see Wigfield; and four studies cited in Deppe and Harackiewicz, p. 869.

37. Many psychologists have written about this phenomenon. One example: Deppe and Harackiewicz.

CHAPTER 5

1. Krugman.

2. Keilman.

3. Those outraged by participation trophies readily concede this point. "By age 4 or 5, children aren't fooled by all the trophies," one journalist says in an essay titled "Losing Is Good for You." It seems reasonable to conclude that if they have no power to mislead, these trophies are unlikely to adversely affect kids' thinking or motivation. Yet somehow the fact that no one is fooled just seems to compound the writer's fury about the fact that kids "automatically get an award" (Merryman).

4. Baumrind 1972, p. 278.

5. Bean, p. 2.

6. I've explored the effects of punishment in some detail in Kohn 1996, 1999a, and 2005a.

7. Stepp.

8. See Kohn 1999a, chapter 6; and 2005a, pp. 34–42, 153–60.

9. That distinction, between effort (or process) and ability (or person) praise, which has attracted considerable attention over the last few years, is derived from the work of Carol Dweck. I have been greatly impressed and influenced by Dweck's broader argument, which spells out the negative effects of leading people to attribute success (or failure) to their intelligence (or its absence). But the critical distinction between effort and ability doesn't map neatly onto the question of praise. First of all, while it's impossible to dispute Dweck's well-substantiated contention that praising kids for being smart is counterproductive, praising them for the effort they've made can also backfire: It may communicate that they're really not very capable and therefore unlikely to succeed at future tasks. (If you're complimenting me just for trying hard, it must be because I'm a loser.) Some studies have supported exactly this concern (see Kohn 1999a, chapter 6).

Second, the more attention we give to the problems of ability-focused praise in particular, the more we're creating the misleading impression that praise in general (or a version that's done "correctly") is harmless or even desirable. Of the various problems I describe here—its status as an extrinsic inducement and a mechanism of control, its message of conditional acceptance, its detrimental effects on intrinsic motivation and achievement—none is limited to the times when we praise someone's ability. In fact, I'm not convinced that this type is any worse than other praise with respect to these deeper issues.

Finally, to the extent that we want to teach the importance of making an effort—the point being that people have some control over their future accomplishments—praise really isn't required at all. Dweck readily conceded this in a conversation we had some years ago. Indeed, she didn't seem particularly attached to praise as a strategy, and she willingly acknowledged its potential pitfalls.

10. Like other sorts of rewards, praise often diminishes the recipient's interest in the task (or commitment to the action) that elicited the praise. It's also likely to interfere with the quality of performance. The effect of a "Good job!" is to devalue the activity itself in the child's mind—for example, reading, drawing, helping—which now comes to be seen as just a means to an end, the end being to receive that expression of approval. If approval *isn't* forthcoming next time, the desire to read, draw, or help is likely to evaporate.

11. Martin Seligman is quite explicit about this: "Praise your child contingent on a success, not just to make him feel better," he counsels (Seligman, p. 288).

Richard Weissbourd, too, decries "too much unconditional praise" (p. 52). Many conservative critics also express indignation that children are praised—and consequently come to expect praise—for what they ought to do just because they've been told. The ideal here is unquestioning obedience. From this perspective, the ultimate nightmare is praise that is "indiscriminate" or given "for nothing"—in other words, not at all conditional. My position is that we should offer unconditional love to children, not unconditional praise. While I'm troubled by the practice of saying "Good job!" to make kids do a better job, I think it's silly to say "Good job!" when they're not doing anything. To object to doling out approval as compensation for turning in an impressive performance at some task isn't the same as arguing for more praise—even the noncontingent kind. (For more, see Kohn 2005a).

12. Johnson. The article lumps together grade inflation, T-ball games where no score is kept, and the decision to increase the number of Academy Award nominees for best picture.

13. Whether it makes sense to say that all children are "special" depends on whether that word is used to denote uniqueness (in which case the statement is true) or some attribute that by definition only a few possess (in which case it's not).

14. This creates an interesting dilemma when those two features diverge. Who should get the prize—individuals who are gifted, or those who are successful?

15. Dries. For another refreshing response to the sport of ridiculing Millennials, see a cartoon by Matt Bors at http://goo.gl/4jHSJ. ("The only thing more lazy than a 20-something is the generational slander that takes place anew every two decades or so . . . ")

16. As I was writing this chapter, *Time* magazine published a cover story called "Millennials: The ME ME ME Generation," which consisted of a series of outlandish generalizations, some complimentary but most disparaging, about 80 million young people (Stein). The writer began by claiming to have found "cold, hard data"—largely consisting of Jean Twenge's claims—and announced at one point, "Millennials got so many participation trophies growing up that a recent study showed that 40% believe they should be promoted every two years, regardless of performance." Even if that statistic is accurate (which means that a majority of Millennials do *not* hold that belief), the attempt to link this point of view with participation trophies has absolutely no basis in fact. Assertions of this kind are quite common; evidence for them is not merely rare but nonexistent.

17. In his book *The Competitive Ethos and Democratic Education*, the late John Nicholls wrote incisively about this issue and how it exposes our core values. If our goal is to help children—*all* children—"develop or exercise their powers as fully as possible or accomplish as much as they can . . . [then] it would be irrational for us to promote competitive or publicly evaluative educational

environments." Even when it meets conventional criteria for being fair, Nicholls adds, competition tends to "increase our preoccupation with how our ability compares with that of our peers and thereby compound[s] inequality of motivation and diminishes the quality of learning and accomplishment" (Nicholls, pp. 117, 158). Ultimately we have to decide whether our priority is to sort children or to support them—to figure out who's better than whom or to help as many kids as possible to succeed.

18. The answer depends on which time periods are being compared and which students we're talking about: Those at a single university? All elite colleges? All colleges and universities? High schools? It also depends on how the data are gathered. Most statistics showing more A's now than at some time in the past are based on student self-reports, which are notoriously unreliable. For a more accurate picture of whether average grades have changed over the years, we'd need to look at official student transcripts. Clifford Adelman, a senior research analyst with the US Department of Education, did just that, reviewing transcripts from more than three thousand institutions. His finding: "Contrary to the widespread lamentations, grades actually declined slightly in the last two decades." A second analysis, which reviewed college transcripts from students who were graduated from high school in 1972, 1982, and 1992, confirmed that there was no significant or linear increase in average grades over that period. (The average GPA for those three cohorts was 2.70, 2.66, and 2.74, respectively.) Even when Adelman looked at "highly selective" institutions, he again found very little change in average GPA over the decades. And a review of other research suggests a comparable lack of support for claims of grade inflation at the high-school level. (For more about these findings, see Kohn 2002 and an annotated guide to the data at www.alfiekohn.org/teaching/gisources.htm.)

19. Maybe students are turning in better assignments. Maybe instructors used to be too stingy with their marks and have become more reasonable. Maybe the concept of assessment itself has evolved, so that today it's more a means for allowing students to demonstrate what they know rather than for sorting them or "catching them out." (The real question, then, is why we spent so many years trying to make good students look bad.) Maybe students aren't forced to take as many courses outside their primary areas of interest in which they didn't fare as well. Maybe struggling students are now able to withdraw from a course before a poor grade appears on their transcripts. (Say what you will about that practice, it challenges the hypothesis that the grades students receive in the courses they complete are inflated.)

20. The two Mansfield quotes are from Scocca and Steinberg, respectively. The Kamber quote is from Toth.

21. Milton et al., p. 225.

22. One odd argument for deprivation is based on a scarcity model. The reasoning is that there are only so many pleasant experiences one can have in one's life, so they shouldn't be used up too soon. If we provide our children with too many "wonderful experiences," then they'll "have nothing to look forward to once they've reached their majority," warns the author of a book called *Spoiled Rotten* (Gosman, p. 49).

23. Holt 1982, p. 267.

24. "I don't want to hear your complaints about anything you're being made to do (or prevented from doing)" is not an unusual sentiment; in fact, it may be exactly what your boss would like to say to you. But that doesn't mean it's admirable to insist, perhaps with a bit of a smirk, that children should just do whatever they're told, regardless of whether it's reasonable or how it makes them feel. If *we* might respond with frustration or resentment to receiving such a message, why would we treat kids that way? "No whining" mostly underscores the fact that the person saying this has more power than the people to whom it's said, and it also communicates that what matters most to this person is his or her convenience; it's obviously easier for anyone in a position of authority if those being ordered to do something comply without objection.

25. Heubert, p. 27. Research on this topic has been conducted by Lorrie Shepard, Ernest House, Robert Hauser, Linda Darling-Hammond, and many others.

26. Natriello, p. 15.

27. Billotti et al.

28. See Lakoff, especially p. 12 and chapter 5.

29. A move in London to discourage the use of red ink for this purpose was predictably denounced as "political correctness" (Philipson). (On the political implications of the phrase "political correctness," see Kohn 2011a.)

CHAPTER 6

1. Mecca.

2. For example: Christopher Lasch ("For Shame: Why Americans Should Be Wary of Self-Esteem") in 1992, Joseph Adelson ("Down with Self-Esteem") in 1996, Chester E. Finn, Jr. ("Narcissus Goes to School") in 1990, Al Shanker ("All Smiles") in 1994, and Charles Krauthammer ("Education: Doing Bad and Feeling Good") in 1990.

3. Of course, some people do compliment kids to help them feel better about themselves. But not all self-esteem boosting consists of praise, and, more important, not all praise is intended to raise self-esteem. As I argued earlier, much of it, like other rewards, is more about reinforcing certain behaviors in an effort to elicit compliance.

4. For example, Martin Seligman's dismissive comments about self-esteem appear alongside his denunciation of "massive grade inflation . . . *competition* becoming a dirty word . . . the demise of rote memorization . . . less plain old hard work" (Seligman, p. 28). And Roy Baumeister, the most prominent academic critic of self-esteem, advises a sympathetic interviewer (in an article titled "When Bad Kids Think They're Great") to "set the rules, reward the child when the child does well, punish the child when he or she does badly" (Milstone).

5. "Poorer mental and physical health . . . ": Trzesniewski et al. 2006. Preadolescents more aggressive: Donnellan et al. Problem eating: McGee and Williams. Depression: Orth et al. 2012: "We replicated previous studies showing that low self-esteem prospectively predicts depression but that the effect of depression on low self-esteem is small or nonsignificant. . . . A similar pattern emerged for measures of dispositional positive and negative affect. . . . In addition, we found that self-esteem was prospectively related to higher levels of relationship satisfaction, job satisfaction, occupational status, salary, and physical health, controlling for prior levels of these variables, but none of these life outcomes had reciprocal effects on self-esteem (or, if significant, the coefficients were small). Moreover, all results held across generations" (p. 1283).

6. Baumeister et al. 2003, pp. 25, 28; Lyubomirsky et al.

7. Baumeister et al. 2003, p. 15; McFarlin and Blascovich.

8. Swann et al., p. 87.

9. O'Mara, p. 184. Also see Valentine et al.

10. Baumeister et al. 2003, p. 14. Oddly, Baumeister continues to tell interviewers that "self-esteem is a result, not a cause" (Stein, p. 28), even though his own review of the research challenges this simplistic statement. Twenge (2006, p. 65), too, offers the unsupported view that "self-esteem does not cause high grades—instead, high grades cause higher self-esteem."

11. One group of researchers argued in the early 1980s that two variables—social class and academic ability—account for most of the variance in self-esteem *and* in performance. See Maruyama et al.

12. DuBois and Tevendale, p. 110. Of course, plenty of other things, too, have an impact on both self-esteem and achievement.

13. O'Mara et al., p. 185.

14. See Kohn 1992, esp. Chapter 5.

15. Children do not come to believe they are important, valued, and capable just because they are told this or made to recite it. But programs that are ineffective and, in some cases, verge on self-parody are sometimes used to discredit the whole enterprise of enhancing kids' self-esteem—indeed, the very *idea* of self-esteem. And some traditionalists don't stop there: They dismiss any school-based efforts to deal with children's emotional lives or address anything beyond

narrowly defined academic skills. The case for attending to students' social and emotional needs at school is overwhelming, even if one is interested only in academic outcomes. For three of many examples, see Flook et al.; Reyes et al.; and Zins et al.

16. First review: Haney and Durlak (quotation on p. 430). Second review: O'Mara et al. (quotation on p. 195).

17. Baumeister has also argued that because (a) men commit more crimes than women and (b) men tend to score higher on measures of self-esteem ("although the difference is not large and may be diminishing in the modern world"), it follows that there's something undesirable about high self-esteem (Baumeister et al. 1996, p. 13). Even more outrageously: Black men now rape white women more often than white men rape black women—a shift that coincided with "efforts to boost self-esteem among Blacks" (ibid., p. 14).

18. Twenge 2006, p. 224. Here she assumes that making demands, which of course is just part of what it means to be a young child, reflects a particular view of the self. She also applies the concept of self-esteem (which was developed with reference to adults and older children) to toddlers, whose basic sense of self isn't even fully formed. And she continues, "Even as children grow older, most are confident and self-assured"—a statement that could charitably be described as bizarre.

19. Otway and Vignoles, p. 104.

20. Gilligan quoted in Weissbourd, p. 13. Interestingly, Baumeister seems to accept another writer's proposition that "to avoid certain negative emotional states, such as shame, dejection, sadness, and disappointment with oneself, the [aggressive] person refuses to contemplate information that reflects unfavorably about the self" (p. 11). What he never explains is how that profile is consistent with having high self-esteem. At another point, he insists that "only the person with a highly favorable opinion of self will be inclined to seek out risky situations to prove his or her merit" (p. 7). But why would such a person need to do so? Those who are easily threatened and inclined to lash out are more likely to hold a tenuous opinion of themselves.

21. Rosenberg quoted in Donnellan et al., p. 333.

22. See p. 201*n*57.

23. Tracy et al., p. 209.

24. "A robust relation between low self-esteem and externalizing problems ... held for different age groups, different nationalities, and multiple methods of assessing self-esteem and externalizing problems" (Donnellan et al.; quotation on p. 333).

25. Ryckman et al.; quotation on p. 91. This replicates another study published four years earlier by Ryckman and a different group of collaborators.

26. Greenberger et al. Three years later, these researchers looked separately at exploitive and non-exploitive entitlement. Self-esteem was negatively correlated with the former and positively correlated with the latter. See Lessard et al.

27. Baumeister et al. 2003, p. 24. Also see pp. 5–6, 21.

28. Self-esteem tends to increase through adulthood until about age sixty (see p. 201n58). As for now-versus-then comparisons, see the research findings from several groups of scholars that contradict Twenge's claims, which I described on pp. 28–29.

29. Lerner, p. 15.

30. Krauthammer.

31. Twenge and Campbell 2008.

32. See Kohn 2000, which, in turn, cites many other sources.

33. You can check this yourself at www.nationsreportcard.gov. Also see Berliner and Biddle; Rothstein; and many writings by the late Gerald Bracey.

34. Kohn 2013.

35. For two of many examples, see Zhao; and the comments of Byong Man Ahn, South Korea's former minister of education, science, and technology, quoted in Cavanagh.

36. It's important to add that self-esteem isn't important *only* for its contribution to academic performance. Quality of life and joy in learning are ends in themselves.

37. Twenge 2006, p. 57; Ehrensaft, p. 123.

38. See pp. 216–17n11.

39. Baumeister et al. 2003, p. 39.

40. Twenge: 2006, p. 66. The columnist: Leo. (Note how he conflates being lovable with being perfect.)

41. Powers, p. 8.

42. Interested readers might look up the work of Gordon Allport as well as findings concerned with the fundamental human impetus to attain a sense of competence (Robert White), to be self-determining (Richard deCharms, Edward Deci, and others), to satisfy our curiosity (D. E. Berlyne), and to "actualize" our potential in various ways (Abraham Maslow).

43. Twenge 2006, p. 66; Powers, p. 8.

44. Kernis et al. 2008, pp. 478, 479. For more about the importance of stability or fragility in evaluating self-esteem, also see Kernis; Kernis et al. 1993; and Seery et al.

45. Kernis et al. 2000, p. 245.

46. On this point, see Tracy et al., especially p. 4; and Deci and Ryan 1995. One difference between the two syndromes, though, is that people with unstable self-esteem may not be aware of that fact, whereas people with contingent

self-esteem know what has to happen in order for them to feel good about themselves (see Kernis et al. 2008, p. 501).

47. For example, see Crocker and Knight; and Crocker and Wolfe.

48. Crocker and Knight, pp. 200, 202.

49. Crocker and Wolfe cite eight studies to substantiate that first list of unhappy consequences, from anxiety to depression (p. 614). Since then, Burwell and Shirk also found that contingent self-esteem, even more than low self-esteem, is a risk factor for depression in adolescents.

50. Helplessness: Burhans and Dweck. (The finding that "children who had expressed a sense of contingent self-worth were significantly more helpless" was replicated in a subsequent study by Kamins and Dweck, described in Dweck, p. 115.) "Maladaptive perfectionism": Soenens and Vansteenkiste. Impact of bullying: Ghoul et al. Drinking: Neighbors et al.

51. Narcissism: Assor and Tal, p. 257. Materialism: Ku et al., pp. 83–84. Effects on parenting: Eaton and Pomerantz; Grolnick et al.; and Ng et al.

52. Miller, p. 58.

53. Chamberlain and Haaga.

54. Also, the reactions of "pleasure following success and disappointment following failure . . . are not colored with defensiveness or self-aggrandizement" in people with stable, unconditional self-esteem (Kernis et al. 2008, p. 500).

55. Harter, p. 101. Emphasis added.

56. See Wuyts et al.

57. Young-Eisendrath, p. 27.

58. Fromm, pp. 41–42.

59. Assor et al.

60. Roth et al.

61. Kindergarteners: Roth and Assor. Young adults: Roth. Teenagers: Assor and Tal. (Quotation on p. 257.)

62. In a study of three hundred middle schoolers, students had lower self-esteem and less intrinsic motivation to learn if they felt their teachers' acceptance of them was contingent on their achievement or on having met the teachers' expectations (Makri-Botsari).

63. Crocker and Wolfe, p. 617.

CHAPTER 7

1. Bowles and Gintis, p. 39.

2. Mischel 1968, especially chapters 2 and 3.

3. A "remarkably consistent finding" in delay-of-gratification studies, at least those designed so that waiting yields a bigger reward, is that "most children and

adolescents do manage to delay." In one such experiment "83 out of the 104 subjects delayed the maximum number of times." This suggests either that complaints about the hedonism and self-indulgence of contemporary youth may be exaggerated or that these studies of self-control are so contrived that *all* of their findings are of dubious relevance to the real world—perhaps because "tiny amounts of snack food . . . may be insufficient incentives to seriously engage the motivational system of preschool children or, at least, to engage tendencies toward impulse overcontrol or undercontrol" (Funder and Block, pp. 1048, 1049).

4. Mischel 1996, p. 209.

5. Mischel 1996, p. 212. See also Mischel et al. 1988, p. 694.

6. Incidentally, other research (with adults) has found that when people opt for a small sum of cash right away instead of waiting for a larger amount, it may simply be due to their mood at the time—sadness is associated with impatience—rather than to an enduring character trait like willpower or the capacity to defer gratification (Lerner et al.).

7. Mischel et al. 1988.

8. A few years before Mischel's experiments, Stanley Milgram convinced ordinary volunteers to deliver what they thought were painful electric shocks to other people when they were instructed to do so by an experimenter in a lab coat as part of a "teaching" exercise. But contrary to popular belief, Milgram's main objective wasn't to prove how readily people will obey authority, even to do things that seem appalling. Rather, he was interested in "how obedience is responsive to modifications in the immediate situation" (Blass, p. 41). As Milgram himself mused, "Often, it is not so much the kind of person a man is as the kind of situation in which he finds himself that determines how he will act" (quoted in Blass, p. 41). For example, will people still cause someone pain if they can hear that person crying out? If he's in the same room with them? If they have to force his hand onto the electrical device? More subjects refused to carry out instructions with each of these iterations of the experiment. The less remote one's victim, the less willing one is to make someone suffer, even if it means defying authority—a rather different moral than the one normally derived from these experiments (Milgram, pp. 34–36).

9. Lehrer 2009a, p. 27.

10. Mischel 1996, p. 212. This uncertainty about the direction of the causal arrow is reminiscent of how helicopter parenting actually may not make kids anxious; instead, anxious kids may elicit that style of parenting, as I pointed out above, on page 68).

11. Mischel 1996, p. 211.

12. Mischel 1996, p. 214. See also Shamosh and Gray.

13. See, for example, Duckworth and Seligman 2005; Duckworth et al. 2012; Tough 2012.

14. Shoda et al.

15. Shoda et al., p. 985. They add that the *ability* to put up with delay so one can make that choice is valuable, but of course this is different from arguing that the exercise of self-control in itself is beneficial.

16. Finkelstein et al.

17. Otto et al., p. 136.

18. Kidd et al.; quotations appear on pp. 110, 113.

19. Moffitt et al. The strength of those associations was reduced when the researchers controlled for socioeconomic status and intelligence, although many of the associations remained statistically significant. The questions used to identify self-control in this study merit a closer look, however. Bundled into that concept were measures of hyperactivity, impulsivity, and aggression—a profile that goes beyond what we generally have in mind when we say that a child "lacks self-discipline" and one more likely to predict difficulties in adult life.

20. Block, pp. 8–9, 195; Block and Block 2006b, p. 318. The late social critic Philip Slater described it this way: "Where internalization is high there is often a feeling that the controls themselves are out of control—that emotion cannot be expressed when the individual would like to express it. Life is muted, experience filtered, emotion anesthetized . . . " (pp. 24–25).

21. Tough 2012 (book), 2009 (article). Two neuroscientists: Aamodt and Wang. Discussions for educators: Rogus, p. 271. Rogus's article appeared in a special issue of an education journal devoted entirely to the topic of self-discipline. Although it featured contributions by a wide range of educational theorists, including some with a distinctly humanistic orientation, none questioned the importance of self-discipline.

22. *Self-Discipline in 10 Days* (Bryant) is for real, and it was not even published by Self-Parody Press.

23. Letzring et al., p. 3.

24. Mischel 1996, p. 198.

25. Peterson and Seligman, p. 515. This sentiment was echoed by Angela Duckworth (2011, p. 2639)—about whom more in a moment.

26. Tangney et al., p. 296.

27. For example, see Zabelina et al.

28. Letzring et al. At the very end of their article, Tangney et al. concede that some people may be rigidly overcontrolled, but the authors immediately and audaciously try to define the problem out of existence: "Such overcontrolled individuals may be said to lack the ability to control their self-control" (p. 314).

29. Block and Block 2006b, p. 318.

30. Less spontaneity: Zabelina et al. Preschoolers: Block and Block 2006a. The studies on drug use and depression (by Block and his colleagues) are summarized in Funder, p. 211. Anorexia: Halse et al. Decisions made quickly: Dickman and Meyer.

31. In fact, "If I have a hard assignment to do, I get started right away" is an actual item on a standard measure of effortful control (EC) used by researchers, who typically assume that EC is a desirable characteristic without qualification.

32. The fact that something resembling self-discipline is required to complete a task doesn't bode well for the likelihood of deriving intellectual benefit from it. Learning, as I mentioned earlier, depends not only on what students do but also on how they regard and construe what they do. This may explain why the data generally fail to show any academic benefit to assigning homework, particularly in elementary or middle school (see Kohn 2006). Yet it's generally assumed that students will somehow benefit from performing tasks they can't wait to be done with, as though their attitudes and goals were irrelevant to the outcome.

33. D. Shapiro, pp. 34, 44.

34. Funder, p. 211.

35. Regarding the way that "disinhibition [is] occasionally manifested by some overcontrolled personalities," see Block, p. 187.

36. Polivy, p. 183. She adds: "This is not to say that one should never inhibit one's natural response, as, for example, when anger makes one want to hurt another, or addiction makes one crave a cigarette." Rather, it means one should weigh the benefits and costs of inhibition in each circumstance. This moderate position contrasts sharply with our society's tendency to endorse self-discipline across the board.

37. Funder, p. 211.

38. "Adaptive human functioning is to be found not in self-control generally but rather in flexible control processes. Effective self-regulation involves the ability to control or to lose control in response to the changing circumstances of the environment and one's own affective reactions and changing priorities" (King, p. 58).

39. Ryan et al., p. 587.

40. Vansteenkiste et al.

41. The broad heading for this model and related empirical investigations is "self-determination theory" (SDT). For details, including a bibliography, see www.selfdeterminationtheory.org.

42. On the connection between conditional self-esteem and the data showing inferior results for introjected internalization, see Assor et al. 2009.

43. See Roth et al.

44. Personal communication, June 2008.

45. See, for example, Baumeister et al. 2007.

46. This was shown in two sets of three experiments each, conducted independently by Moller et al. and Muraven et al. And it builds on research showing that people are more successful at activities that require self-discipline, such as losing weight, quitting smoking, or exercising, when they feel less controlled.

47. In a series of studies, only people who already thought of willpower as a limited resource—or who were led by the experimenter to believe this—showed ego depletion. They did as well or better on a second task if they were told instead "Sometimes, working on a strenuous mental task can make you feel energized for further challenging activities" (Job et al.).

48. Emblematic of this shift is Paul Tough's 2012 book *How Children Succeed*, which opens with a declaration that what matters most for children isn't their academic proficiency; it's qualities like "persistence, self-control, curiosity, conscientiousness, grit, and self-confidence" (p. xv). But that's the last the reader hears about curiosity or self-confidence, neither of which appears in the index. By contrast, there are lengthy entries for "self-control" and "grit," which occupy Tough for much of the book.

49. Duckworth et al. 2007, p. 1100.

50. The first quote is from Duckworth 2013; the second is from Perkins-Gough, p. 16.

51. Duckworth quoted in Lehrer 2009b, p. D2.

52. For example, one educator has written a pamphlet called *Fostering Grit* that includes a six-step strategy for teaching students to persist at anything they do, regardless of the value of the task. The author's premise, moreover, is that "teaching children how to respond to frustration and failure requires that they experience frustration and failure," so they are deliberately made to experience these things (Hoerr 2013).

53. This point also applies to self-discipline. The late Fred Rothbaum, a psychologist at Tufts University, speculated that Milgram's experimental subjects had to exercise considerable self-discipline in order to obey orders to shock someone, forcing themselves to overcome their natural inclination to avoid causing harm (personal communication, June 2008).

54. McFarlin et al.; quotation on p. 152. Also see King.

55. Streep and Bernstein, pp. 1, 3, 212.

56. Miller and Wrosch, p. 773.

57. Dillard, p. 161.

58. Smith quoted in Duckworth 2013.

59. This pathology flourishes in a culture that not only celebrates competitive triumph—succeeding at the price of others' failure—but valorizes athletes,

including children, who persist in competing despite having been hurt, notwithstanding the risk of permanent injury. Call it self-destructive grit. Like the kind that is destructive to others, this desperate need to win is often driven by a particularly deep-seated version of conditional self-esteem. It was captured by Lance Armstrong's (perhaps unintentionally) revealing phrase "losing equals death."

60. Duckworth et al. 2007, studies 4 and 5.

61. Duckworth et al. 2011, p. 175; and Duckworth et al. 2007, study 6.

62. Krashen.

63. Duckworth and Seligman 2005, 2006. Self-discipline was mostly assessed by how the students described themselves, or how their teachers and parents described them, rather than as a function of something they actually did. The sole behavioral measure—making them choose either a dollar today or two dollars in a week—correlated weakly with the other measures and showed the smallest gender difference.

64. See Kohn 1999a, 1999b.

65. Hogan and Weiss, p. 148.

66. Wolfe and Johnson.

67. In one of their articles, Duckworth and Seligman (2006) maintained that self-discipline "gives girls the edge": They have more of it than boys and consequently get higher grades. The implication is that girls in our culture are socialized (more successfully than boys) to control their impulses and do what they're told, to the point that they're rewarded with higher marks. Is that really cause for celebration?

68. Lakoff, pp. 68, 165. What is less logical—but surely, by now, unsurprising—is that self-discipline would be embraced just as warmly by liberals and endorsed uncritically in virtually every article on the subject to appear in the popular press.

69. Tough 2011, p. 85.

70. The aphorism is really rather silly. As Christopher Hitchens observed, "There are all too many things that could kill you, don't kill you, and then leave you considerably weaker." It was popularized in late-twentieth-century America by the movie *Conan the Barbarian,* which was directed by war enthusiast and self-described "right-wing extremist" John Milius, and also by Watergate burglar-in-chief G. Gordon Liddy.

71. Duckworth 2011, p. 2639.

72. McCullough et al.; and Bartkowski et al., respectively.

73. Brooks 2008.

74. Baumeister quoted in Milstone. In the same interview, he said that telling children "they are great no matter what they do . . . creates narcissism." Such

children develop a sense of entitlement and "believe they're good even when they're not." As we've seen, there isn't a shred of evidence for these claims.

75. Goldman, pp. 136, 137, 139. This article was published in 1996, by the way, not 1896.

76. For example, see Reiner; and Tough 2012. Virtually every article in the popular press about such schools and programs offers an uncritical, even glowing, account of treating children of color this way. Many contain the by now *de rigueur* reference to the marshmallow studies (relying on widespread misconceptions about them) and to Angela Duckworth's studies of grit. Such schools— which are extremely popular among affluent education reformers, though rarely for their own children—are typically characterized not only by a boot-camp approach to discipline but also by a highly structured, test-oriented curriculum and a style of teaching focused more on memorizing facts and practicing skills than on understanding ideas. This kind of instruction was aptly described by the late Martin Haberman as "the pedagogy of poverty."

77. Herman, p. 46. He goes on to fault Baumeister and a colleague for attributing "the current problems of the United States . . . to a decline in self-control and personal responsibility," a claim he describes as better suited to "a Republican keynote address" than to an academic monograph.

78. Mischel et al. 1972, p. 217.

79. Wikström and Treiber, pp. 243, 251.

80. Competition: Sherif et al. Prison: See www.prisonexp.org for details of Philip Zimbardo's classic Stanford Prison Experiment. Cheating: *Character Education Inquiry*, Book 1, p. 400.

81. In a national survey of Americans' beliefs about the causes of economic inequality, the only three items thought to be "very important" by a majority of respondents all dealt with the individual: lack of money-management skills, lack of effort, and lack of ability on the part of the poor. (This survey was reported in a book by James Kluegel and Eliot Smith that was cited by Berliner and Biddle, pp. 153–54.)

Regarding obesity: "Unfortunately, behavior changes won't work on their own without seismic societal shifts, health experts say, because eating too much and exercising too little are merely symptoms of a much larger malady. The real problem is a landscape littered with inexpensive fast-food meals; saturation advertising for fatty, sugary products; inner cities that lack supermarkets; and unhealthy, high-stress workplaces. . . . 'If you take a changed person and put them in the same environment, they are going to go back to the old behaviors,' says Dr. [Dee W.] Edington . . . director of the Health Management Research Center at the University of Michigan" (Singer).

82. Gillies.

83. See, for example, CBS News.

84. See Rogers.

85. Gottfredson and Hirschi. Quotation appears on p. xvi. For a critique of this theory, see the essay by Gilbert Geis and other chapters in Goode.

86. Brooks 2006.

87. Tough 2012, p. 195.

88. If we look at financial assets rather than total assets, the top 1 percent owns more than *nine* times what the bottom 80 percent owns. And these disparities have been widening rather than narrowing over the last three decades (Domhoff). Moreover, "America is not only less equal, but also less mobile": Children born at the bottom in this country are more likely to stay there than are children in other industrialized countries (DeParle).

89. One of these posters features a dramatic image of the pyramids along with this caption: "ACHIEVEMENT—You can do anything you set your mind to when you have vision, determination, and an endless supply of expendable labor." Another depicts a packet of fast-food French fries; it says, "POTENTIAL—Not everyone gets to be an astronaut when they grow up." On a third poster, a leaping salmon is about to wind up in the jaws of a bear: "AMBITION—The journey of a thousand miles sometimes ends very, very badly." For more, see www.despair.com. If you find these offensive rather than funny, the chances are you haven't liked this book.

90. Of course it's understandable that we'd want to do something about the fact that something like a million American students leave high school every year without graduating—and the dropout rate is substantially higher for African American and Latino students. But do we address the structural features of school that students understandably find alienating, or do we just tell kids to put up with school as it's currently configured because they'll earn more money if they stick it out? If we can't give kids a better reason to stay in school than financial gain, if we reduce education to nothing more than a tedious prerequisite to collecting a credential, then we've essentially conceded school's lack of intrinsic value. In a practical sense, moreover, researchers find that "highlighting the monetary benefits that education can bring . . . could very well discourage youths from fully engaging with learning" (Ku et al., p. 84).

91. Kozol, p. 35. It would be interesting to see the results of a research study that counted the number of positive-thinking materials and self-control training sessions at a school, and then assessed certain other features of that school. My hypothesis: The popularity of inspirational slogans, grit workshops, and the like will be correlated with a lower probability that students are invited to play a meaningful role in decision-making, as well as less evidence of an emphasis

on critical thinking threaded through the curriculum and a less welcoming attitude toward questioning authority.

92. Lieberman.

93. Bowles and Gintis, p. 39.

94. Sizer, p. xi.

95. The first three quotes are from Duckworth and Seligman 2006, p. 199; the last is from Duckworth et al. 2012, p. 441. Notice that the emphasis in that last phrase is on observable behavior rather than the needs and motives that define the child's experience of the situation. Notice, too, that the child has no role in defining what constitutes "proper" behavior.

96. Hartnett, p. 63. See also the example offered on pp. 87–88.

97. Duckworth et al. 2012, p. 448.

98. Duckworth contends that "habit and character are essentially the same thing" (quoted in Tough 2012, p. 94). This is an odd equation because many habits obviously have nothing to do with character. But is it even true that most of what we'd call character could be described as habit—which by definition means behaviors that are performed automatically, without reflection?

99. Willingham, p. 23.

CHAPTER 8

1. The concept of autonomy, too, can be conceived as either "reflective" or "reactive." See Koestner and Losier.

2. In profiling several courageous resisters, the writer Eyal Press noted that none fit the profile of "iconoclasts who don't share the moral code to which most of their fellow citizens subscribe [or] who delight in thumbing their noses at whatever authority figure will pay them mind." Rather, his resisters regarded as "inviolable" "the values and ideals of the societies they lived in or the organizations they belonged to." They weren't cynical and they weren't absolute individualists. It's precisely because they accepted important values espoused by the countries or groups of which they were part that they refused to go along when people in those groups violated those principles (Press, p. 180).

3. Baumrind 1996, p. 408. Similarly, Roy Baumeister and his colleagues assert that "an optimal fit between self and environment . . . can be substantially improved by altering the self to fit the world" (Tangney et al., p. 272). For "world," read "this society" or even "this school (or workplace)."

4. The decision to engage in political activism as a young adult may indeed be influenced by how one was raised, as we'll see on page 189, but it doesn't seem to result from *permissive* parenting.

5. Diamond. His parody was a response to a newspaper ad that listed the symptoms of ODD ("argues with adults," "actively defies rules") and invited parents who thought they had such children to allow them to be given an experimental medication.

6. Jordan.

7. Math teacher: Bohl, p. 23. College student: quoted in Marano, p. 245.

8. Schemo.

9. Slouka, p. 11.

10. See Kohn 2005a, pp. 6, 54, and 222n6.

11. Dix et al.; quotation on p. 1218. For another caution about "the compulsively compliant child," see Block, p. 195.

12. Quenqua. Details about the incident were also drawn from these two accounts: http://ow.ly/oQdGJ and http://ow.ly/oQdCE.

13. Meier, p. 4; Bensman, p. 62.

14. "Moral rebels . . . may think that they are only taking a stand against the status quo, but bystanders who did not take that stand can take this rebellion as a personal threat. This suggests that the root of resentment may be that the rebel's choice implicitly condemns the perceiver's own behavior" and in effect "threatens the positive self-image of individuals who did not rebel" (Monin et al., pp. 76–77).

15. Bernstein.

16. See Kohn 1990 and, for a brief summary, Kohn 2005a, chapter 10.

17. Various research findings on this point are reviewed in Kohn 1990, Chapter 3.

18. I've written about this distinction in an article called "The Limits of Teaching Skills" (Kohn 1997b).

19. Block et al.

20. See p. 72.

21. For more on this idea, which was sparked by Marilyn Watson, see Kohn 2005a, pp. 196–97.

22. Gerbner et al.

References

Aamodt, Sandra, and Sam Wang. "Building Self-Control, the American Way." *New York Times*, February 19, 2012: SR5.

Ackerman, Robert A., Edward A. Witt, M. Brent Donnellan, Kali H. Trzesniewski, Richard W. Robins, and Deborah A. Kashy. "What Does the Narcissistic Personality Inventory Really Measure?" *Assessment* 18 (2011): 67–87.

Adams, Caralee. "'Soft Skills' Seen as Key Element for Higher Ed." *Education Week*, November 14, 2012a: 1, 14.

———. "K-12 and College Completion Rates Set Record." *Education Week*, November 14, 2012b: 4.

Allen, Scott, and Karl L. Wuensch. "Effects of an Academic Failure Experience on Subsequent Performance on Anagram and Paired-Associate Tasks." *Journal of Genetic Psychology* 154 (1993): 53–60.

Alwin, Duane F. "From Obedience to Autonomy: Changes in Traits Desired in Children, 1924–1978." *Public Opinion Quarterly* 52 (1988): 33–52.

———. "Changes in Qualities Valued in Children in the United States, 1964 to 1984." *Social Science Research* 18 (1989): 195–236.

——— . "From Childbearing to Childrearing: The Link Between Declines in Fertility and Changes in the Socialization of Children." *Population and Development Review*, vol. 22, *Supplement: Fertility in the United States*, 1996: 176–96.

Applebome, Peter. "Children Place Low in Adults' Esteem, a Study Finds." *New York Times*, June 26, 1997.

"Are We Trapped in a Child-Centered World?" *Newsweek*, November 28, 1960.

Arnett, Jeffrey Jensen. "Suffering, Selfish, Slackers? Myths and Reality About Emerging Adults." *Journal of Youth and Adolescence* 36 (2007): 23–29.

———. "Storm and Stress Redux: Review of *Generation Me*." *American Journal of Psychology* 121 (2008): 675–82.

———. "Oh, Grow Up! Generational Grumbling and the New Life Stage of Emerging Adulthood." *Perspectives on Psychological Science* 5 (2010): 89–92.

Arnett, Jeffrey Jensen, and Elizabeth Fishel. *When Will My Grown-Up Kid Grow Up? Loving and Understanding Your Emerging Adult*. New York: Workman, 2013.

Arnett, Jeffrey Jensen, and Joseph Schwab. *Poll of Emerging Adults: Thriving, Struggling & Hopeful*. Worcester, MA: Clark University, December 2012. Available at www.clarku.edu/clarkpoll.

Assor, Avi, Yaniv Kanat-Maymon, and Guy Roth. "Parental Conditional Regard: Psychological Costs and Antecedents." In *Human Motivation and Interpersonal Relationships: Theory, Research, and Applications*, edited by Netta Weinstein. New York: Springer-Verlag, 2014.

Assor, Avi, Guy Roth, and Edward L. Deci. "The Emotional Costs of Parents' Conditional Regard: A Self-Determination Theory Analysis." *Journal of Personality* 72 (2004): 47–88.

Assor, Avi, and Karen Tal. "When Parents' Affection Depends on Child's Achievement: Parental Conditional Positive Regard, Self-Aggrandizement, Shame and Coping in Adolescents." *Journal of Adolescence* 35 (2012): 249–60.

Assor, Avi, Maarten Vansteenkiste, and Avi Kaplan. "Identified Versus Introjected Approach and Introjected Avoidance Motivations in School and in Sports: The Limited Benefits of Self-Worth Strivings." *Journal of Educational Psychology* 101 (2009): 482–97.

Astin, Alexander W., Leticia Oseguera, Linda J. Sax, and William S. Korn. *The American Freshman: Thirty-Five Year Trends*. Los Angeles: UCLA Higher Education Research Institute, 2002.

Aucoin, Don. "For Some, Helicopter Parenting Delivers Benefits." *Boston Globe*, March 3, 2009.

Aunola, Kaisa, and Jari-Erik Nurmi. "Maternal Affection Moderates the Impact of Psychological Control on a Child's Mathematical Performance." *Developmental Psychology* 40 (2004): 965–78.

Baldwin, Mark W., and Lisa Sinclair. "Self-Esteem and 'If . . . Then' Contingencies of Interpersonal Acceptance." *Journal of Personality and Social Psychology* 71 (1996): 1130–41.

Barber, Brian K. "Parental Psychological Control: Revisiting a Neglected Construct." *Child Development* 67 (1996): 3296–3319.

————, editor. *Intrusive Parenting: How Psychological Control Affects Children and Adolescents*. Washington, DC: American Psychological Association, 2002.

Bartkowski, John P., Xiaohe Xu, and Martin L. Levin. "Religion and Child Development." *Social Science Research* 37 (2008): 18–36.

Bauerlein, Mark. "Boredom's Paradox." *Education Week*, August 7, 2013: 31.

Baumeister, Roy F., Jennifer D. Campbell, Joachim I. Krueger, and Kathleen D. Vohs. "Does High Self-Esteem Cause Better Performance, Interpersonal Success, Happiness, or Healthier Lifestyles?" *Psychological Science in the Public Interest* 4 (2003): 1–44.

Baumeister, Roy F., Laura Smart, and Joseph M. Boden. "Relation of Threatened Egoism to Violence and Aggression: The Dark Side of High Self-Esteem." *Psychological Review* 103 (1996): 5–33.

Baumeister, Roy F., Kathleen D. Vohs, and Dianne M. Tice. "The Strength Model of Self-Control." *Current Directions in Psychological Science* 16 (2007): 351–55.

Baumrind, Diana. "Effects of Authoritative Parental Control on Child Behavior." *Child Development* 37 (1966): 887–907.

————. "Some Thoughts About Childrearing." In *Influences on Human Development*, edited by Urie Bronfenbrenner. Hinsdale, IL: Dryden Press, 1972.

————. "The Discipline Controversy Revisited." *Family Relations* 45 (1996): 405–14.

————. "Differentiating between Confrontive and Coercive Kinds of Parental Power-Assertive Disciplinary Practices." *Human Development* 55 (2012): 35–51.

Bean, Philip. *Punishment: A Philosophical and Criminological Inquiry*. Oxford: Martin Robertson, 1981.

Beecher, Marguerite, and Willard Beecher. *Parents on the Run*. New York: Julian Press, 1955.

Belkin, Lisa. "Let the Kid Be." *New York Times Magazine*, May 31, 2009: 19–20.

————. "Defining a Successful Parent." *New York Times* Motherlode blog, July 19, 2010. Available at: http://parenting.blogs.nytimes.com/2010/07/19/defining-a-successful-parent.

Bell, Silvia M., and Mary D. Salter Ainsworth. "Infant Crying and Maternal Responsiveness." *Child Development* 43 (1972): 1171–90.

Bensman, David. *Central Park East and Its Graduates: Learning by Heart*. New York: Teachers College Press, 2000.

Berliner, David C., and Bruce J. Biddle. *The Manufactured Crisis: Myths, Fraud, and the Attack on America's Public Schools*. Reading, MA: Addison-Wesley, 1995.

Bernstein, David. "Beating 'Compliance Acquiescence Disorder' in School." *Washington Post* Answer Sheet blog, October 5, 2012. Available at http://ow.ly/oPjF2.

Bernstein, Gaia, and Zvi H. Triger. "Over-Parenting." *University of California Davis Law Review* 44 (2011): 1221–1279.

Billotti, David et al. "A New Rite of Passage: Third Grade" (letters to the editor). *New York Times*, March 18, 2004.

Bird, Joseph, and Lois Bird. *Power to the Parents.* New York: Doubleday, 1972.

Blass, Thomas. "From New Haven to Santa Clara: A Historical Perspective on the Milgram Obedience Experiments." *American Psychologist*, January 2009: 37–45.

Block, Jack. *Personality as an Affect-Processing System: Toward an Integrative Theory.* Mahway, NJ: Erlbaum, 2002.

Block, Jack, and Jeanne H. Block. "Nursery School Personality and Political Orientation Two Decades Later." *Journal of Research in Personality* 40 (2006a): 734–49.

———. "Venturing a 30-Year Longitudinal Study." *American Psychologist*, May–June 2006b: 315–27.

Block, Jeanne H., Norma Haan, and M. Brewster Smith. "Socialization Correlates of Student Activism." *Journal of Social Issues* 25 (1969): 143–77.

Boas, Ralph Philip. Introduction. *Youth and the New World: Essays from the Atlantic Monthly*, edited by Ralph Philip Boas. Boston: Atlantic Monthly Press, 1921.

Boggiano, Ann K., Marty Barrett, and Teddy Kellam. "Competing Theoretical Analyses of Helplessness: A Social-Developmental Analysis." *Journal of Experimental Child Psychology* 55 (1993): 194–207.

Bohl, Jeffrey. "Problems That Matter: Teaching Mathematics as Critical Engagement." *Humanistic Mathematics Network Journal*, no. 17 (1998): 23–31.

Bowles, Samuel, and Herbert Gintis. *Schooling in Capitalist America: Educational Reform and the Contradictions of Economic Life.* New York: Basic Books, 1976.

Boylan, Jennifer Finley. "A Freshman All Over Again." *New York Times*, August 23, 2012: A21.

Bracey, Gerald. "April Foolishness: The 20th Anniversary of 'A Nation at Risk.'" *Phi Delta Kappan*, April 2003: 616–21.

Briggs, L. B. R. et al. *Report of the Committee on Raising the Standard.* Cambridge, MA: Harvard College, January 16, 1894.

Brooks, David. "Marshmallows and Public Policy." *New York Times*, May 7, 2006: WK13.

———. "The Art of Growing Up." *New York Times*, June 6, 2008: A23.

———. "Description Is Prescription." *New York Times*, November 26, 2010: A27.

Bryant, Theodore. *Self-Discipline in 10 Days.* Seattle: HUB Publishing, 2011.

Burhans, Karen Klein, and Carol S. Dweck. "Helplessness in Early Childhood: The Role of Contingent Worth." *Child Development* 66 (1995): 1719–38.

Burnett, James H. III. "What If Spanking Works?" *Boston Globe Magazine,* June 17, 2012: 16–21.

Burwell, Rebecca A., and Stephen R. Shirk. "Self Processes in Adolescent Depression: The Role of Self-Worth Contingencies." *Journal of Research on Adolescence* 16 (2006): 479–90.

Cable, Mary. *The Little Darlings: A History of Child Rearing in America.* New York: Charles Scribner's Sons, 1975.

Capron, Earl W. "Types of Pampering and the Narcissistic Personality Trait." *Journal of Individual Psychology* 60 (2004): 76–93.

Cavanagh, Sean. "South Korean Official Advises Caution in Following His Country's Model." *Education Week* State EdWatch blog, March 27, 2011. Available at: http://ow.ly/4C7r2.

CBS News. "Meet 'Generation Plastic.'" May 17, 2007. Available at http://goo.gl/PfecQ1.

Chamberlain, John M., and David A. F. Haaga. "Unconditional Self-Acceptance and Psychological Health." *Journal of Rational-Emotive and Cognitive-Behavior Therapy* 19 (2001): 163–76.

Character Education Inquiry. *Studies in the Nature of Character* Volume 1: *Studies in Deceit.* New York: Macmillan, 1928.

Chirkov, Valery, Richard M. Ryan, Youngmee Kimi, and Ulas Kaplan. "Differentiating Autonomy from Individualism and Independence." *Journal of Personality and Social Psychology* 84 (2003): 97–110.

"Class Rank." *NACAC* [National Association for College Admission Counseling] *Research to Practice Brief,* Issue 3, 2007. Available at http://goo.gl/Q2SRv.

Cohen, Patricia, Judith S. Brook, Jacob Cohen, C. Noemi Velez, and Marc Garcia. "Common and Uncommon Pathways to Adolescent Psychopathology and Problem Behavior." In *Straight and Devious Pathways from Childhood to Adulthood,* edited by Lee N. Robins and Michael Rutter. Cambridge, England: Cambridge University Press, 1990.

Combs, Arthur W. "A Perceptual View of the Adequate Personality." In *Perceiving, Behaving, Becoming: Lessons Learned,* edited by H. Jerome Freiberg. Alexandria, VA: ASCD, 1999.

Comer, Cornelia A. P. "A Letter to the Rising Generation." *Atlantic Monthly,* February 1911: 145–54.

Covington, Martin V. *Making the Grade: A Self-Worth Perspective on Motivation and School Reform.* Cambridge, England: Cambridge University Press, 1992.

Crain, William. *Reclaiming Childhood*. New York: Times Books, 2003.

Cramer, Phoebe. "Young Adult Narcissism: A 20-Year Longitudinal Study of the Contribution of Parenting Styles, Preschool Precursors of Narcissism, and Denial." *Journal of Personality* 45 (2011): 19–28.

Crocker, Jennifer, and Katherine M. Knight. "Contingencies of Self-Worth." *Current Directions in Psychological Science* 14 (2005): 200–203.

Crocker, Jennifer, and Connie T. Wolfe. "Contingencies of Self-Worth." *Psychological Review* 108 (2001): 593–623.

Cross, Gary. *The Cute and the Cool: Wondrous Innocence and Modern American Children's Culture*. Oxford: Oxford University Press, 2004.

Csikszentmihalyi, Mihaly, and Judith LeFevre. "Optimal Experience in Work and Leisure." *Journal of Personality and Social Psychology* 56 (1989): 815–22.

Day, Randal D., and Laura M. Padilla-Walker. "Mother and Father Connectedness and Involvement During Early Adolescence." *Journal of Family Psychology* 23 (2009): 900–904.

Deci, Edward L., and Richard M. Ryan. "Human Autonomy: The Basis for True Self-Esteem." In *Efficacy, Agency, and Self-Esteem*, edited by Michael H. Kernis. New York: Plenum, 1995.

DeMause, Lloyd. *Emotional Life of Nations*. New York: Karnac, 2002.

DeParle, Jason. "Harder for Americans to Rise from Economy's Lower Rungs." *New York Times*, January 5, 2012: A1.

Deppe, Roberta K., and Judith M. Harackiewicz. "Self-Handicapping and Intrinsic Motivation: Buffering Intrinsic Motivation from the Threat of Failure." *Journal of Personality and Social Psychology* 70 (1996): 868–76.

Diamond, Norm. "Defiance Is Not a Disease." *Rethinking Schools*, Summer 2003: 13.

Dickman, Scott J., and David E. Meyer. "Impulsivity and Speed-Accuracy Tradeoffs in Information Processing." *Journal of Personality and Social Psychology* 54 (1988): 274–90.

Dillard, Annie. "To Fashion a Text." In *Inventing the Truth*, edited by William Zinsser. Rev. ed. Boston: Houghton Mifflin, 1998.

Dix, Theodore, Amanda D. Stewart, Elizabeth T. Gershoff, and William H. Day. "Autonomy and Children's Reactions to Being Controlled." *Child Development* 78 (2007): 1204–21.

Domhoff, G. William. "Wealth, Income, and Power." February 2013. Posted at http://whorulesamerica.net/power/wealth.html.

Donnellan, M. Brent, and Kali H. Trzesniewski. "How Should We Study Generational 'Changes'—Or Should We? A Critical Examination of the Evidence for 'Generation Me.'" *Social and Personality Psychology Compass* 3 (2009): 1–10.

Donnellan, M. Brent, Kali H. Trzesniewski, Richard W. Robins, Terrie E. Moffitt, and Avshalom Caspi. "Low Self-Esteem Is Related to Aggression, Antisocial Behavior, and Delinquency." *Psychological Science* 16 (2005): 328–35.

Dries, Kate. "The Truth About Millennials (in Boomer Eyes)." *New York Times* Booming blog, May 28, 2013. Available at http://ow.ly/lv7Le.

DuBois, David L., and Heather D. Tevendale. "Self-Esteem in Childhood and Adolescence: Vaccine or Epiphenomenon?" *Applied and Preventive Psychology* 8 (1999): 103–17.

Duckworth, Angela L. "The Significance of Self-Control." *Proceedings of the National Academy of Sciences* 108 (2011): 2639–40.

———. "True Grit." [Association for Psychological Science] *Observer*, April 2013.

Duckworth, Angela Lee, Teri A. Kirby, Eli Tsukayama, Heather Berstein, and K. Anders Ericsson. "Deliberate Practice Spells Success: Why Grittier Competitors Triumph at the National Spelling Bee." *Social Psychological and Personality Science* 2 (2011): 174–81.

Duckworth, Angela L., Christopher Peterson, Michael D. Matthews, and Dennis R. Kelly. "Grit: Perseverance and Passion for Long-Term Goals." *Journal of Personality and Social Psychology* 92 (2007): 1087–1101.

Duckworth, Angela L., Patrick D. Quinn, and Eli Tsukayama. "What *No Child Left Behind* Leaves Behind: The Roles of IQ and Self-Control in Predicting Standardized Achievement Test Scores and Report Card Grades." *Journal of Educational Psychology* 104 (2012): 439–51.

Duckworth, Angela L., and Martin E. P. Seligman. "Self-Discipline Outdoes IQ in Predicting Academic Performance of Adolescents." *Psychological Science* 16 (2005): 939–44.

———. "Self-Discipline Gives Girls the Edge: Gender in Self-Discipline, Grades, and Achievement Test Scores." *Journal of Educational Psychology* 98 (2006): 198–208.

Dweck, Carol S. *Self-Theories: Their Role in Motivation, Personality, and Development*. Philadelphia: Taylor & Francis, 2000.

Eaton, Missa Murry, and Eva M. Pomerantz. "When Parents' Self-Worth Is Contingent on Children's Performance: Implications for Parents' Mental Health." Presentation at the Biennial Meeting of the Society for Research in Child Development, Atlanta, GA. April 2005.

Eccles, Jacquelynne S., Christy M. Buchanan, Constance Flanagan, Andrew Fuligni, Carol Midgley, and Doris Yee. "Control Versus Autonomy During Early Adolescence." *Journal of Social Issues* 47 (1991): 53–68.

Ehrenreich, Barbara. *Fear of Falling: The Inner Life of the Middle Class*. New York: Pantheon, 1989.

Ehrensaft, Diane. *Spoiling Childhood: How Well-Meaning Parents Are Giving Children Too Much—But Not What They Need.* New York: Guilford Press, 1997.

Eibach, Richard P., and Lisa K. Libby. "Ideology of the Good Old Days: Exaggerated Perceptions of Moral Decline and Conservative Politics." In *Social and Psychological Bases of Ideology and System Justification*, edited by J. T. Jost et al. New York: Oxford University Press, 2009.

Eibach, Richard P., Lisa K. Libby, and Thomas D. Gilovich. "When Change in the Self Is Mistaken for Change in the World." *Journal of Personality and Social Psychology* 84 (2003): 917–31.

Elliot, Andrew J., and Judith M. Harackiewicz. "Approach and Avoidance Achievement Goals and Intrinsic Motivation: A Mediational Analysis." *Journal of Personality and Social Psychology* 70 (1996): 461–75.

Erol, Ruth Yasemin, and Ulrich Orth. "Self-Esteem Development from Age 14 to 30 Years: A Longitudinal Study." *Journal of Personality and Social Psychology* 101 (2011): 607–19.

Fingerman, Karen L., Yen-Pi Chang, Eric D. Wesselmann, Steven Zarit, Frank Furstenberg, and Kira S. Birditt. "Helicopter Parents and Landing Pad Kids: Intense Parental Support of Grown Children." *Journal of Marriage and Family* 74 (2012): 880–96.

Finkelstein, Amy, Erzo F. P. Luttmer, and Matthew J. Notowidigdo. "What Good Is Wealth Without Health? The Effect of Health on the Marginal Utility of Consumption." Working paper #14089. Cambridge, MA: National Bureau of Economic Research, June 2008.

Flacks, Richard. "Who Protests: The Social Bases of the Student Movement." In *Protest! Student Activism in America*, edited by Julian Foster and Durward Long. New York: William Morrow, 1970.

Flook, Lisa, Rena L. Repetti, and Jodie B. Ullman. "Classroom Social Experiences as Predictors of Academic Performance." *Developmental Psychology* 41 (2005): 319–27.

Fogarty, James A. *Overindulged Children.* Raleigh, NC: Liberty Publishing, 2003.

Foster, Joshua D., W. Keith Campbell, and Jean M. Twenge. "Individual Differences in Narcissism: Inflated Self-Views Across the Lifespan and Around the World." *Journal of Research in Personality* 37 (2003): 469–86.

Fromm, Erich. *The Art of Loving.* New York: Harper Colophon, 1956.

Funder, David C. "On the Pros and Cons of Delay of Gratification." *Psychological Inquiry* 9 (1998): 211–12.

Funder, David C., and Jack Block. "The Role of Ego-Control, Ego-Resiliency, and IQ in Delay of Gratification in Adolescence." *Journal of Personality and Social Psychology* 57 (1989): 1041–50.

Garber, Judy, Nancy S. Robinson, and David Valentiner. "The Relation Between Parenting and Adolescent Depression: Self-Worth as a Mediator." *Journal of Adolescent Research* 12 (1997): 12–33.

Gardner, Phil. "Parent Involvement in the College Recruiting Process: To What Extent?" *CERI Research Brief.* Collegiate Employment Research Institute, Michigan State University, 2007.

Gehring, John. "Dodge Ball Takes a Drubbing in Several School Districts." *Education Week*, February 21, 2001: 6.

Gentile, Brittany, Jean M. Twenge, and W. Keith Campbell. "Birth Cohort Differences in Self-Esteem, 1988–2008: A Cross-Temporal Meta-Analysis." *Review of General Psychology* 14 (2010): 261–68.

George, Cossondra. "My Coercive Classroom." *Teacher* magazine online, May 6, 2009.

Gerbner, George, Larry Gross, Michael Morgan, Nancy Signorielli, and James Shanahan. "Growing Up with Television: Cultivation Processes." In *Media Effects: Advances in Theory and Research*, edited by Jennings Bryant and Dolf Zillmann. Hillsdale, NJ: Erlbaum, 1994.

Gershoff, Elizabeth Thompson. "Corporal Punishment by Parents and Associated Child Behaviors and Experiences: A Meta-Analysis and Theoretical Review." *Psychological Bulletin* 128 (2002): 539–79.

Gershoff, Elizabeth T., and Susan H. Bitensky. "The Case Against Corporal Punishment of Children." *Psychology, Public Policy, and the Law* 13 (2007): 231–72.

Ghoul, Assia, Erika Y. Niwa, and Paul Boxer. "The Role of Contingent Self-Worth in the Relation Between Victimization and Internalizing Problems in Adolescents." *Journal of Adolescence* 36 (2013): 457–64.

Gibbs, Nancy. "Parents and Children: Who's in Charge Here?" *Time*, August 6, 2001. Available at www.time.com/time/magazine/article/0,9171,1000465,00.html.

———. "The Growing Backlash Against Overparenting." *Time*, November 30, 2009. Available at www.time.com/time/magazine/article/0,9171,1940697,00.html.

Gillies, Val. "Social and Emotional Pedagogies: Critiquing the New Orthodoxy of Emotion in Classroom Behavior Management." *British Journal of Sociology of Education* 32 (2011): 185–202.

Givertz, Michelle, and Chris Segrin. "The Association Between Overinvolved Parenting and Young Adults' Self-Efficacy, Psychological Entitlement, and Family Communication." *Communication Research* DOI 10.1177/0093650212456392. Published online August 20, 2012.

Glassman, Mark. "Five Myths About Millennials." *Washington Post*, August 30, 2013.

Goldman, Louis. "Mind, Character, and the Deferral of Gratification." *Educational Forum* 60 (1996): 135–40.

Goldstein, Susanne. "Here's How to Deal with Millennials Who Aren't Ready to Face Real Challenges." *Business Insider*, August 17, 2012. Available at http://ow.ly/lJoB4.

Goode, Erich, ed. *Out of Control: Assessing the General Theory of Crime.* Stanford, CA: Stanford University Press, 2008.

Goodlad, John I. *A Place Called School: Prospects for the Future.* New York: McGraw-Hill, 1984.

Gosman, Fred G. *Spoiled Rotten: Today's Children and How to Change Them.* New York: Villard Books, 1992.

Gottfredson, Michael R., and Travis Hirschi. *A General Theory of Crime.* Stanford, CA: Stanford University Press, 1990.

Gray, Peter, and David Chanoff. "Democratic Schooling: What Happens to Young People Who Have Charge of Their Own Education?" *American Journal of Education* 94 (1986): 182–213.

Greenberger, Ellen, Jared Lessard, Chuansheng Chen, and Susan P. Farruggia. "Self-Entitled College Students: Contributions of Personality, Parenting, and Motivational Factors." *Journal of Youth and Adolescence* 37 (2008): 1193–1204.

Grille, Robin. *Parenting for a Peaceful World.* Alexandria, NSW, Australia: Longueville, 2005.

Grolnick, Wendy S. *The Psychology of Parental Control: How Well-Meant Parenting Backfires.* Mahwah, NJ: Erlbaum, 2003.

Grolnick, Wendy S., Carrie E. Price, Krista L. Beiswenger, and Christine C. Sauck. "Evaluative Pressure in Mothers: Effects of Situation, Maternal, and Child Characteristics on Autonomy Supportive Versus Controlling Behavior." *Developmental Psychology* 43 (2007): 991–1002.

Gromoske, Andrea N., and Kathryn Maguire-Jack. "Transactional and Cascading Relations Between Early Spanking and Children's Social-Emotional Development." *Journal of Marriage and Family* 74 (2012): 1054–68.

Halse, Christine, Anne Honey, and Desiree Boughtwood. "The Paradox of Virtue: (Re)thinking Deviance, Anorexia, and Schooling." *Gender and Education* 19 (2007): 219–235.

Halverson, Charles F., Jr. "Remembering Your Parents: Reflections on the Retrospective Method." *Journal of Personality* 56 (1988): 435–43.

Haney, Penny, and Joseph A. Durlak. "Changing Self-Esteem in Children and Adolescents: A Meta-Analytic Review." *Journal of Clinical Child Psychology* 27 (1998): 423–33.

Hardyment, Christina. *Dream Babies: Three Centuries of Good Advice on Child Care.* New York: Harper & Row, 1983.

Hart, Craig H., D. Michele DeWolf, Patricia Wozniak, and Diane C. Burts. "Maternal and Paternal Disciplinary Styles: Relations with Preschoolers' Playground Behavioral Orientations and Peer Status." *Child Development* 63 (1992): 879–92.

Harter, Susan. "Causes and Consequences of Low Self-Esteem in Children and Adolescents." In *Self-Esteem: The Puzzle of Low Self-Regard*, edited by Roy F. Baumeister. New York: Plenum, 1993.

Hartnett, Kevin. "Character's Content." *The Pennsylvania Gazette*, May–June 2012: 59–64.

Hays, Sharon. *The Cultural Contradictions of Motherhood*. New Haven, CT: Yale University Press, 1996.

Herman, C. Peter. "Thoughts of a Veteran of Self-Regulation Failure." *Psychological Inquiry* 7 (1996): 46–50.

Hersey, John. "Why Do Students Bog Down on First R?" *Life*, May 24, 1954.

Heubert, Jay P. "First, Do No Harm." *Educational Leadership*, December 2002–January 2003: 26–30.

Higher Education Research Institute. "The American Freshman: National Norms for 2007." *HERI Research Brief*, January 2008. Available at http://heri.ucla.edu/PDFs/pubs/briefs/brief-012408-07FreshmanNorms.pdf.

Hill, Patrick L., and Brent W. Roberts. "Narcissism, Well-Being, and Observer-Rated Personality Across the Lifespan." *Social Psychological and Personality Science* 3 (2012): 216–23.

Hoagland, Edward. "Last Call." *Harper's*, May 2010: 33–41.

Hoerr, Thomas R. "Got Grit?" *Educational Leadership*, March 2012: 84–85.

———. *Fostering Grit*. Alexandria, VA: ASCD, 2013.

Hoffman, Martin, and Herbert D. Saltzstein. "Parent Discipline and the Child's Moral Development." *Journal of Personality and Social Psychology* 5 (1967): 45–57.

Hogan, Robert, and Daniel S. Weiss. "Personality Correlates of Superior Academic Achievement." *Journal of Counseling Psychology* 21 (1974): 144–49.

Holt, John. *How Children Fail*. Rev. ed. New York: Delta, 1982.

———. *Escape from Childhood: The Needs and Rights of Children*. New York: Dutton, 1974.

Hoover, Eric. "Survey of Students' Views Complicate Spin on 'Helicopter Parents.'" *Chronicle of Higher Education*, January 24, 2008.

"Hopscotch? Well, Maybe." *Los Angeles Times*, November 28, 2004.

Hudson, Jennifer L., and Helen F. Dodd. "Informing Early Intervention: Preschool Predictors of Anxiety Disorders in Middle Childhood." *PLoS ONE*, 7 (August 2012): 1–7.

Hulbert, Ann. *Raising America*. New York: Knopf, 2003.

Jencks, Christopher. "Is It All Dr. Spock's Fault?" *New York Times Magazine,* March 3, 1968.

Job, Veronika, Carol S. Dweck, and Gregory M. Walton. "Ego Depletion—Is It All in Your Head? Implicit Theories About Willpower Affect Self-Regulation." *Psychological Science* 21 (2010): 1686–93.

Johnson, Steve. "At This Year's Oscars, Everyone's a Winner." *Chicago Tribune,* February 23, 2010.

Jordan, Tina. "J. K. Rowling Outs Dumbledore." *Entertainment Weekly,* October 20, 2007.

Joussemet, Mireille, Richard Koestner, Natasha Lekes, and Renee Landry. "A Longitudinal Study of the Relationship of Maternal Autonomy Support to Children's Adjustment and Achievement in School." *Journal of Personality* 73 (2005): 1215–35.

Joussemet, Mireille, Renee Landry, and Richard Koestner. "A Self-Determination Theory Perspective on Parenting." *Canadian Psychology* 49 (2008): 194–200.

Juster, F. Thomas. "Preferences for Work and Leisure." In *Time, Goods, and Well-Being,* edited by F. Thomas Juster and Frank P. Stafford. Ann Arbor: University of Michigan Institute for Social Research, 1985.

Keilman, John. "A Downside to High Teen Self-Esteem?" *Chicago Tribune,* July 4, 2010.

Kernis, Michael H. "Toward a Conceptualization of Optimal Self-Esteem." *Psychological Inquiry* 14 (2003): 1–26.

Kernis, Michael H., Anita C. Brown, and Gene H. Brody. "Fragile Self-Esteem in Children and Its Associations with Perceived Patterns of Parent-Child Communication." *Journal of Personality* 68 (2000): 225–52.

Kernis, Michael H., David P. Cornell, Chien-Ru Sun, Andrea Berry, and Thomas Harlow. "There's More to Self-Esteem Than Whether It Is High or Low: The Importance of Stability of Self-Esteem." *Journal of Personality and Social Psychology* 65 (1993): 1190–1204.

Kernis, Michael H., Chad E. Lakey, and Whitney L. Heppner. "Secure Versus Fragile High Self-Esteem as a Predictor of Verbal Defensiveness." *Journal of Personality* 76 (2008): 477–512.

Kidd, Celeste, Holly Palmeri, and Richard N. Aslin. "Rational Snacking: Young Children's Decision-Making on the Marshmallow Task Is Moderated by Beliefs About Environmental Reliability." *Cognition* 126 (2013): 109–14.

Kim, Su Yeong, Yijie Wang, Diana Oroczo-Lapray, Yishan Shen, and Mohammed Murtuza. "Does 'Tiger Parenting' Exist? Parenting Profiles of Chinese Americans and Adolescent Developmental Outcomes." *Asian American Journal of Psychology* 4 (2013): 7–18.

King, Laura A. "Who Is Regulating What and Why? Motivational Context of Self-Regulation." *Psychological Inquiry* 7 (1996): 57–60.

Kins, Evie, Bart Soenens, and Wim Beyers. "Parental Psychological Control and Dysfunctional Separation-Individuation." *Journal of Adolescence* 35 (2012): 1099–1109.

Knafo, Ariel, and Robert Plomin. "Parental Discipline and Affection and Children's Prosocial Behavior: Genetic and Environmental Links." *Journal of Personality and Social Psychology* 90 (2006): 147–64.

Kochanska, Grazyna, Nazan Aksan, and Jennifer J. Carlson. "Temperament, Relationships, and Young Children's Receptive Cooperation with Their Parents." *Developmental Psychology* 41 (2005): 648–60.

Koestner, Richard, and Gaëtan F. Losier. "Distinguishing Reactive Versus Reflective Autonomy." *Journal of Personality* 64 (1996): 465–94.

Kohn, Alfie. *The Brighter Side of Human Nature: Altruism and Empathy in Everyday Life.* New York: Basic Books, 1990.

———. *No Contest: The Case Against Competition.* Rev. ed. Boston: Houghton Mifflin, 1992.

———. *Beyond Discipline: From Compliance to Community.* Alexandria, VA: ASCD, 1996.

———. "How Not to Teach Values: A Critical Look at Character Education." *Phi Delta Kappan*, February 1997a: 429-39. Available at www.alfiekohn.org /teaching/hnttv.htm.

———. "The Limits of Teaching Skills." *Reaching Today's Youth*, Summer 1997b. Available at www.alfiekohn.org/teaching/lts.htm.

———. *Punished by Rewards: The Trouble with Gold Stars, Incentive Plans, A's, Praise, and Other Bribes.* Rev. ed. Boston: Houghton Mifflin, 1999a.

———. *The Schools Our Children Deserve: Moving Beyond Traditional Classrooms and "Tougher Standards."* Boston: Houghton Mifflin, 1999b.

———. *The Case Against Standardized Testing: Raising the Scores, Ruining the Schools.* Portsmouth, NH: Heinemann, 2000.

———. "The Dangerous Myth of Grade Inflation." *Chronicle of Higher Education*, November 8, 2002: B7-9. Available at www.alfiekohn.org/teaching/gi.htm.

———. *Unconditional Parenting: Moving from Rewards and Punishments to Love and Reason.* New York: Atria, 2005a.

———. "Getting-Hit-on-the-Head Lessons." *Education Week*, September 7, 2005b: 52, 46–47. Available at www.alfiekohn.org/teaching/edweek/bguti. htm.

———. *The Homework Myth: Why Our Kids Get Too Much of a Bad Thing.* Cambridge, MA: Da Capo, 2006.

———. "'Politically Correct'—The Lazy Bully's Label of Choice." *Huffington Post*, January 18, 2011a. Available at http://bit.ly/f2uneY.

———. "The Case Against Grades." *Educational Leadership*, November 2011b: 28–33. Available at www.alfiekohn.org/teaching/tcag.htm.

———. "'We're Number Umpteenth!': The Myth of Lagging U.S. Schools." *Washington Post* Answer Sheet blog, May 3, 2013. Available at http://ow.ly /kFKUN.

Kolbert, Elizabeth. "Spoiled Rotten: Why Do Kids Rule the Roost?" *New Yorker*, July 2, 2012.

Konrath, Sara H., Edward H. O'Brien, and Courtney Hsing. "Changes in Dispositional Empathy in American College Students Over Time: A Meta-Analysis." *Personality and Social Psychology Review* 15 (2011): 180–98.

Kozol, Jonathan. *The Shame of the Nation: The Restoration of Apartheid Schooling in America.* New York: Crown, 2005.

Krashen, Stephen. "Reading Improves Students' Spelling." *Education Week*, December 11, 2002: 33.

Krauthammer, Charles. "Education: Doing Bad and Feeling Good." *Time*, February 5, 1990: 78.

Krevans, Julia, and John C. Gibbs. "Parents' Use of Inductive Discipline: Relations to Children's Empathy and Prosocial Behavior." *Child Development* 67 (1996): 3263–77.

Krugman, Paul. "A Tale of Two Moralities." *New York Times*, January 14, 2011: A23.

Ku, Lisbeth, Helga Dittmar, and Robin Banerjee. "Are Materialistic Teenagers Less Motivated to Learn?" *Journal of Educational Psychology* 104 (2012): 74–86.

Lahey, Jessica. "Why Parents Need to Let Their Children Fail." *The Atlantic* blog, January 29, 2013. Available at http://goo.gl/tO4H6.

Lakoff, George. *Moral Politics: How Liberals and Conservatives Think.* 2nd ed. Chicago: University of Chicago Press, 2002.

Lamborn, Susie D., Nina S. Mounts, Laurence Steinberg, and Sanford M. Dornbusch. "Patterns of Competence and Adjustment among Adolescents from Authoritative, Authoritarian, Indulgent, and Neglectful Families." *Child Development* 62 (1991): 1049–65.

Lareau, Annette. *Unequal Childhoods: Class, Race, and Family Life.* Berkeley, CA: University of California Press, 2003.

Lear, Martha Weinman. *The Child Worshipers.* New York: Crown, 1963.

Lehrer, Jonah. "Don't! The Secret of Self-Control." *New Yorker*, May 18, 2009a: 26–32.

———. "The Truth About Grit." *Boston Globe*, August 2, 2009b: D1–2.

LeMoyne, Terri, and Tom Buchanan. "Does 'Hovering' Matter? Helicopter Parenting and Its Effect on Well-Being." *Sociological Spectrum* 31 (2011): 399–418.

Leo, John. "The Trouble with Self-Esteem." *U.S. News and World Report*, April 2, 1990: 16.

Lerner, Barbara. "Self-Esteem and Excellence: The Choice and the Paradox." *American Educator*, Winter 1985: 10–16.

Lerner, Jennifer S., Ye Li, and Elke U. Weber. "The Financial Costs of Sadness." *Psychological Science* 24 (2013): 72–79.

Lessard, Jared, Ellen Greenberger, Chuansheng Chen, and Susan Farruggia. "Are Youths' Feelings of Entitlement Always 'Bad'?: Evidence for a Distinction Between Exploitive and Non-exploitive Dimensions of Entitlement." *Journal of Adolescence* 34 (2011): 521–29.

Letzring, Tera D., Jack Block, and David C. Funder. "Ego-control and Ego-resiliency: Generalization of Self-Report Scales Based on Personality Descriptions from Acquaintances, Clinicians, and the Self." *Journal of Research in Personality* 39 (2005): 395–422.

Levine, Madeline. "Raising Successful Children." *New York Times*, August 5, 2012: SR8.

Lewis, Catherine C. "The Effects of Parental Firm Control: A Reinterpretation of Findings." *Psychological Bulletin* 90 (1981): 547–63.

Lewis, Harry. "The Racial Theory of Grade Inflation." *Harvard Crimson*, April 23, 2001.

Liberman, Mark. "Psycho Kids Today." Post on *Language Log* blog, November 12, 2012. Available at: http://languagelog.ldc.upenn.edu/nll/?p=4311.

———. "'. . . A Generation of Deluded Narcissists'?" Posted on *Language Log* blog, January 13, 2013. Available at: http://languagelog.ldc.upenn.edu/nll/?p=4413.

Lieberman, Matthew D. "The Hidden Doublespeak of Willpower and Self-Control." *Psychology Today* blog, April 23, 2012. Available at http://goo.gl/0AuEO.

Liu, Amy, Jessica Sharkness, and John H. Pryor. *Findings from the 2007 Administration of Your First College Year (YFCY): National Aggregates*. Los Angeles: Higher Education Research Institute, UCLA, May 2008.

Locke, Judith Y., Marilyn A. Campbell, and David Kavanagh. "Can a Parent Do Too Much for Their Child?: An Examination by Parenting Professionals of the Concept of Overparenting." *Australian Journal of Guidance and Counselling* 22 (2012): 249–65.

Luster, Tom, Kelly Rhoades, and Bruce Haas. "The Relation between Parental Values and Parenting Behavior." *Journal of Marriage and Family* 51 (1989): 139–47.

Lyubomirsky, Sonja, Chris Tkach, and M. Robin Dimatteo. "What Are the Differences Between Happiness and Self-Esteem?" *Social Indicators Research* 78 (2006): 363–404.

MacKenzie, Michael J., Eric Nicklas, Jane Waldfogel, and Jeanne Brooks-Gunn. "Spanking and Child Development Across the First Decade of Life." *Pediatrics* 132 (November 2013): e1118–25.

Maier, Thomas. *Dr. Spock: An American Life.* New York: Basic, 2003.

Makri-Botsari, E. "Causal Links Between Academic Intrinsic Motivation, Self-Esteem, and Unconditional Acceptance by Teachers in High School Students." In *International Perspectives on Individual Differences*, vol. 2: *Self Perception*, edited by Richard J. Riding and Stephen G. Rayner. Westport, CT: Ablex, 2001.

Mamen, Maggie. *The Pampered Child Syndrome.* Rev. ed. Philadelphia: Jessica Kingsley, 2006.

Mansfield, Harvey C. "Grade Inflation: It's Time to Face the Facts." *Chronicle of Higher Education,* April 6, 2001: B24.

Marano, Hara Estroff. *A Nation of Wimps: The High Cost of Invasive Parenting.* New York: Broadway, 2008.

Marrero, Tony. "Hernando School Board Balks at Giving Zeroes a Pass." *Tampa Bay Times,* July 8, 2009.

Maruyama, Geoffrey, Rosalyn A. Rubin, and G. Gage Kingsbury. "Self-Esteem and Educational Achievement: Independent Constructs with a Common Cause?" *Journal of Personality and Social Psychology* 40 (1981): 962–75.

Mathews, Jay. "New Study Gives Hovering College Parents Extra Credit." *Washington Post*, November 5, 2007.

McAdams, Dan P., Michelle Albaugh, Emily Farber, Jennifer Daniels, Regina L. Logan, and Brad Olson. "Family Metaphors and Moral Intuitions: How Conservatives and Liberals Narrate Their Lives." *Journal of Personality and Social Psychology* 95 (2008): 978–90.

McCullough, Michael E., and Brian L. B. Willoughby. "Religion, Self-Regulation, and Self-Control." *Psychological Bulletin* 135 (2009): 69–93.

McFarlin, Dean B., Roy F. Baumeister, and Jim Blascovich. "On Knowing When to Quit: Task Failure, Self-Esteem, Advice, and Nonproductive Persistence." *Journal of Personality* 52 (1984): 138–55.

McFarlin, Dean B., and Jim Blascovich. "Effects of Self-Esteem and Performance Feedback on Future Affective Preferences and Cognitive Expectations." *Journal of Personality and Social Psychology* 40 (1981): 521–31.

McGee, Rob, and Sheila Williams. "Does Low Self-Esteem Predict Health Compromising Behaviours Among Adolescents?" *Journal of Adolescence* 23 (2000): 569–82.

McLeod, Bryce D., Jeffrey J. Wood, and John R. Weisz. "Examining the Association Between Parenting and Childhood Anxiety: A Meta-Analysis." *Clinical Psychology Review* 27 (2007): 155–72.

Mecca, Andrew M., Neil J. Smelser, and John Vasconcellos, eds. *The Social Importance of Self-Esteem*. Berkeley, CA: University of California Press, 1989.

Meier, Deborah. *The Power of Their Ideas: Lessons for America from a Small School in Harlem*. Boston: Beacon, 1995.

Merryman, Ashley. "Losing Is Good for You." *New York Times*, September 25, 2013: A27.

Mikulincer, Mario, Phillip R. Shaver, Omri Gillath, and Rachel A. Nitzberg. "Attachment, Caregiving, and Altruism: Boosting Attachment Security Increases Compassion and Helping." *Journal of Personality and Social Psychology* 89 (2005): 817–39.

Milgram, Stanley. *Obedience to Authority*. New York: Harper Colophon, 1975.

Miller, Alice. *The Drama of the Gifted Child*. Rev. ed. New York: Basic, 1994.

Miller, Gregory E., and Carsten Wrosch. "You've Gotta Know When to Fold 'Em: Goal Disengagement and Systematic Inflammation in Adolescence." *Psychological Science* 18 (2007): 773–77.

Milstone, Carol. "When Bad Kids Think They're Great." *National Post* [Canada], March 23, 1999.

Milton, Ohmer, Howard R. Pollio, and James A. Eison. *Making Sense of College Grades*. San Francisco: Jossey-Bass, 1986.

Mintz, Steven. *Huck's Raft: A History of American Childhood*. Cambridge, MA: Harvard University Press, 2006.

Mischel, Walter. *Personality and Assessment*. New York: Wiley, 1968.

———. "From Good Intentions to Willpower." In *The Psychology of Action: Linking Cognition and Motivation to Behavior*, edited by Peter M. Gollwitzer and John A. Bargh. New York: Guilford, 1996.

Mischel, Walter, Ebbe B. Ebbesen, and Antonette Raskoff Zeiss. "Cognitive and Attentional Mechanisms in Delay of Gratification." *Journal of Personality and Social Psychology* 21 (1972): 204–18.

Mischel, Walter, Yuichi Shoda, and Philip K. Peake. "The Nature of Adolescent Competencies Predicted by Preschool Delay of Gratification." *Journal of Personality and Social Psychology* 54 (1988): 687–96.

Moffitt, Terrie E., Louise Arseneault, Daniel Belsky, Nigel Dickson and Robert J. Hancox et al. "A Gradient of Childhood Self-Control Predicts Health, Wealth, and Public Safety." *Proceedings of the National Academy of Sciences* 108 (2011): 2693–98.

Mogel, Wendy. *The Blessings of a Skinned Knee*. New York: Scribner, 2001.

Moller, Arlen C., Edward L. Deci, and Richard M. Ryan. "Choice and Ego Depletion: The Moderating Role of Autonomy." *Personality and Social Psychology Bulletin* 32 (2006): 1024–36.

Monin, Benoît, Pamela J. Sawyer, and Matthew J. Marquez. "The Rejection of Moral Rebels: Resenting Those Who Do the Right Thing." *Journal of Personality and Social Psychology* 95 (2008): 76–93.

Munich, Richard L., and Matthew A. Munich. "Overparenting and the Narcissistic Pursuit of Attachment." *Psychiatric Annals* 39 (2009): 227–35.

Muraven, Mark, Marylène Gagné, and Heather Rosman. "Helpful Self-Control: Autonomy Support, Vitality, and Depletion." *Journal of Experimental Social Psychology* 44 (2008): 573–85.

Murayama, Kou, and Andrew J. Elliot. "The Competition-Performance Relation: A Meta-Analytic Review and Test of the Opposing Processes Model of Competition and Performance." *Psychological Bulletin* 138 (2012): 1035–70.

National Survey of Student Engagement. *Experiences That Matter: Enhancing Student Learning and Success*—Annual Report 2007. Center for Postsecondary Research, Indiana University at Bloomington, 2007.

Natriello, Gary. "Failing Grades for Retention." *School Administrator*, August 1998: 14–17.

Neighbors, Clayton, Mary E. Larimer, Irene Markman Geisner, and C. Raymond Knee. "Feeling Controlled and Drinking Motives Among College Students." *Self and Identity* 3 (2004): 207–24.

Nelson, Margaret K. *Parenting Out of Control: Anxious Parents in Uncertain Times*. New York: New York University Press, 2010.

Neyfakh, Leon. "The Armored Child." *Boston Globe*, August 14, 2011.

Ng, Florrie Fei-Yin, Eva M. Pomerantz, and Ciping Deng. "Why Are Chinese Mothers More Controlling Than American Mothers? 'My Child Is My Report Card.'" *Child Development* 85 (2014).

Nicholls, John G. *The Competitive Ethos and Democratic Education*. Cambridge, MA: Harvard University Press, 1989.

O'Brien, Keith. "The Empathy Deficit." *Boston Globe*, October 17, 2010.

O'Mara, Alison J., Herbert W. Marsh, Rhonda G. Craven, and Raymond L. Debus. "Do Self-Concept Interventions Make a Difference?" *Educational Psychologist* 41 (2006): 181–206.

Orenstein, Peggy. "The Toxic Paradox." *New York Times Magazine*, February 8, 2009: 17–18.

Orlick, Terry. *The Cooperative Sports and Games Book*. New York: Pantheon, 1978.

Orth, Ulrich, Richard W. Robins, and Keith F. Widaman. "Life-Span Development of Self-Esteem and Its Effects on Important Life Outcomes." *Journal of Personality and Social Psychology* 102 (2012): 1271–88.

Orth, Ulrich, Kali H. Trzesniewski, and Richard W. Robins. "Self-Esteem Development from Young Adulthood to Old Age: A Cohort-Sequential Longitudinal Study." *Journal of Personality and Social Psychology* 98 (2010): 645–58.

Otto, A. Ross, Arthur B. Markman, and Bradley C. Love. "Taking More, Now: The Optimality of Impulsive Choice Hinges on Environment Structure." *Social Psychological and Personality Science* 3 (2012): 131–38.

Otway, Lorna J., and Vivian L. Vignoles. "Narcissism and Childhood Recollections: A Quantitative Test of Psychoanalytic Predictions." *Personality and Social Psychology Bulletin* 32 (2006): 104–16.

Padilla-Walker, Laura M., and Larry J. Nelson. "Black Hawk Down? Establishing Helicopter Parenting as a Distinct Construct from Other Forms of Parental Control During Emerging Adulthood." *Journal of Adolescence* 35 (2012): 1177–90.

Pappano, Laura. "There's Dissension on the Ranks." *Boston Globe*, February 1, 2004: B6.

Penn, Mark J. *Microtrends*. New York: Twelve, 2007.

Perkins-Gough, Deborah. "The Significance of Grit: A Conversation with Angela Lee Duckworth." *Educational Leadership*, September 2013: 14–20.

Peterson, Christopher, and Martin Seligman. *Character Strengths and Virtues*. New York: Oxford University Press, 2004.

Phelps, Jonathan. "Honors Night Nixed at Ipswich Middle School." *Salem News*, March 21, 2013.

Philipson, Alice. "Teachers Told They Must Not Use Red Ink . . . " *London Telegraph*, April 22, 2013. Available at http://ow.ly/kJ67O.

Pinker, Steven. *The Better Angels of Our Nature: Why Violence Has Declined*. New York: Viking, 2011.

Polivy, Janet. "The Effects of Behavioral Inhibition." *Psychological Inquiry* 9 (1998): 181–204.

Pomerantz, Eva M., Elizabeth A. Moorman, and Scott D. Litwack. "The How, Whom, and Why of Parents' Involvement in Children's Academic Lives: More Is Not Always Better." *Review of Educational Research* 77 (2007): 373–410.

Posner, Rick. *Lives of Passion, School of Hope: How One Public School Ignites a Lifelong Love of Learning*. Boulder, CO: Sentient Publications, 2009.

Powers, John. "Feeling Good (for Nothing)." *Boston Globe Magazine*, January 24, 1993: 7–8.

Press, Eyal. *Beautiful Souls: Saying No, Breaking Ranks, and Heeding the Voice of Conscience in Dark Times*. New York: Farrar, Straus & Giroux, 2012.

Pryor, John H., Linda DeAngelo, Laura Palucki Blake, Sylvia Hurtado, and Serge Tran. *The American Freshman: National Norms—Fall 2011*. Los Angeles: UCLA Higher Education Research Institute, 2011.

Quenqua, Douglas. "Young Students Against Bad Science." *New York Times,* September 3, 2013: D7.

Ramsey, Angela, P. J. Watson, Michael D. Biderman, and Amy L. Reeves. "Self-Reported Narcissism and Perceived Parental Permissiveness and Authoritarianism." *Journal of Genetic Psychology* 157 (1996): 227–38.

Reese, Robin D. "Booting the Dodge Ball." *Education Week,* March 14, 2001.

Reiner, Andrew. "Believing Self-Control Predicts Success, Schools Teach Coping." *Washington Post Magazine,* April 11, 2013.

Rettner, Rachael. "'Helicopter' Parents Have Neurotic Kids." *Today*.com. 2010. Available at www.today.com/id/37493795/ns/health-kids_and_parenting.

Reyes, Maria R., Marc A. Brackett, Susan E. Rivers, Mark White, and Peter Salovey. "Classroom Emotional Climate, Student Engagement, and Academic Achievement." *Journal of Educational Psychology* 104 (2012): 700–712.

Reynolds, John R., and Chardie L. Baird. "Is There a Downside to Shooting for the Stars?" *American Sociological Review* 75 (2010): 151–72.

Rhee, Kyung E., Julie C. Lumeng, Danielle P. Appugliese, Niko Kaciroti, and Robert H. Bradley. "Parent Styles and Overweight Status in First Grade." *Pediatrics* 117 (2006): 2047–54.

Ricker, Audrey. *Backtalk.* New York: Touchstone, 1998.

Roberts, Brent W., Grant Edmonds, and Emily Grijalva. "It Is Developmental Me, Not Generation Me: Developmental Changes Are More Important Than Generational Changes in Narcissism." *Perspectives on Psychological Science* 5 (2010): 97–102.

Rogers, Heather. *Gone Tomorrow: The Hidden Life of Garbage.* New York: New Press, 2005.

Rogus, Joseph F. "Promoting Self-Discipline: A Comprehensive Approach." *Theory Into Practice* 24 (1985): 271–76.

Rohner, Ronald P. "The Parental 'Acceptance-Rejection Syndrome': Universal Correlates of Perceived Rejection." *American Psychologist,* November 2004: 830–40.

Roosevelt, Max. "Student Expectations Seen as Causing Grade Disputes." *New York Times,* February 18, 2009: A15.

Rosenfeld, Alvin, and Nicole Wise. *The Over-Scheduled Child: Avoiding the Hyper-Parenting Trap.* New York: St. Martin's Griffin, 2000.

Roth, Guy. "Perceived Parental Conditional Regard and Autonomy Support as Predictors of Young Adults' Self- Versus Other-Oriented Prosocial Tendencies." *Journal of Personality* 76 (2008): 513–33.

Roth, Guy, and Avi Assor. "Parental Conditional Regard as a Predictor of Deficiencies in Young Children's Capacities to Respond to Sad Feelings." *Infant and Child Development* 19 (2010): 465–77.

Roth, Guy, Avi Assor, Christopher P. Niemiec, Richard M. Ryan, and Edward L. Deci. "The Emotional and Academic Consequences of Parental Conditional Regard." *Developmental Psychology* 45 (2009): 1119–42.

Rothstein, Richard. *The Way We Were?* New York: Century Foundation Press, 1998.

Rutherford, Markella B. "Children's Autonomy and Responsibility: An Analysis of Childrearing Advice." *Qualitative Sociology* 32 (2009): 337–53.

Ryan, Richard M., Scott Rigby, and Kristi King. "Two Types of Religious Internalization and Their Relations to Religious Orientations and Mental Health." *Journal of Personality and Social Psychology* 65 (1993): 586–96.

Ryckman, Richard M., Bill Thornton, and J. Corey Butler. "Personality Correlates of the Hypercompetitive Attitude Scale." *Journal of Personality Assessment* 62 (1994): 84–94.

Samuelson, Robert J. "The Trophy Syndrome." *Newsweek*, December 20, 1992.

Samuolis, Jessica, Kiera Layburn, and Kathleen M. Schiaffino. "Identity Development and Attachment to Parents in College Students." *Journal of Youth and Adolescence* 30 (2001): 373–84.

Schemo, Diana Jean. "In Small Town, 'Grease' Ignites a Culture War." *New York Times*, February 11, 2006.

Schiffrin, Holly H., Miriam Liss, Haley Miles-McLean, Katherine A. Geary, Mindy J. Erchull, and Taryn Tashner. "Helping or Hovering? The Effects of Helicopter Parenting on College Students' Well-Being." *Journal of Child and Family Studies.* DOI 10.1007/10826013-9716-3. Published online February 9, 2013.

Scocca, Tom. "The Great Grade-Inflation Lie." *Boston Phoenix*, April 24, 1998: 4–7.

Seery, Mark D., Jim Blascovich, Max Weisbuch, and S. Brooke Vick. "The Relationship Between Self-Esteem Level, Self-Esteem Stability, and Cardiovascular Reactions to Performance Feedback." *Journal of Personality and Social Psychology* 87 (2004): 133–45.

Segrin, Chris, Alesia Woszidlo, Michelle Givertz, Amy Bauer, and Melissa Taylor Murphy. "The Association Between Overparenting, Parent-Child Communication, and Entitlement and Adaptive Traits in Adult Children." *Family Relations* 61 (2012): 237–52.

Seligman, Martin E. P. *The Optimistic Child.* Boston: Houghton Mifflin, 1995.

Sengupta, Somni. "'Big Brother'? No, It's Parents." *New York Times*, June 26, 2012: A1, B4.

Settersten, Richard A., Jr. "Worry More About Under-Involved Parents." *New York Times* Room for Debate (online symposium), July 14, 2012. Available at http://ow.ly/iXyn6.

Shamosh, Noah A., and Jeremy R. Gray. "Delay Discounting and Intelligence: A Meta-Analysis." *Intelligence* 38 (2008): 289–305.

Shapiro, David. *Neurotic Styles.* New York: Basic, 1965.

Shapiro, Evan. "What's the Matter with Kids Today?" *Huffington Post*, November 19, 2012. Available at www.huffingtonpost.com/evan-shapiro/whats-the -matter-with-kid_1_b_2157862.html.

Shaw, Robert. *The Epidemic: The Rot of American Culture, Absentee and Permissive Parenting, and the Resultant Plague of Joyless, Selfish Children.* NY: Regan Books, 2003.

Sherif, Muzafer, O. J. Harvey, B. J. White, W. R. Hood, and C. W. Sherif. *Intergroup Conflict and Cooperation: The Robbers' Cave Experiment.* Norman, OK: University Book Exchange, 1961.

Shoda, Yuichi, Walter Mischel, and Philip K. Peake. "Predicting Adolescent Cognitive and Self-Regulatory Competencies from Preschool Delay of Gratification." *Developmental Psychology* 26 (1990): 978–86.

Silva, Jennifer M. "Young and Isolated." *New York Times*, June 23, 2013: SR7.

Singer, Natasha. "Fixing a World That Fosters Fat." *New York Times*, August 22, 2010: BU3.

Sizer, Theodore R. *Horace's Compromise: The Dilemma of the American High School.* Rev. edition. Boston: Houghton Mifflin, 1992.

Slater, Philip. *The Pursuit of Loneliness: American Culture at the Breaking Point.* Boston: Beacon, 1970.

Slouka, Mark. "Democracy and Deference." *Harper's*, June 2008: 9–13.

Small, Meg L., Nicole Morgan, Caitlin Abar, and Jennifer L. Maggs. "Protective Effects of Parent-College Student Communication During the First Semester of College." *Journal of American College Health* 59 (2011): 547–54.

Smollar, David. "Eliminating a Grade of F Raises Tempest in S. D. Schools." *Los Angeles Times*, July 15, 1991.

Soenens, Bart, Koen Luyckx, Maarten Vansteenkiste, Patrick Luyten, Bart Duriez and Luc Goossens. "Maladaptive Perfectionism as an Intervening Variable Between Psychological Control and Adolescent Depressive Symptoms." *Journal of Family Psychology* 22 (2008): 465–74.

Soenens, Bart, and Maarten Vansteenkiste. "A Theoretical Upgrade of the Concept of Parental Psychological Control: Proposing New Insights on the Basis of Self-Determination Theory." *Developmental Review* 30 (2010): 74–99.

Soenens, Bart, Maarten Vansteenkiste, Willy Lens, Koen Luyckx, Luc Goossens, Wim Beyers, and Richard M. Ryan. "Conceptualizing Parental Autonomy Support." *Developmental Psychology* 43 (2007): 633–46.

Soenens, Bart, Maarten Vansteenkiste, and Patrick Luyten. "Toward a Domain-Specific Approach to the Study of Parental Psychological Control." *Journal of Personality* 78 (2010): 217–56.

Soenens, Bart, Maarten Vansteenkiste, Patrick Luyten, Bart Duriez, and Luc Goossens. "Maladaptive Perfectionistic Self-Representations: The Mediational Link Between Psychological Control and Adjustment." *Personality and Individual Differences* 38 (2005): 487–98.

Somers, Patricia, and Jim Settle. "The Helicopter Parent." *College & University* 86 (2010): 18–27.

Sparks, Sarah D. "Advocacy Tactics Found to Differ by Families' Class." *Education Week*, August 29, 2012: 1, 11.

Spock, Benjamin. *Common Sense Book of Baby and Child Care*. New York: Duell, Sloan and Pearce, 1946.

———. "Don't Blame Me!" *Look*, January 26, 1971: 37–38.

Statistics Canada. *National Longitudinal Survey of Children and Youth: Home Environment, Income, and Child Behaviour*. February 21, 2005. Available at www.statcan.gc.ca/daily-quotidien/050221/dq050221b-eng.htm.

Stearns, Peter N. *Anxious Parents: A History of Modern Childrearing in America*. New York: New York University Press, 2003.

Stein, Joel. "Millennials: The Me Me Me Generation." *Time*, May 20, 2013: 26–34.

Steinberg, Jacques. "Woe Is Harvard, Where All Are Above Average." *New York Times*, December 5, 2001: A14.

Stephens, Nicole M., Stephanie A. Fryberg, Hazel Rose Markus, Camille S. Johnson, and Rebecca Covarrubias. "Unseen Disadvantage: How American Universities' Focus on Independence Undermines the Academic Performance of First-Generation College Students." *Journal of Personality and Social Psychology* 102 (2012): 1178–97.

Stepp, Laura Sessions. "A Full Head of Esteem." *Washington Post*, February 21, 1995.

Stevens, V., I. De Bourdeauhuij, and P. Van Oost. "Relationship of the Family Environment to Children's Involvement in Bully/Victim Problems at School." *Journal of Youth and Adolescence* 31 (2002): 419–28.

Stevenson, Harold W. "'Oscars' Made of Tin." *New York Times*, October 11, 1994: A21.

Stipek, Deborah J. *Motivation to Learn: From Theory to Practice*. 2nd ed. Boston: Allyn & Bacon, 1993.

Strage, Amy, and Tamara Swanson Brandt. "Authoritative Parenting and College Students' Academic Adjustment and Success." *Journal of Educational Psychology* 91 (1999): 146–56.

Strayer, Janet, and William Roberts. "Children's Anger, Emotional Expressiveness, and Empathy." *Social Development* 13 (2004): 229–54.

Streep, Peg, and Alan B. Bernstein. *Mastering the Art of Quitting*. Boston: Da Capo, 2013.

Suarez, Ana Veciana. "There's Glory for No. 1, But Competition's Hard." *Miami Herald*, June 1, 2003.

Sullivan, Rachel. "Helicopter Parenting Causes Anxious Kids." *ABC Science* [Australian]. August 20, 2012.

Swann, William B., Jr., Christine Chang-Schneider, and Katie Larsen McClarty. "Do People's Self-Views Matter? Self-Concept and Self-Esteem in Everyday Life." *American Psychologist*, February-March 2007: 84–94.

Tangney, June, Roy Baumeister, and Angie Luzio Boone. "High Self-Control Predicts Good Adjustment, Less Pathology, Better Grades, and Interpersonal Success." *Journal of Personality* 72 (2004): 271–324.

Taylor, Catherine A., Jennifer A. Manganello, Shawna J. Lee, and Janet C. Rice. "Mothers' Spanking of 3-Year-Old Children and Subsequent Risk of Children's Aggressive Behavior." *Pediatrics* 125 (2010): 1057–65.

Toth, Lisa. "On the Rise." [University of Oregon] *Daily Emerald*, June 7, 2002.

Tough, Paul. "Can the Right Kinds of Play Teach Self-Control?" *New York Times Magazine*, September 27, 2009.

———. "The Character Test." *New York Times Magazine*, September 18, 2011: 38–46, 85.

———. *How Children Succeed: Grit, Curiosity, and the Hidden Power of Character.* Boston: Houghton Mifflin Harcourt, 2012.

Tracy, Jessica L., Joey T. Cheng, Richard W. Robins, and Kali H. Trzesniewski. "Authentic and Hubristic Pride: The Affective Core of Self-Esteem and Narcissism." *Self and Identity* 8 (2009): 196–213.

Trollope, Mrs. [Frances]. *Domestic Manners of the Americans.* London: Whittaker, Treacher, & Co., 1832.

Trzesniewski, Kali H., and M. Brent Donnellan. "Rethinking 'Generation Me': A Study of Cohort Effects From 1976–2006." *Perspectives in Psychological Science* 5 (2010): 58–75.

Trzesniewski, Kali H.; M. Brent Donnellan, Terrie E. Moffitt, Richard W. Robins, Richie Poulton, and Avshalom Caspi. "Low Self-Esteem During Adolescence Predicts Poor Health, Criminal Behavior, and Limited Economic Prospects During Adulthood." *Developmental Psychology* 42 (2006): 381-90.

Trzesniewski, Kali H., M. Brent Donnellan, and Richard W. Robins. "Do Today's Young People Really Think They Are So Extraordinary? An Examination of Secular Trends in Narcissism and Self-Enhancement." *Psychological Science* 19 (2008a): 181–88.

———. "Is 'Generation Me' Really More Narcissistic Than Previous Generations?" *Journal of Personality* 76 (2008b): 903–17.

Twenge, Jean M. *Generation Me.* New York: Free Press, 2006.

———. "The Evidence for Generation Me and Against Generation We." *Emerging Adulthood* 1 (2013a): 11–16.

———. "Overwhelming Evidence for Generation Me: A Reply to Arnett." *Emerging Adulthood* 1 (2013b): 21–26.

Twenge, Jean M., and W. Keith Campbell. "Increases in Positive Self-Views Among High School Students." *Psychological Science* 19 (2008): 1082–86.

———. *The Narcissism Epidemic: Living in the Age of Entitlement*. New York: Free Press, 2010.

Twenge, Jean M., and Joshua D. Foster. "Birth Cohort Increases in Narcissistic Personality Traits Among American College Students, 1982–2009." *Social Psychological and Personality Science* 1 (2010): 99–106.

Ungar, Michael. "Overprotective Parenting: Helping Parents Provide Children the Right Amount of Risk and Responsibility." *American Journal of Family Therapy* 37 (2009): 258–71.

Valentine, Jeffrey C., David L. DuBois, and Harris Cooper. "The Relation Between Self-Beliefs and Academic Achievement: A Meta-Analytic Review." *Educational Psychologist* 39 (2004): 111–33.

Vansteenkiste, Maarten, Joke Simons, Willy Lens, Bart Soenens, and Lennia Matos. "Examining the Motivational Impact of Intrinsic Versus Extrinsic Goal Framing and Autonomy-Supportive Versus Internally Controlling Communication Style on Early Adolescents' Academic Achievement." *Child Development* 76 (2005): 483–501.

Vinson, Kathleen Elliott. "Hovering Too Close: The Ramifications of Helicopter Parenting in Higher Education." Suffolk University Law School Legal Studies Research Paper 12–05, January 10, 2012.

Wagner, Jenny, Denis Gerstorf, Christiane Hoppmann, and Mary A. Luszcz. "The Nature and Correlates of Self-Esteem Trajectories in Late Life." *Journal of Personality and Social Psychology* 105 (2013): 139–53.

Wang, Qian, Eva M. Pomerantz, and Huichang Chen. "The Role of Parents' Control in Early Adolescents' Psychological Functioning: A Longitudinal Investigation in the United States and China." *Child Development* 78 (2007): 1592–1610.

Warner, Judith. "No More Mrs. Nice Mom." *New York Times Magazine*, January 16, 2011: 11.

Watson, P. J., Susan E. Hickman, Ronald J. Morris, J. Trevor Milliron, and Linda Whiting. "Narcissism, Self-Esteem, and Parental Nurturance." *Journal of Psychology* 129 (1995): 61–73.

Watson, P.J., Tracy Little, and Michael D. Biderman. "Narcissism and Parenting Styles." *Psychoanalytic Psychology* 9 (1992): 231–44.

Weiss, Laura H., and J. Conrad Schwarz. "The Relationship between Parenting Types and Older Adolescents' Personality, Academic Achievement, Adjustment, and Substance Use." *Child Development* 67 (1996): 2101–14.

Weissbourd, Richard. *The Parents We Mean to Be: How Well-Intentioned Adults Undermine Children's Moral and Emotional Development.* Boston: Houghton Mifflin, 2009.

Wente, Margaret. "Why Kids Need to Fail to Succeed in School." [Toronto] *Globe and Mail*, October 9, 2012.

Wigfield, Allan. "Children's Attributions for Success and Failure: Effects of Age and Attentional Focus." *Journal of Educational Psychology* 80 (1988): 76–81.

Wikström, Per-Olof H., and Kyle Treiber. "The Role of Self-Control in Crime Causation." *European Journal of Criminology* 4 (2007): 237–64.

Willingham, Daniel T. "Can Teachers Increase Students' Self-Control?" *American Educator*, Summer 2011: 22–27.

Wolf, De'Sha S., Linda J. Sax, and Casandra E. Harper. "Parental Engagement and Contact in the Academic Lives of College Students." *NASPA* [National Association of Student Personnel Administrators] *Journal* 46 (2009): 325–58.

Wolfe, Raymond N., and Scott D. Johnson. "Personality as a Predictor of College Performance." *Educational and Psychological Measurement* 55 (1995): 177–85.

Wood, Jeffrey J. "Parental Intrusiveness and Children's Separation Anxiety in a Clinical Sample." *Child Psychiatry and Human Development* 37 (2006): 73–87.

Wuyts, Dorien, Maarten Vansteenkiste, Bart Soenens, and Avi Assor. "An Examination of the Controlling Dynamics Involved in Parental Child-Invested Contingent Self-Esteem." Unpublished manuscript, 2013.

Wyden, Peter. *Suburbia's Coddled Kids.* Garden City, NY: Doubleday, 1962.

Young-Bruehl, Elisabeth. *Childism: Confronting Prejudice Against Children.* New Haven, CT: Yale University Press, 2012.

Young-Eisendrath, Polly. *The Self-Esteem Trap.* New York: Little, Brown, 2008.

Zabelina, Darya L., Michael D. Robinson, and Cali L. Anicha. "The Psychological Tradeoffs of Self-Control." *Personality and Individual Differences* 43 (2007): 463–73.

Zelizer, Viviana A. *Pricing the Priceless Child: The Changing Social Value of Children.* Princeton, NJ: Princeton University Press, 1994.

Zhao, Yong. "Flunking Innovation and Creativity." *Phi Delta Kappan*, September 2012: 56–61.

Zhou, Qing, Nancy Eisenberg, Sandra H. Losoya, Richard A. Fabes, Mark Reiser, Ivanna K. Guthrie, Bridget C. Murphy, Amanda J. Cumberland, and Stephanie A. Shepard. "The Relations of Parental Warmth and Positive Expressiveness to Children's Empathy-Related Responding and Social Functioning." *Child Development* 73 (2002): 893–915.

Zimmermann, Friederike, Kerstin Schütte, Päivi Taskinen, and Olaf Köller. "Reciprocal Effects Between Adolescent Externalizing Problems and Measures of Achievement." *Journal of Educational Psychology* 105 (2013): 747–61.

Zins, Joseph E., Roger P. Weissberg, Margaret C. Wang, and Herbert J. Walberg, eds. *Building Academic Success on Social and Emotional Learning: What Does the Research Say*. New York: Teachers College Press, 2004.

Zuk, Marlene. "The Evolutionary Search for Our Perfect Past." *New York Times*, January 20, 2009: D5.

Index